Gene Logsdon's
Moneysaving Secrets

Gene Logsdon's

Moneysaving Secrets

A Treasury of
Salvaging, Bargaining,
Recycling,
and Scavenging Techniques

Illustrations by Gene Mater
Photographs by Gene Logsdon
and the Rodale Press Photography Department

Rodale Press, Emmaus, Pennsylvania

Edited by Cheryl Winters Tetreau
Designed by Glen Burris

Library of Congress Cataloging-in-Publication Data
Logsdon, Gene.
    Gene Logsdon's moneysaving secrets.

    Includes index.
    1. Do it yourself work.   2. Building materials—
Recycling.   3. House furnishings—Recycling.
4. Shopping.   5. Handicraft.   I. Title.
TT149.L63   1986   643'.7   86–6522
ISBN   0–87857–624–X   hardcover
ISBN   0–87857–625–8   paperback

2 4 6 8 10 9 7 5 3 1   hardcover
2 4 6 8 10 9 7 5 3 1   paperback

Contents

18534

Acknowledgements

Writing this book reminds me of canoeing down an unknown river. Once more I climbed into that trusty craft called Rodale Press and headed downstream, professing to know where I was headed. Carol Hupping, one of my editors, sat behind me using her paddle as a rudder to steer me between rocks of obscure writing and over submerged logs of non sequiturs. Cheryl Winters Tetreau, my other editor, sat in front, furiously paddling around shallows of unmet deadlines. I, in the middle, had but to keep up the pace and not shift around into intriguing backwaters not pertinent to the subject at hand.

On shore, publisher Tom Woll, other editors—particularly Bill Hylton and Ray Wolf—and chief photographer Tom Gettings all shouted words of encouragement and advice. As we whipped and twisted through white water, researchers, marketers, and production workers, all members of the Rodale team, stood at every bend to point out the safest channels for us to shoot.

Finally we left the torrential rapids of creation and eased into the still, deep waters of completion. Two weeks late, but hey, we never capsized once. There were moments when I panicked and paddled the wrong way, even jabbed my editors in the ribs inadvertently. But they knew how to get even, throwing water of editorial realism upon my most precious rhetorical oaring maneuvers. The facts that got washed overboard and the errors that did not get bailed out are entirely my fault, but any commas, misplaced modifiers, and so forth, that drifted like flotsam to land where they were least expected, I blame on my editors—so there. After all, as middle paddler in a canoe, my main job is to act as ballast, and I have true talent for that.

Last but not least, when I came ashore each night, tired and wet, there was my wife as always, with dry clothes, good food, warm heart, and words of encouragement. My thanks to all.

Introduction

While visiting newlyweds who had just set up housekeeping, I remarked on the cute little round table in their breakfast nook. They laughed and lifted the tablecloth that hung generously over the sides. To my surprise, their "table" was in reality one of those big wooden spools made to hold heavy wire or cable for shipping. It did indeed make an adequate table, if not for a kitchen, then certainly perfect for a recreation room or children's playroom. Cost? Zilch. "We spotted a whole bunch of them at a building site and the man said we could have one," said my friend. "We went back for more, but they were all gone."

Yankee ingenuity is not dead in this country. It may in fact be thriving more vigorously than ever, since there are more ways in our seemingly throwaway society to exercise it. One of my neighbors, desiring a chicken coop, was appalled to find out the lumber he needed was going to cost him more than $400. You can buy a lot of eggs for that much money. You can buy a lot of eggs with just the *interest* on that money. He mentioned his problem to the roofer who was reroofing his house. No sweat, the roofer said. He knew where an old but well-kept chicken coop could be bought for less than $100. All he had to do was move it.

No problem. My neighbor traded a day's labor and the promise of fresh eggs for the use of a friend's truck and they moved the little building easily. The coop would have made a dandy tool shed or a potting shed for a gardener. There are thousands of unused little buildings like this one on farmsteads all over the country, awaiting Yankee ingenuity.

While my neighbor was talking to the roofer, I was eyeballing the old metal he was removing from the roof. It was standing-seam tin roofing, without nail holes in it, and it was actually in good shape, considering its age. What was my neighbor going to do with it? He told me the junkman would hardly give him anything for it. I asked if I could have a few lengths. He was glad to get rid of it. And what did I want it for? To cover the ricks of firewood I was seasoning in the woodlot. The roofing was exactly the right width. If I bought new metal or plastic panels for this purpose, they would cost me at least $50 to cover all my wood.

In his barn, an acquaintance of mine built a hay mow using 2×6s and 2×8s from pallets he got for free from the glass factory where his wife works.

The line fence between us has sections of used telephone poles for cornerposts that I got for free. I was able to buy some of the fencing at a farm sale for less than a third of its true value. The fencing is 9-gauge wire throughout and even though it is used, it will last longer than I will live.

It occurred to me, observing all this scrounging going on around me, that a helpful book on the subject might be worthwhile. No sooner had the idea suggested itself than I began to find examples everywhere I looked. My son came home from work and said he had met a man who made rocking chairs—*nice* rocking chairs—out of pallet wood. The man also had framed an addition on his house mostly from the same kind of wood. And that reminded me that I knew a farmer who had a sideline business of tearing apart used pallets and making smaller ones out of them for resale. (A pallet costs about $6, and when you buy something shipped in them you directly or indirectly pay for them.)

While visiting relatives in Louisville, Kentucky, I found young Danny Downs busily at work in his blacksmith shop next to his father's woodworking shop in their backyard barn. Danny is a master scrounger because he has to be. Just out of high school, he has no money to launch himself in business, so he turns scrap metal into useful and beautiful objects. He can't even afford to buy the tools of his trade, so he makes most of them. Even his first forge was made of scraps—angle iron and an old tire rim half-filled with clay. He made his tongs from scrap steel rod and his many hammers from old jackhammer blades, with the handles from pieces of ash or hickory firewood.

"What other people consider a pile of trash beside the road is a gold mine to me," he says. "People throw away all the raw materials I need." All he had to buy was an anvil and eventually a real forge—both secondhand, of course. After only a few simple lessons in tempering and annealing, he can make common steel harder, or hard steel softer, so the possibilities for re-creation are endless.

When I was visiting him, he had just finished making a pair of wrought iron tables. Actually, he made only the legs. The tops were old hot air registers, obsolete now, but very attractive in their new role. Part (or all) of the challenge and allure of saving money through recycling and scrounging is to do so elegantly.

And so to this book. I've tried hard to describe moneysaving ways that are both practical and tasteful. But occasionally I've slipped a few ideas in just for fun, when my editors weren't looking. For example, it is a fact of science that compost—good old decaying compost—generates electricity. And upon that fact, human ingenuity is, as always, busily at work. A fellow in Grenada builds and sells what he calls garbage batteries. And that's just what they are—containers of compost connected by copper wires. Garbage batteries will as yet run only a couple of light bulbs or a radio and may not (yet) be either practical or elegant for Americans, but I knew you'd want to know about them. So, here they are, along with all the other moneysaving ideas I've learned from others or discovered on my own. Perhaps they will inspire you to even greater heights of Yankee ingenuity!

CHAPTER 1

Decorating on a Shoestring

A New York penthouse featured recently in *House and Garden* magazine contained a rather crude seventeenth-century country bench on one side of the sofa and a Post Modern abstract sculpture executed in 1969 on the other. In the bathroom, an ancient stone ram's head spigot spit water into a nineteenth-century pedestal sink while, hardly a room away, a table glowed in iridescent Du Pont car paint. In other words, as far as interior design goes these days, anything goes, and if it was going good at some earlier period (any earlier period), it will go even better now. Art Deco is back; Victorian is flourishing; Modern (which dates from the 1920s) vies with Post Modern, which isn't particularly modern, either, in the sense of new. Nor do you have to be consistent. You can do one room one way, another room another way—if it pleases you (and especially if no one else has thought of it yet), it's okay with today's guardians of high style. In the home of one very wealthy family, a living room is dominated by a brass firemen's pole and lots of gleaming metal cabinetry. The style involved is described as "using Modern to achieve a space-age decor." In another house, an ancient painted French wheelbarrow stands under a wrought iron chandelier in front of new leaded-glass windows. In another home, a young couple eats in a restaurant booth rescued from a 1930s diner. This is very "Decoesque," in the language of the hour.

If this hodgepodge of styles has a generality, it is that any and all materials are potentially usable for furniture and interior decorating: metal, wood, stone, masonry, rubber, tin, even plastic, like the Lucite furniture that enjoyed a brief vogue in the '50s. And what *that* means is you don't have to be rich to get into the game. It's a recycler's paradise, where imagination, which costs nothing, makes the rules. Federico Forquet is considered one of the most discriminating of Italian designers. Much of the wall space in his home is covered with framed arrangements of dried grass and ferns. Exquisite, yet an idea within the financial means of anyone with the gumption to collect plants along the roadside. Given a choice, I suppose we'd all choose a bathtub made of onyx over the standard fare, but just about as much acclaim for originality will be heaped upon the decorators with more imagination than money who revitalize and install a copper-lined wooden tub or find a way to move one of those huge, old Victorian monsters with claw feet from a salvage yard into their home. My vote for the most imaginative piece of "furniture" is an elaborate brass and copper espresso coffee maker friends of ours installed in their living room. Very Decoesque. It is a great conversation piece. Newcomers often believe it to be a whiskey still. We have other friends who do have a cute old copper still, which they plan by and by to shine up and move to their living room.

ANYTHING GOES

There are slick recycling ideas in nearly every home where imagination rises above the humdrum: Kitchen counters covered with old schoolhouse blackboards and polished to a smooth, gleaming silkiness; a trestle table with a top made from a salvaged bowling alley; cabinets entirely faced with weathered barn siding; an old gas station pump installed in a rec room, just for fun; a wall covered with old roofing slates, waxed and polished. The common denominator in all these ideas is that the materials were available *free*.

The most imaginative recyclers I happen to know are Joan and Bill Downs of Boston, Kentucky. "I do the imagining and Bill does the recycling," says Joan. Their patio is made of rectangular and square slabs of marble sunk in concrete. Marble?

"You would have to ask," Joan says. "I, ah, found it in the men's room of an old hotel being torn down in Louisville."

"Yeah," Bill adds dryly. "I thought I could get it all in two truck loads, but it took five trips and one flat tire."

Joan wanted a table on the veranda of their comfortable old southern home—something capable of seating a lawn party should

rain threaten; something that could sit in the open year in and year out and not require much maintenance. While slumming around flea markets and salvage yards one day, she spied a candy maker's white stone table top. Just the thing, she thought. But it would take ten wrestlers to move it. Bill came to the rescue. "I sawed it into three pieces with a Carborundum saw blade," he says. "Back home we made three identical tables that fit against each other and formed one long monster."

And what about the legs? You have to see them to believe them. They are the black iron legs from three old sewing machines.

In the kitchen, Joan hangs woven baskets from a butcher-shop meat hook and an old enamelware bean pot from the breast chain of a horse harness. Right inside the entrance door, there's a three-tiered set of glass insulators, taken from a telephone pole, that are used now to hang hats on.

The lazy Susan in the kitchen is made from the top of an old whiskey barrel, sanded and stained to reveal the beautiful grain. (Whiskey barrels are almost always made from high-quality white oak.) There are letters stamped into the barrel top identifying the original contents. Joan left these dark to contrast with the wood for easy readability. For napkin holders, she uses wooden pony stirrups.

In the living room there's a rare walnut sanctuary table that Joan

bought cheaply at an auction. Some of the fragile carvings on the bottom of the table apron had broken off during the years. But Bill made new ones that are difficult to tell from the original. Sure, it's not the priceless antique it would have been in its original state, but if you can't tell the difference between repair and original, what difference does it make? For a recycler, the pleasure of the deft repair may be greater than the pleasure of finding a perfect original.

THE ART DECO LOOK

The Art Deco rage is a particularly happy hunting ground for recyclers because there's plenty of it to be dug out of attics and secondhand shops cheaply or even for free. What Art Deco is, is not always easy to say. Almost anything in the decorative arts made between 1925 and 1940 eventually gets tagged Art Deco—or anything made up through the '50s that looks like it might have been made in 1930. The name comes from the 1925 Paris design show known as Exposition International des Arts Decoratifs et Industriele Modernes. The idea of the show was to exhibit works of artists and designers who somehow made Modernism (the "new" art and architecture of that time) appealing to the masses. It consisted of lots of metal, geometrical patterns, straight lines, rounded corners and edges, and spiral staircases "pulsating with Jazz Age energy." Some descriptions of the Art Deco look can be fairly meaningless—like this quote from an editor of *Progressive Architecture* after viewing the 1985 entries in its annual furniture and lighting competition: "The historicist and postmodernist is fading, and there are more modernist-looking pieces as well as a greater emphasis on the fifties. The fifties influence was not the kitsch stuff but more the mass production aspects." Even an art historian is going to have trouble with verbiage like that.

But to take an example: In the mid-1930s, the now-famous designer Alvar Aalto was designing lacquered metal furniture that is much in vogue again. Literally tons of cheap metal furniture that today is "very Decoesque" was made in the '30s, inspired by Aalto and others. By 1960, most of it was junked or stored away or used for lawn furniture until it rusted out. Now it is fashionable. A word to the wise recycler is sufficient.

The fastest way to get on the inside of the Art Deco revival, or any other revival, is to get a copy of what is known as the *Brown Book: A Directory of Information* (The National Trust for Historic Preservation, 1785 Massachusetts Avenue N.W., Washington, DC 20036). It contains a comprehensive list of preservation groups in the United States, including various Art Deco societies. You can order the book for $17.95 plus $2.50 postage.

One place to look for treasures is in hotels of the 1920s and '30s scheduled for razing. Or be on the lookout for diners from the 1930s, or in just about any attic. If it looks like lawn furniture, don't worry. Lacquer it and use it inside. Even old wicker furniture, once used outside, is now *de rigueur* in the home, but paint it white or some pastel color.

THE OFFICE LOOK

Another furniture style now emerging in the homes of younger couples intent on saving money might be called "Old Office." As offices modernize for the computer age, perfectly good desks, tables, chairs, and shelves are suddenly *persona non grata,* and many times the boss is only too glad to give his faithful workers this stuff if they will tote it away. So people are decorating their apartments with swivel chairs, drafting tables, and file cabinets in a way that Aalto might have approved of even if Mother doesn't. When, for example, plastic mail trays replaced the wire ones (heaven only knows why), the latter often found their recycling way into kitchens to become potato and onion bins, or into the powder room to hold towels, or perhaps into the foyer to do what they always did: hold mail.

A hot seller at stores right now is computer furniture—straight, blocky, simple, plain-surfaced stuff that looks as if it were made out of old doors fastened together. As a matter of fact, you can save a lot of money by making your own—out of old doors. Even paneled doors work nicely if they are cut down to size evenly—the margins around the panels kept to pleasing proportions. The doors then are glued and screwed together, some vertically for "legs" and some horizontally for table or desk tops; then the whole thing is painted. Easy, practical, and if you have an eye for proportion, attractive. For ideas, look at computer furniture in catalogs.

Common hollow-core interior doors make economical computer furniture and shelving, even if you buy them new. There are a few tricks to using them. When cutting down to size, make use of as much of the finished edges as possible. Where you must cut through an open edge, mask the hollow with a moulding strip or cut a piece of pine board to fit. Insert the board into the edge (about 2 inches is sufficient), glue, and clamp. If you use strips of hollow door for shelves and plug the edges with moulding only, you might need extra support if you plan on putting anything heavy on your shelves. Put a 1 by 2-inch vertical support board every 2 feet between shelf sides—in other words allow no more than 2 feet of shelf space without a support. Actually, this is a good idea even when using solid inch boards for shelves.

Old panel doors can also be used quite exquisitely to make window or wall seats that box in and hide floor radiators. Or use them to surround that big, old Victorian tub to give it a built-in look.

THE COUNTRY LOOK

Another hot fashion in home interiors is the "country look." Though it may end in the country, the fashion began as urban nostalgia. Genuine country people are still startled when a condo-dwelling friend begs them for their old corn sheller languishing in the barn or for a much-used manure fork. Such items can give an apartment an aura of down-home timelessness referred to, simply, as "country." The term is best defined as a state of mind that finds beauty and happiness in a cross between Not-So-Early American and Yesterday's Barnyard. All the obsolete paraphernalia of civilization that our grandmothers and mothers threw out the back door forty years ago is being dragged back in through the front by the grown-up grandchildren: butter churns, milk bucket benches, woodboxes, milking stools, rough pine tables, oak iceboxes, harness vises, pie safes, dry sinks, grain cradles, winnowing sieves, cheeseboxes—even the twig chairs grandma was ashamed for company to sit on and made grandpa stow away in the hayloft just as soon as she had saved enough egg money to buy the latest metal and plastic dinette set. Nor do yesterday's throwaways have to be in good condition to become part of the modern home decor. If the boards on the table are warped so badly you can't find a level place to pour a cup of coffee, so much the better. Mice gnawings make a piece authentic. If the original paint, however flaky, still shows, and especially if it's blue, the higher the price. Any dirt stains that won't wipe off with a summary whisk of a wire brush are "patina."

Why Americans have become so enamored of the country look is not easy to explain. We all seem to yearn for some simpler era that we imagine occurred before our time or that we think we experienced briefly as children. This romanticism is given added impetus by the practical revival of woodstoves and self-sufficient gardening and by an economic climate where cottage industry goods again can almost compete in the marketplace with factory-made.

Introducing the Artful Pennypincher

However historians will explain the phenomenon, one thing is certain: The original perpetrator of Not-So-Early American and Yesterday's Barnyard was a dyed-in-the-wool, 100 percent pure, Artful Pennypincher. He or she perceived that fine, truly old Early American pieces—the value of which has been driven up by scarcity, an increasing number of collectors, and too many tax-financed museums—were beyond their financial resources. So were good reproductions, and anyway, reproductions are not much fun, especially when they're expensive. On the other hand, Not-So-Early American (anything made or used before you were 10 years old) was free for the finding or cheap at flea markets and auctions. All it took was a lively enough imagination to envision an object now lying in a junk pile or mildewing away in an attic transformed to beauty when enshrined properly in one's living room. Once a person rescues, say, an old wooden seed corn dryer from the dusty corner of a forgotten barn and sees how grand it looks by the fireplace festooned with ears of drying popcorn, one is hooked for life.

Every day is Christmas for the Artful Pennypincher who is decorating a home. Every turn in the road may turn up something free or ridiculously cheap that may enhance a home's decor and that might grow in value. Since many of these objects were simply made in the first place, the Artful Pennypincher who does not get in on the ground floor (before a particular piece vaults heavenward in price) can make a facsimile quite easily. In either case, the result is a house full of stylish but quite inexpensive furniture and accessories.

You don't have to be enthralled with the country look *per se* to profit from it. The country collectors have legitimized the use of almost anything of worldly interest in interior decorating. One lady, an antiques dealer herself, has installed an old carpenter's bench, complete with vises at both ends, for her kitchen work island. If you find that hard to believe, start thumbing through the pages of *Country Living* magazine (whose editorial offices are in that oh-so-countryfied place called New York City). Even the label from a pair of Finck's Detroit Special Overalls ("The Man Who Thinks, Invests in Finck's. They Wear Like a Pig's Nose.") is *haute couture* today. If you find a pair of these overalls, the thing to do is to hang them prominently on the wall as decoration.

One of the most imaginative accessories I've noticed is a wooden rack consisting of several narrow pieces of wood spaced about a foot apart, each about 4 feet long, joined by two side boards. The rack is suspended horizontally from the ceiling, and woven baskets hang from it. It is identified as a "fragment from a chicken coop." I am fairly certain it is, or was, a section of chicken roost.

Turning a piece of a chicken coop into a kitchen rack is what makes the country look so much fun—you find some new use for an old object its maker never dreamed of. Let us step inside the home of

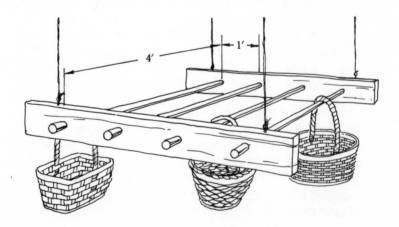

Mrs. Art(ful) Pennypincher. There in the entranceway is a dented tin milk can, circa 1938, used as an umbrella stand. Country people as a rule don't use umbrellas, but never mind. Mrs. Pennypincher has several walking sticks in her umbrella stand, too, delightfully spiraled sticks formed not by hand carving or some expensive jig on a lathe, but naturally, by a vine constricting the sapling around which it was growing when Mrs. Pennypincher found it in the woods. In the kitchen is an ancient cast-iron cookstove, but look closely. It has been electrified. On the exposed ceiling beams of the kitchen (the beams came out of an old barn) are rows of steel hay hooks and meat carcass hooks from which pots and pans hang handily. The work island in the center of the kitchen is a display counter Mrs. Pennypincher rescued from the back room of a hardware store going out of business—for $25 and the hassle of moving it. The glass bins all around the sides of the counter are filled with seeds of various colors and sizes. The ceiling lights in the kitchen are old electric fixtures, also from the hardware store. A collection of graniteware nests on shelves that originally were used for milk buckets in a farm dairy. A wooden paper roller from a butcher shop serves as an attractive shelf and towel rack when turned upside down. On the work island sits an old tool carrier used as a silverware tray. Kitchen cabinets are done in unfinished barn siding. The sink is a remodeled dry sink.

A metal bushel grain basket by the fireplace holds wood. The rug in front of the fireplace is braided from scraps of wool (which won't burn if a spark lands on it). Most of the rugs in the house are rag rugs woven by Mrs. Pennypincher. One is dyed with beet juice. An old flat-topped, brass-bound chest scrounged from grandma's attic serves as a coffee table. Two game tables are telephone cable spools turned on end. Lamp bases throughout the house are old crockery jugs. A milking stool becomes a footstool. A tobacco basket holds a potted plant. A printer's tray hung on the wall serves as a shadow-box cabinet for a collection of miniatures, some of them very simple but effective: a robin's egg in a tiny basket glued together from pieces cut from a berry basket; three tiny sheep cut from a piece of barn roof tin; a small stone cleverly painted to look like a pig; a toy spinning top made from an acorn.

Flower vases are old bottles, the clear glass turned pale amethyst with age. Sleigh bells jingle when the front door is opened. As I admire her imagination, Mrs. Pennypincher serves beverages in glasses set in an old graniteware muffin tray.

Accessories of a purely decorative nature reflect the same deft skill at artistic recycling. A framed piece of old sheet music hangs between two ancient skeleton keys on the wall. The frame is from a weathered barn board and the music and keys from a flea market, where they were bought for less than $2. But the effect on the wall is striking. A bleached cow skull, a grain sickle, and a wooden-toothed hand rake make a stunning trio on another wall. A patchwork wall hanging rivets the eye. There are more visually appealing items: a windowsill of bird nests, a candle sconce of pierced tin made from a tin can but looking like a genuine antique, a wire egg basket full of pine cones, a wreath of twisted grapevines, an old store sign (the name coincidentally that of the township in which the house stands), a high shelf trimmed with a piece of decorative gingerbread salvaged from an old house, a wooden rug beater, flour and sugar sacks stuffed with old, cut-up nylon stockings, tied shut with gaily colored ribbon and used as throw pillows. Then there's a farmer's straw hat on a wall nail, and two corn knives, blades crossed, above the fireplace mantle. The mantle itself is a beam rescued from an old barn. The iron seat from a horse-drawn cultivator hangs above a door. Scattered about are silhouettes of farm animals cut from old pine boards and painted. (These sell for about $15 at fancy stores. Fasten the silhouette to a stick pedestal and it becomes "folk art"—very popular and worth another $10.)

The popularity of the country look is propitious for real country people, albeit a bit amusing. Their life-style supplies them with the proper decor automatically and saves them money in a way even the Internal Revenue Service would find impossible to tax. Until I began reading magazines that cater to the well-heeled pursuers of the country look, I did not realize that the baskets of hickory nuts on our kitchen counter were *de rigueur* in decorating. In fact, I'd been growling to my wife about putting them away someplace out of sight. Our woodstove is for keeping us warm in winter, not to create an aura. We use a woodbox—surprise—to hold wood.

Our spice and herb cabinet holds spices and herbs. The cheap pine cupboard that I made years ago with a hammer and a handsaw evolved out of financial desperation, and I got into the habit of apologizing to visitors for the crude workmanship displayed in it. Now the cupboard is right in style, and I shrug off compliments by saying that we "picked it up for a song at a sale." If only I had painted it blue instead of varnishing it. With the paint flaking off as it would be by now, I could probably get a couple hundred bucks for it, especially since the doors have warped so badly.

The horse cultivator sitting in the corner of my office no longer draws quizzical stares from visitors—they figure it is part of the country look. The truth is, I use that thing occasionally and hope someday to have a workhorse so I can use it to do all my cultivating. I keep it in my office because it is very old and I want to protect it as best as possible from the elements. There's a milking stool next to it that I used for a milking stool until I found a better one. The foot scraper outside the door, made from a recycled part of a junked disk cultivator, is used every day. When my wife scolds me for leaving a hoe in the hallway (handy for a quick half-hour in the garden when I need a break from my typewriter), I simply say "decor" for an excuse. We use our flour mill all the time. Unfortunately, it is in the basement where no one can see it.

In the homes of other country people I can find 100 ideas for the country-look decorator: a spinning wheel in use, a loom with a half-made towel in the harnesses, a quilting frame set up, a basket of eggs not yet put in the refrigerator, an old-fashioned cupboard with its pull-out enamelware table extended for rolling out dough, a wood-burning cookstove actually cooking, a big graniteware coffeepot steaming on the stove, if not for coffee or tea water, then to put much needed humidity into the air of the wood-heated winter rooms. Pots and pans hang from the ceiling handy for use, not just for decoration. I've seen a porch with a foot-powered grindstone on it—to sharpen tools with, not for looks. Nearby, a scythe, hoe, and shovel hang on pegs, handy for use. A south kitchen window may be full of herbs in pots—decorative, but also ready to be used. Then there's the flagstone floor found only after six layers of linoleum were removed, and chairs bought for a dollar each at sales, then mended and repainted or varnished into cherished antiques. I know of a kitchen that houses an oak trestle table that was given free to the owners twenty years ago and that has a row of lidded canning jars at the back of a counter, each half filled with a different kind of bean or other seed—very nice, and the cost was negligible.

FINDING YOUR OWN
HOUSEHOLD ACCESSORIES

The trick to recycling Yesterday's Barnyard (or workshop, grocery store, factory, or whatever) into interesting and attractive interior decoration is the ability to recognize the potential of items when you see them. Potential money-saving accessories lie around us all the time, becoming obsolete, going out of style, or for some other reason discarded by society. Last evening, as I exited our old Carnegie Library (a new library is in the planning stages), I happened to notice for the first time the "crash-bar" door latch. I have pushed open that door hundreds of times, and hundreds more times I've opened similar doors on school buildings. The bar on these doors is almost as wide as the door itself and when pushed, activates the latch. Such doors, as you know, are much easier to open than doors with knobs and so are often found on older public buildings. On this particular door, the entire crash bar assembly is made of brass. It would make a beautiful towel rack in the most sumptuous bathroom, once the brass was cleaned and shined. No doubt hundreds of such doors go for salvage when old buildings are torn down or automatic electric-eye doors are put in.

All That Glitters . . .

It is tempting to make a rule that almost anything made of brass (or copper or wrought iron) has potential in home decorating. But beauty is a function of taste, and there are no rules in the bewildering world of human taste. The current popularity of brass, copper, wrought iron, solid wood, and even tin may be a revolt against the overwhelming ubiquitousness of plastic.

Tin was the plastic of an earlier era and everything made of it was, almost by definition, cheap—tin cans, tin trays, tin signs, tin boxes. Now, of course, many of these items are much sought after by collectors and enjoy places of honor as household decoration. The tin Coca-Cola tip trays are now valued from $35 to as much as $2,500 for the scarcer ones. Cigarette tins, especially the "Lucky Strike Green Has Gone to War" ones, are also becoming valuable. How do you tell, *now,* which cheap throwaways will be tomorrow's treasures? Scarcity is only one ingredient. There must also be something unique about the piece: a distinctive label, or some historical or nostalgic significance. Lucky Strike Green has both. The girls painted on the Coca-Cola trays provide the uniqueness. A sure winner for the same kind of canonization in the future are the tin containers of "Bag Balm," still marketed and commonly found on farms. These tins meet the qualifications on all counts. They are square, rather than round. The lid is removable. The label is printed on, not papered. The name, "Bag Balm," is unique, to say the least. The product has been in use for a long time, not just as an ointment for sore cow teats, but also very effective for chapped hands. Finally, the tin is an instant hit with the country-look fashion, since the lid shows a cow's head surrounded by adorable pink clover blossoms. The tin itself is green. The ointment even helps slow down the onslaught of rust.

Even if I turn out to be wrong about Bag Balm containers, that is the kind of thinking and instinct you should develop as an Artful Pennypincher. Rule nothing out, *if it pleases you*. Even linoleum is now being looked upon kindly by interior decorators re-creating the "authentic" Not-So-Early-American look.

Starting Your Search

The most logical place to begin a search is at flea markets and auctions (see Chapter 6). Antique shops are good for ideas and occasionally for a good buy, but once an object has arrived in the antiques market, it has been discovered, so to speak, and the price has already risen higher than the moneysaver may wish to spend.

It is seldom worthwhile, in my experience, to search strange areas beyond one's own locale, although that observation flies in the face of popular wisdom. The farther out into the country you go, the more suspicious country dwellers seem to be, having been harassed before by treasure hunters and bargain beaters. If you show interest in the most insignificant primitive piece in their barns, they immediately attach an inflated value to it. And because you are a stranger, they probably won't sell to you at any price. The day of the naive country hick is gone.

Everything you need to accessorize your house imaginatively and cheaply is invariably available in your own community. My reaping sickle was found in a hollow wall of a house being remodeled and given to me by the owner, who knew my interests. Carpenters, plumbers, roofers, real estate agents, and similar service professionals are your best contacts in this regard. They get inside houses. I know a man who has decorated his recreation room with tin and glassware he collects as a hobby through his business of replacing furnaces. He gets into all kinds of cellars and crawl spaces. As he takes out the old furnace, he asks the homeowner for other pieces of "junk" that look interesting to him. Nine times out of ten, they will give him old bottles or tin signs for free or only a pittance.

And that is the other side of the complex human character. On the one hand, we will hold on to some triviality in the face of more money than it is worth. On the other hand, when we get into the throwing-away mood, strange things happen. In *The Garage Sale Manual* by Jean and Jim Young (Praeger Publishers, New York, 1973), the authors recount a story of a friend who found a Tiffany lamp at the local dump. Miraculously, it was unbroken. So valuable was it that when the friend took it to a dealer, the latter did not believe his story and was able to trace the lamp to its original owner. Robbery was suspected. But the owner insisted that the finder keep it. She *had* thrown that old lamp away, and good riddance.

I can't vouch for that story, but I can vouch for one even stranger. In a large midwestern city, which shall remain unnamed, church authorities made a decision to abandon an old church that had over the years become surrounded by ghettos. Some valuable items were removed, but others unaccountably were left behind. A few people who were aware of the situation were allowed to rescue some things—part of the communion rail ended up as a handsome balustrade of an upper floor balcony in a cathedral-ceilinged home, for example. The sanctuary lamp became a stunning accessory in another private home. But much was simply left to vandals. They smashed beautiful candlesticks and statues. They tore the pipe organ apart and threw parts of it out of the choir loft. They beat a marble baptismal font to pieces with hammers. Dressed in richly brocaded vestments, they played Superman in the streets. Apart from the travesty of culture such scenes evoke, it was a horrible waste. But a few Artful Penny-pinchers, alert to human foible in their own community, were able to benefit before the tragedy occurred.

Cities and villages are much more likely sites for such sensational opportunities than the country. In cities, not just churches but hotels, factories, schools, warehouses, theaters, and old homes are constantly being demolished to make way for the new. As business flees the villages, sadly enough, more and more shops on "Main Street" close up. But often those shops are not as vacant as they appear. Find out who's in charge. If you can get permission to beat the demolition crews, the renovators, or other interested parties to the sites, you can come away with all sorts of things—from fireplaces to irreplaceable hardwood moulding, and sometimes whole roomfuls of treasure other people couldn't be bothered to haul away.

Obviously, you can accomplish such matters best in the territory you are familiar with. It's not only who you know, but what you know. There is a village hardware store I have been sworn to secrecy about that has been going out of business for about twenty years. That is, little new stuff is brought in and little effort made to sell the old. The store still has the original gas lights hanging in it. Not much of real value remains on the shelves, but they are still full of fairly old merchandise of a kind interesting to Yesterday's Barnyard lovers. But you have to know about it.

For the nine years I lived in a suburb being overwhelmed by the outpouring population of Philadelphia, I often walked past a dilapidated shed in the heart of a little village. Inside was a complete nineteenth-century blacksmith shop that looked as if the owner had just stepped out for lunch. It could so easily have been vandalized or the tools stolen that those of us who knew and cared about it kept very quiet. I suppose by now it has gone to a museum or been sold, but for years there was an opportunity available to the enterprising recycler, if not a young blacksmith. But you had to have your roots down in that community to even know about the place, much less to have a chance to bring it out into the light of day.

Another reason for thinking local is that every region has its own unique collectibles of little value elsewhere but of intense local interest. You can have the best of both worlds finding such items cheap or for free and then being the envy of the local interior decorating world. Just a few days ago I got a call from a woman who decorates her beautiful home mostly in Yesterday's Barnyard. She had a tip. The local feed mill had found a whole stack of flour sacks, brand new and never used, that came from the last flour mill in our village. The sacks had the name of the flour mill on them, the name of the village, and the name of the flour—Wyandot Maid. Best of all, in the middle of the lettering was a large picture in full color of what an early 1900s gristmill owner thought an Indian maid should look like. I judge the sacks to be late 1930-ish since the maid looks rather like a Hollywood movie actress of that era with a band and feather in her hair. No matter. Lots of us think she's gorgeous and oh-so-country. The feed mill does not understand the run on their sacks, which they have actually been *using!*

My sack now hangs on my office wall (above a wooden fork) and pleases me not so much because of the country look but because it has historical significance. Our Wyandot County was the last reservation of the Wyandot Indians before they were forced to go to Oklahoma, and for a century thereafter, nearly every other business that opened in town worked "Wyandot" or "Indian" or both into their names or labels. It also proves this town still supplied its own flour when I was a kid, which gives me hope that it might do so again some day. Cost of my newly found wall hanging? Zilch. The people at the feed mill are kind enough to give them away.

In the final analysis, ignore all rules of collecting and put in your home only that which pleases *you*. Fashions come and go. Stuffed and mounted animal heads, considered for a while to be tasteless, are now back in style. Likely as not, what appeals to you will appeal to many other people anyway. Start a trend, don't follow one. I saw an old child's potty-chair the other day with a houseplant in it. Who would ever have thought. . . .

PLANT CONTAINERS

An essential ingredient of Post Modernism in interior decorating is lots of potted plants, especially in the powder room. I recently attended a party in an apartment where one almost needed a machete to find his way to the bathroom. But the junglelike effect, which I would be more inclined to call Post Pliocene, was soothing to the spirit and not without practical advantages. Seated upon the toilet, one was so wreathed in ferns that closing the door seemed almost unnecessary. But what astounded me most was the child's training potty in the corner, which had been turned into a plant container. The plant appeared to be particularly healthy, which made me wonder, mischievously, if a child with more literal common sense than adults might have tried to use the receptacle for what it was originally intended.

Apart from that, the apartment's verdancy was magnificent and often arose from humble but imaginative ideas. For one thing, an old step ladder had been cleaned, stripped and repainted a white enamel, transforming it into a stunning plant ladder. A plant too large and ungainly to move easily by lifting was ensconced in an old barbecue kettle—the kind that is on wheels. The plant could be moved handily out onto the balcony in summer. The barbecue kettle, legs and all, had been completely redone in shiny black lacquer, and the inside bottom, where it was in danger of rusting through, had been lined with several layers of aluminum foil before the dirt was put in.

With chrome being a favorite accent in both Art Deco revival and Post Modernism, I will not be at all surprised to one day see an inside window box contrived from one of those voluptuously curved, late-1940s automobile bumpers. Early examples of the more expensive plastics such as the Lucite furniture and accessories of the 1950s are being dragged out of attics either for their original use or as containers of one kind or another, plants included. (Remember that if you grow a plant in a container without drainage holes, you must water very sparingly. Excessively wet soil will kill most houseplants as quickly as no water at all.)

Another free-for-the-finding plant container that goes well with modern or traditional decor is a piece of driftwood or a rock with a naturally formed cavity in it. Even without convenient cavities large enough for a flowerpot, driftwood lends itself exceedingly well to many dried flower arrangements—an art that has no rules to success except your own imagination.

WOODBOXES AND WOOD RACKS

Many metal containers make handy and handsome woodboxes by the hearth. Copper and brass kettles or buckets are the most popular but are expensive. Sometimes you can buy a beat-up one with a hole or two in it for much less than the going price (anywhere from $50 to $150 or more). Holes or even a missing handle are somewhat inconsequential for holding wood. You can put a piece of cardboard in the bottom to keep wood dirt from dribbling out on the floor. The wood will hide the cardboard.

When you're looking for old buckets, remember that tarnished brass has a dull grey brown patina, while old copper gives itself away every time with a greenish cast. When in doubt about brass, shave into it with a pocketknife. Brass is soft enough to cut a bit, and the undersurface will shine bright yellow. Save anything made of brass or copper. Even as junk it is of value. To clean the metals, use a recommended polisher, or try a mixture of lemon juice and salt. Some people lacquer the surface to keep it bright. A good job of lacquering, however, is difficult even for professionals, and you might find a periodic polishing to be more to your satisfaction. Or let the piece tarnish. A brightly glittering wood holder can be a distraction.

The copper boilers used of old on wash days are fairly easy to find and are cheaper than the buckets. They also make interesting wood holders. Metal bushel baskets are appropriate, too, and quite common. You can buy them new, in fact, for around $10 at farm supply stores and from mail-order farm suppliers, even though they are obsolete except on the smallest farms. Only a few old dedicated fools like me handle corn in bushel baskets anymore.

A wooden wheelbarrow, old or new, makes an attractive wood holder and is also a handy way to get wood into the house. Just make sure the wheel is clean before you run it over the rug. As a wood holder, your barrow serves you the whole year and is kept out of the weather in winter.

Various metal log racks on the market, especially the circular ones, can be duplicated cheaply with interesting pieces of Yesterday's

Barnyard. You need to know how to weld or know someone who does. A rack made of two wheels of a junked side-delivery hay rake will make a stunning conversation stopper. Cut half or more of the spokes out, and use what you need of them for the stand. Space the wheels about a foot apart at the bottom, weld together at the top as in the illustration here, and weld on the stand using spokes cut out of the wheels.

If your fireplace or woodstove is in a nice, large room, you may want to consider an old milk-can cart from Yesterday's Barnyard (still considered junk but not for long) for an unusual but useful wood rack. The wood is ranked on the low cart bed and the tall wheels act as side braces.

Of course, the logical container to use for a woodbox is a woodbox. There are old ones spending their declining years on country porches where they serve as repositories for work shoes and boots, or potatoes and onions, or trash. Others, especially ones with hinged lids, now reside in old barns where they were used to store grain concentrates for chickens or livestock and now stand empty or full of scrap wire.

You can easily build one that looks old by using weathered boards. Pine is the traditional wood to use, but if you have to use new wood, you might consider cedar, which is darker and rougher and so looks old. Weathered barn siding is excellent for woodboxes. Cut the corners at 45-degree bevels to hide fresh-cut edges. A post at each inside corner then provides support to nail to.

Where fresh-cut edges can't be hidden, you can darken them if you like. Fresh-cut edges of old pine won't stand out so clearly if covered with walnut stain. Rub on some finely powdered wood ashes first to make the color greyer. If the old boards you use have traces of the original paint, this makes them all the more desirable among collectors. You can mimic faded paint by dabbing on glazes used in antiquing and then wiping them off quickly so that only a little paint remains in the seams of the grain. Some of the new colored penetrating stains work fine for this, too. You can't quite duplicate the genuine

thing, however, but the result might please you more than no color at all. Whatever you do, always experiment on scrap wood first.

To add the finishing touch to your "old" woodbox, use old nails. Straighten a crooked nail by laying it on a hard flat surface, with the bend toward you, and tapping it with a hammer. The nails don't have to be perfectly straight if you are using pine, cedar, or other softwood. But if you are using old oak, even new nails will often bend when you try to drive them in. Wetting the nail with saliva sometimes helps, though liquid soap is better. Often when using old hardwood, you will first have to drill a hole three-fourths the length of the nail. The diameter of the hole should be slightly smaller than that of the nail.

Whenever I reuse nails, I'm reminded of the story told about a man in our town who has long since passed away. When he hit a nail with a glancing blow, sending it flying into the air, he was so frugal that he would stop work and hunt for the nail until he found it. The man's name was Harrison Smith. He became rich and donated the land for our city park. His frugality gained him something greater than wealth—local immortality.

Wooden containers meant for other duty make interesting woodboxes. Traditionally, farmers have always fed grain to pigs in what they call self-feeders. These were (before metal took over) wooden bins with slanted sides that opened into troughs at the bottom. The bin was filled from above and as the pigs ate, the grain fell down into

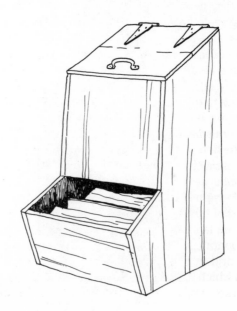

the troughs. Refilling was an occasional job instead of a daily chore. Most of these feeders are too large to bring inside your house. But occasionally, where a farmer was feeding only a few pigs, he'd make a small feeder maybe 3 feet wide and 4 feet high. These make darling woodboxes, especially the kind that fit against a wall. No one has started collecting hog feeders yet, so keep your eyes open and your lips sealed. One that has seen good use will take a heap of cleaning around the bottom, but if it has pleasing proportions, there's a jewel lying under that mud and manure. And if you don't burn wood, the bin will make an excellent children's toy box. Loose marbles, dice, and other small objects will come out into the trough instead of getting lost down in the depths of the box. Come to think of it, *any* woodbox would make a fairly good toy box, or a back porch receptacle for boots and shoes, or a potato and onion bin. And so the world turns.

LIGHT FIXTURES

You can make lamp bases out of anything—and some people do. The tastefulness of all these creations is a matter of doubt, but beauty remains irrevocably in the eye of the beholder. At least pottery lamp bases seem appropriate for any occasion, and for interior decorators of the country-look school, they're most appropriate if made from old (or new) crockery, especially crock jugs. Turning such a jug into a lamp is quite easy now that you can buy lamp socket kits at department stores. (Angelo Brothers Company, 10981 Decatur Rd., Philadelphia, PA 19154 is a source if you can't find them locally.) The kit consists of socket assembly, the "harp" that protects the bulb and to which the shade attaches, and a threaded nipple at the base of the socket. Normally, either the nipple is turned into threads in the lamp base or is bolted to the base. But the easiest way to convert jugs is to use a cork that fits very snugly in the jug mouth. Bore a hole into the center of the cork smaller than the nipple, and jam the nipple or turn it tightly into the hole, then stick the cork into the jug. If you want to be *really* country, use a corncob instead of a cork. When I was a child, the crock jugs of water we brought to the field were always stoppered with corncobs (and wrapped in a wet burlap sack to keep the water cool for a longer period of time).

To finish the lamp, you can drill a hole into the side of the jug close to the bottom for the electric cord. (You'll need a tungsten carbide bit to drill the hole.) Most decorators find it easier to use a lamp socket in which the electric cord exits at the side rather than the base of the socket. The cord then runs down the outside of the lamp base but is generally not very noticeable if kept to the back side of the lamp.

Crock jugs linger in nearly every cellar that's more than 75 years old and sell cheap (usually) at auctions because they are not rare yet. Corncobs are free. And with the addition of a socket, a light bulb, and a shade, you're in business.

Glass bottle lamp bases are also very popular. Any old bottle with an interesting color or shape, or historical significance, will do. Short, squat bottles are more stable than tall skinny ones because they have broader bases. Try filling the bottle with nuts or colorful seeds—I've seen beans, corn, and even alfalfa seed used effectively. The seeds are quite attractive, especially in clear glass bottles, and add weight and stability to the lamp base.

In glass bottle lamps, as in jug lamps, the socket nipple is inserted in a cork as previously described. Use a socket with a side exit for the cord to avoid having to make a hole in the base. Drilling a hole in glass requires either a diamond bit, with turpentine used as a lubricant, or a tungsten carbide drill.

A Tin Candle Sconce

A folk art tin candle sconce is easy to make and hard to tell from an antique one. You need a tin snips and a flat piece of old tin. The underside of an old piece of standing-seam barn roofing has just about the perfect reflective patina—not too shiny, not too dull. Early sconces were cut out in hundreds of designs, often not very well proportioned. The illustrations here show a few samples copied from very old sconces.

Folk art objects are often more spontaneous creations than technically skillful ones, and where artistic skill is present, the spontaneity gives a delightful result. Thus a sconce in folk art tradition avoids the more difficult and technically proper ways of working tin, such as hemming the edges on curved shapes and soldering. Often soldering is avoided for the simple reason that solder wasn't available in earlier times. So one is free to improvise.

Your sconce shield might easily be cut in the shape of an owl. The edges will be rough (burred) and very sharp after cutting. Be sure to file off the burred edges or hammer them blunt. Then crimp the edges for strength and decoration. This is easily done with pliers— needle-nose pliers work best. Just grip the tin in the jaws of the pliers and roll the jaws sideways. With a little practice, you will be able to do several different designs by varying the amount of crimp you put in the tin. (A good description of how to hem edges and solder joints in tin work can be found in *Make It! Don't Buy It* from Rodale Press.)

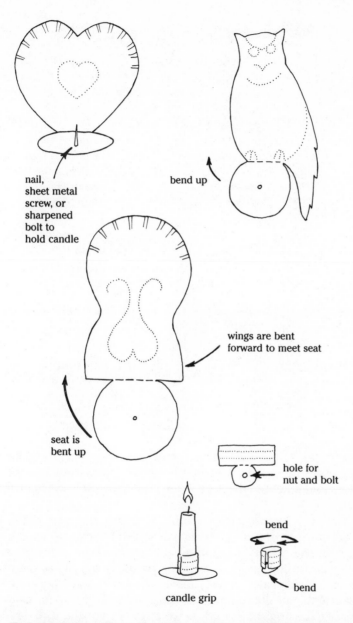

nail,
sheet metal
screw, or
sharpened
bolt to
hold candle

bend up

wings are bent
forward to meet seat

seat is
bent up

hole for
nut and bolt

bend

bend

candle grip

To hold the candle to the base, you do not have to solder on a socket holder, although that is the proper way. Here are several alternatives: Drive a nail up through the base and seat the candle on it; melt a little wax on the base and set the candle in it; or drive a screw through a hole made by a smaller nail and turn the candle down on

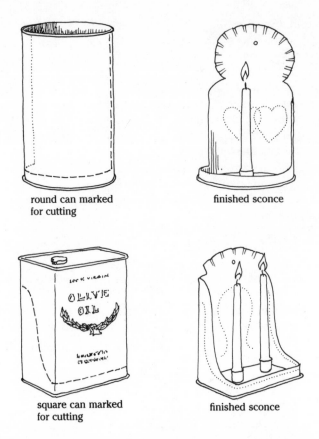

round can marked
for cutting

finished sconce

square can marked
for cutting

finished sconce

the screw for a tighter fit. Or run a small bolt through the hole, having first ground the end of the bolt to a fine point. Screw a nut down on the bolt to hold it tight to the base. Then push the candle down over the point.

Now you have a sconce without soldering. The last part of the project is the most fun—piercing a design in the tin with an awl or a supply of sharp nails. Lay the tin out flat on a hard piece of wood. Draw your design on it. Then, following the design lines, put holes with hammer and awl (or nail) about ⅛ to ¼ inch apart. If you wish to remain authentically country, use hearts for your design; or be a free spirit like the original folk artists were, and make your own designs.

A sconce made from a tin can is another easy accomplishment. A 2-quart or larger can works better than small ones unless you are using only a small candle. With a tin snips, cut away most of the can except the back (which will be the sconce) down to about 1 inch from the bottom. (See drawing on previous page.) You won't be able to cut precisely to the line around the base, but must approach it gradually. First cut down from the top to the base line on both sides. Then cut down through the waste, curving toward the corners until you have cleared enough waste to give the tin snips enough room to complete the horizontal base cut. Cut the back of the sconce to whatever outer shape pleases you, pierce the tin in the design of your choice, make a holder for the candle as described above, crimp the edge of the sconce, and you are finished.

Imagination can engender light fixtures out of wildly unrelated objects. A current favorite uses old musical horns like that bugle your granduncle once thought he wanted to play and that has ever since been gathering dust in the family attic. Set the instrument on a coffee table or mantel, horn end down and, after removing the mouthpiece, put a candle in the top and you will have achieved a surprisingly artful candlestick.

A lover of old brass found, of all things, some old plumbing traps—like those found under the sink—made of the metal. He thought long and hard about what to do with them. Inspiration finally came. Attaching the straight end to a block of wood and the wood to the wall, he created a candlestick that became the envy of all the country chic lovers in the neighborhood. Or do you call that plumber's chic?

WALL COVERINGS

The cheapest way to decorate a painted drywall or plaster wall is to stencil it, an old art form now again in fashion. Stenciling preceded wallpaper and continued as a substitute and imitation for wallpaper where the latter was too expensive except for the wealthy. Now we have come full circle. You can buy wallpapers today that imitate stenciling.

Essentially, wall stenciling involves painting a repeated pattern on the wall, using a stencil for a design rather than painting freehand. The stencil or stencils used can be cut out of cardboard, tin, leather, varnished paper, or plastic. The preferred material is architect's linen, available from art supply stores. Use a stencil knife, razor blade, or other sharp, thin-bladed knife to cut the patterns out. To get ideas for the designs, study stenciled walls depicted in home furnishing magazines, or look for books on stenciling. In addition, you need a stubby-bristled stencil brush to paint through the stencil, or strips of velour to dab the paint through with your finger. Be sure you leave plenty of margin around the stencil pattern to avoid getting paint on the wall where you don't want it.

In most cases, the stencil pattern is painted only around the wall borders. You can space the repeated pattern or patterns equidistantly from each other by eye. If, however, you intend to cover all the wall, or most of it, you may first need to mark cross-hatch lines on the wall to locate equidistant horizontal and vertical planes so you can maintain the proper distances between the patterns. Use a level or a simple plumb line and square to section off the wall.

Plaster takes stenciling the best. Drywall should first be painted, preferably with an oil-based paint. As for the paint to actually stencil with, the original stencilers used milk paint. You can buy it from Country Way (206 Summit Place Drive, Dunwoody, GA 30338). If you have your own cow, you can make milk paint without too much trouble. Recipes vary, but practitioners have found this one satisfactory: Mix 5 parts raw skimmed milk to 1 part lime, and add 3 parts water along with enough powdered dry color dye to obtain the color desired.

Most modern stencilers prefer to use quick-drying lacquers rather than milk paint. There's less fuss and much less chance of smudging the wall as you move the stencil. If a pattern calls for two or three different colors and forms, you must wait for the first to dry before applying the second.

Stenciling can be a stunning way to decorate furniture and toleware, too. Stenciled Hitchcock chairs are very valuable—but there's no reason you can't do your own.

Fabric Hangings

Much has been written about quilts (perhaps too much), but the interest in them appears to be insatiable. Patchwork quilts have indeed become the most profitable way ever invented to recycle scrap. As they increase in price, quilts are more often displayed on walls today than on beds, which has led to a trend in fabric wall hangings.

As a wall decoration, a quilt need not be large enough for a bed, nor does it necessarily have to be a true quilt. It can be as small as a framed picture, or consist of only the upper layer of a quilt pieced together but not yet quilted to a lining and backing. It can even be a top waiting to be quilted. A couple of small quilts might enhance a wall better than a full-size one. And these small quilts would still be usable for a baby bed, or to drape over the back of a sofa, a practice as stylish at the moment as it was in Victorian times. If you want to cover all or most of the wall, the quilt top is lighter to hang and certainly cheaper to make than a completed quilt, while achieving nearly the same effect.

Making a Crazy Quilt

You can make a crazy quilt or a patchwork quilt almost entirely of recycled materials without using a quilt frame or quilting. The pieces come from old clothing that has been washed, of course, with buttons, seams, and badly worn areas removed. Try to use as many different kinds of fabric as you have available, even velvet and silk scraps, just like the Victorians did. Rather than being sewn to each other, the pieces are sewn onto a backing. Use an old sheet for backing by cutting it into 12-inch squares. Place the pieces on a square of backing and shift them around until you have worked out a design (or lack thereof) that pleases you. This is the creative part of the work. Pieces should overlap ½ inch all around. Once arranged, take one piece at a time from its position and transfer it to the same position on another square, so you don't get the pieces mixed up. Start at one corner. Stitch around the piece with the sewing machine. Do not turn the

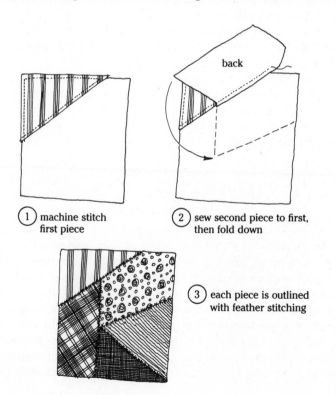

back

1 machine stitch first piece

2 sew second piece to first, then fold down

3 each piece is outlined with feather stitching

edges of this first piece under. Lay the second piece face down on top of the first piece and machine-sew the edge where they overlap, as in the illustration. When you turn the second piece right side up in its proper position, you turn under the unfinished edge where the two pieces join.

Continue sewing on all the pieces in the same manner. Curved pieces and oddly angled pieces may have to be turned under by hand and blind-stitched, as in applique work. When the squares are all finished, embroider around the edges of the patches. (A feather stitch makes a nice bold outline.) Next, sew squares into a strip the length of the quilt, following the same procedure as when sewing the patches together. Next embroider these seams the same way as the patch borders. Sew the strips together just as you sewed the squares, and embroider these seams. The quilt top is finished.

For backing you can use old drapes sewn together or a colored sheet—whatever you have. Lay the quilt top on the floor, right side up, and lay the backing on top of it, back side up. Pin, baste, and machine-sew three sides as if you were making a giant sack. Then turn it right side out, effectively hiding the sewn edges. Now turn under the fourth edge and blind stitch by hand.

The backing is tied rather than quilted to the front. Tying is much faster, though the finished quilt will not be valued as highly by collectors. To tie, lay the quilt out on the floor again, right side up, and with a piece of chalk and a yardstick, mark dots at 4-inch intervals. Thread a crochet needle with crochet cotton. Work with a double strand of yarn. Poke your needle through at the first dot and come back up right next to it (about ¼ inch away). Then proceed on to the second dot, do the same, and proceed on until you run out of yarn. Cut the double strand halfway between each dot, tie a knot at each dot, and trim the ends uniformly, about ½ inch long. Continue until the quilt is finished. On your wall or on your bed, it will give you much satisfaction.

Making a Padded Quilt

To make a padded quilt that's nearly as light and warm as a down comforter, quilters have learned to use worn-out panty hose for cheap padding. The easiest way to do this is to use a design that calls for 4-inch squares. Cut the squares from your scrap fabric. Sew two of them together on three sides to make a little sack, leaving about a ⅝-inch seam allowance. Be sure to sew the squares together inside out. Clip the corners off (but not through the stitching, of course) and turn the little sack right side out. Take one pair of panty hose, cut off the elastic waistband (save that for plant ties if you are a gardener), and stuff it evenly into the little sack. Then sew the fourth side shut using a small overcast stitch. Repeat that procedure until you have as many little 4-inch "pillows" as you need to make the comforter. Sew the "pillows" into pairs. Then sew the pairs to other pairs to make blocks of four. Then sew the blocks of four to other blocks of four, and so on until the comforter is complete. Sewing the blocks together this way is better, say quilters, than the normal way of sewing them into strips and then strips to strips. That customary way allows the nylon padding to stretch out of shape too much. The comforter can be made reversible or a backing can be added. (Panty hose also makes excellent stuffing for homemade pillows. See page 83.)

Another hint: Conventional fabric scraps and remnants are not the only raw material for quilts. A quilter in Idaho made two quilts decorated with emblems from farm caps, sewed to squares from old jeans.

A Quilt Display Frame

A homeowner near Sunbury, Ohio, showed me the clever frame her son made for displaying quilts on walls without taking up the whole wall. Essentially, the quilt is wrapped on two rollers that are inserted into a wooden frame. The frame is slightly wider than the width of the quilt and just long enough so that the viewer can see about 2 feet of the quilt at a time. By turning either of the rollers, another section of quilt is rolled into view. It's neat and not difficult to make. All you need is a box frame large enough to accommodate the quilt and about 6 inches deep. Holes in the sides of the frame accept the roller axles. Pins keep them from sliding out of the holes. Knobs to turn the rollers are glued on.

The rollers themselves can be rounded down from any wood stock on a lathe, or they can be two short lengths of 2×4 glued together and then hand-formed with a drawknife. Your work doesn't have to be perfect, since the quilt hides the rollers from view. In tacking the quilt edge to the roller, it's best to put a strip of tougher cloth under and over the tacked area as a precaution against tearing the quilt, in case it should ever be unrolled too far.

FLOOR COVERINGS FROM SCRAPS

You can weave, braid, or crochet beautiful rugs using rags, and the only cost is your time. Or you can piece together carpet scraps to make stunning accent rugs. And if you have saved a supply of scrap felt, appliqued felt rugs are almost too pretty to put on a floor.

A Knotted Shag Rug

Knotted shag rugs from rags are not as well known as other rag rugs but are of particular interest to the moneysaver because they are made by recycling very small pieces of cloth. In this version of rug-making, you start with what has to be the simplest loom ever invented—nothing more than two pieces of board and nails that hold two strings tight. You knot small pieces of scrap cloth on the strings to form a shag strand that is then coiled and stitched together, as in making a braided rug.

To make the loom, saw a 16-inch length from a 1 × 6 and saw another piece 4 inches long. Nail the small piece to the larger one as shown in the illustration, positioning the small piece about 5 inches from one end of the larger piece. Drive two 10d finishing nails midway between the 4-inch board and the end of the flat board. On top of the 4-inch board, drive two pairs of small finishing nails partway into the wood, each pair in line with one of the larger nails on the flat board below. The paired nails should be about 1 inch from each other. At the end of the flat board opposite the large nails, drive one 10d nail, centered. The two large nails will hold spools of thread. The two pairs of smaller nails are tighteners to hold the string or thread taut. The bottom nail is the anchor.

To string your "loom," set the spools in place on the large nails, pull enough string off each to reach the bottom anchor nail, and wrap each around its respective pair of nail tighteners in figure-eight fashion. Pull the strings taut and tie them to the bottom nail. Now you are ready to tie on or weave the short pieces of scrap rags to make a strand.

Cut the rag strips to uniform lengths. For a 1-inch-thick rug, the strips should be ½ inch wide and 2½ inches long.

Knot each strip on the loom strings. To do so, hold a strip between the thumb and forefinger of each hand above the two tight strings. Bring the ends down around the strings and then back up between the strings on the lower side (the side nearest the anchor nail). Pull tight and slide the piece down to the anchor nail (see drawing). Repeat with more scraps until the string is as full up to the upright as you can get it. Then loosen the strings from the tighteners, lift the knotted strand off the anchor nail, pull another appropriate length of string from the spools, hitch them to the tighteners, pull the

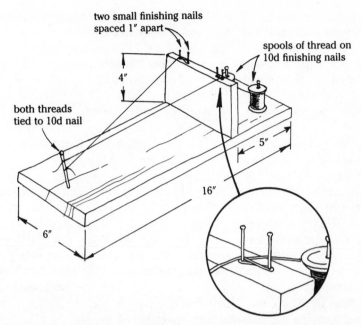

two small finishing nails
spaced 1″ apart

spools of thread on
10d finishing nails

4″

both threads
tied to 10d nail

5″

16″

6″

strand tight, and replace it on the anchor nail behind one of the last knots tied. Then continue tying on the scrap pieces as before.

When your knotted strip is a few feet long, you should begin coiling it into a rug so it doesn't get all tangled up. Coil it the same way you would a braided rug—either round or oval. To determine the size of an oval rug, subtract the desired finished width from the desired finished length to give you the right length of the starting center strip. Thus an oval rug 30 inches wide by 48 inches long should have a center strip 18 inches long. Whipstitch the coils together, using double carpet thread or similarly strong string.

A Woven Hoop Rug

Woven rugs are as easy to make as potholders. A woven hoop rug, or wagon wheel rug, can be startlingly beautiful. The name, wagon wheel rug, came about because often the "loom" upon which the rug was made was a wagon wheel rim. There is no reason why the same rims can't be employed today. Hardly a farm auction goes by that such wheels are not sold, on or off the wagon. Many of the wheels have deteriorating wooden parts and sell cheaply. Barrel hoops have been used as hoop looms, too, and even plastic Hula-Hoops have been recruited to do the job! If you can get someone to attach legs to your hoop, all the better. Otherwise you have to prop the hoop up with chairs, or whatever, to a comfortable work height.

With the hoop ready, the first step is to tie on the "spokes." Tie four rag strips across the hoop dividing the area roughly into eight equal parts. Leave about 4 inches of each strip sticking out beyond the knot on the hoop. Since it is necessary to have an uneven number of spokes to complete the weaving properly, a ninth strip must be added. Tie or sew it to the center of the other strips and then out to the rim. (The spokes are actually warp strips, which are stationary. You weave the weft strips over and under the warp strips.)

Start weaving in the weft strips at the center, under one warp strip and over the next. After weaving a few rounds, the space between the warp strips gets too wide for tight weaving and you have to add more warps. Tie the new warp to the rim of the hoop, then take it back and loop it under the last weft strip, then back out to the rim again. You might need to add more than one warp at a time. Continue weaving until the space between the warps again becomes too wide. Add more warp strips. When the outer limits of the hoop are reached, untie the rug from the hoop, machine-stitch the outside edge to hold the last line of weaving in place and trim the fringe off evenly.

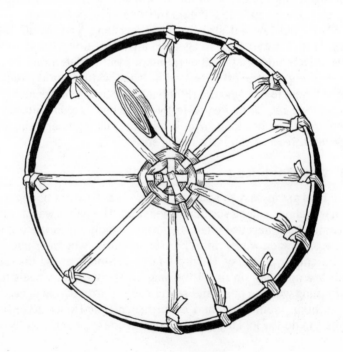

A square frame works as well as a hoop (better really, but the results are not always so eye-catching), and the rug is made in squares by simply weaving under and over, as in a potholder. The squares are later joined to make a larger rug. You can easily nail together a box frame for a small rug, or use any wooden box. Drive 7- or 8-penny nails partway into the edge, ½ inch apart, along two opposite edges of your wooden frame or box. This spacing works well when you're using heavy cotton string for warp, but when using a wide strip of fabric, loop it around two nails and then skip a nail between each looping. Cut your weaving strips about 6 inches longer than the frame so you have about 3 inches on each side for fringe. Or you can use long rag strips to go back and forth continuously to produce a closed edge instead of fringe.

When using fabric strips as weft, roll the edges inward to enclose them. (In addition, the rolled weft makes an exceedingly long-wearing carpet.) Machine-stitch across the ends to hold the weavings in place. When string is used as warp, the loops are usually cut through when the rug is finished, knotted to hold the weavings in place, then trimmed evenly to make fringe.

A Carpet Scrap Rug

Moneysavers find artful ways of using up all those scraps left over from years of installing carpeting. They cut out designs in various colors and textures, much like making a patchwork quilt, only using bigger sizes of various geometric or random patterns. These are then glued (with latex adhesives) to canvas, jute, burlap, or any heavy fabric backing, or can be held together with carpet tape (available from carpet shops). A worn-out rug can be turned over and used for backing or the unworn parts cut up for use in a new rug. Some folks turn over small old rugs and *paint* a design on the backing. This requires latex paint. It works only with uncoated backings, not latex-covered backings. Such upside-down rugs serve well as entry mats.

To cut carpet, draw the design on the back with crayon, then cut with a mat knife, razor blade, or other sharp knife. Cut just through the backing, then pull apart.

Carpet scraps can be glued with mastic right to a floor. If you don't have enough of your own scraps, you can buy them at considerable savings over a whole rug. Square pieces are higher-priced than randomly shaped ones. If you know a carpet layer, you should be able to get all the scraps you want for next to nothing, at least until the rest of the neighborhood learns how easy it is to make rugs with them.

Appliqued Felt Rugs

Felt scraps are difficult to find in quantities large enough for a practical-size rug. Therefore, there are more small felt rugs hanging on walls than being used as rugs, even though they can be exceedingly durable. Adaptations of the traditional button rug are the most practical use of felt scraps because only small pieces of felt are needed.

For a felt button rug, felt scraps are cut into circles of various sizes (although other geometric shapes could be used as well), then sewn to a heavy wool or felt backing—any piece of heavy fabric might do. The circles or other geometric shapes are usually stacked two, three, or more layers thick, each shape slightly smaller than the one below it and all in widely different colors. Often the circles are notched into flower blossom shapes for an even gaudier display. The stacks of circles, flowers, or other shapes are spaced in rows or randomly sewn on the backing.

Several different stitches might be employed to attach the stacks of felt pieces, depending on how tightly you wish to sew the stacks down—tighter for a rug than for a wall hanging. Some sewers use a French knot—three strands of embroidery floss tied into a knot—on top of each stack and also tied behind the backing. One such knot in the center might suffice for a wall hanging, but something like an overcast stitch around the outside of each felt piece will be needed to hold it firmly enough for a rug. Or you could use a buttonhole stitch around the border of each piece. It's very slow work but makes a very durable rug.

Cutting the circles or flowers is also time-consuming. Steel dies that are used to cut holes in leather will cut felt circles but do not come in a variety of sizes necessary for a button rug. What you need is a pneumatic press for cutting gaskets, but alas, they aren't available to most of us. You'll have to settle for cutting two or three circles at a time with a scissors. To cut flower shapes, divide the circles by eye in halves and then in halves again. Then cut out notches. Perfect symmetry is neither necessary nor desirable.

If you have a button collection, a unique way to display it is to sew the buttons onto a felt button rug to make a wall hanging. That way you also display an authentic button rug (which really did have buttons sewn on).

CHAIRS AND TABLES

The famous woodworker Wharton Esherick was a master recycler who could not only find a use for everything, but make a work of art out of it to boot. (His home is now a museum—Box 595, Paoli, PA 19301, phone (215) 644-5822—open on weekends and well worth visiting.) Needing a curved handrail for his hand-carved spiral staircase, he found that sections cut from the forked tongues of pony carts were just perfect, except for one unusual turn. After hunting a long time without success for a piece of naturally curved wood that would be just right for the railing, he used a mastodon tusk a friend brought him from Alaska.

Faced with some curved logs most carpenters would have deemed fit only for firewood, Esherick split them down the middle

and used them for roof rafters on his workshop, curve out on one side, curve in on the other. The result was not a queer, lopsided building as might be expected, but a strangely proportional yet asymmetrical structure that seems so alive one expects it to move at any instant. But his most famous work using scrap materials was the chairs he built in 1924 for a theatrical group short on money, as most theatrical groups are. He built the chairs out of two barrels' worth of reject hammer handles he'd gotten for free. You can see a couple of them in his museum-home today.

Esherick is the artful pennypincher's patron saint, especially in today's climate of economizing creativity. As he's shown, tables and chairs don't *have* to be simply tables and chairs as we know them. A chair is something to sit on and a table's only real requirement is to be a more or less level surface upon which to set things. You can be thinking in terms of an end table, card table, butcher block table, game table, tea caddy, side bar, kitchen island, coffee table, lamp table, dinner table—whatever does the job in a pleasing manner. The most interesting (and cheapest) butcher block I've seen lately is a huge chunk of sycamore log stump set up on legs.

When it comes to dining room tables, most people will choose a rather formal one. But for the many other smaller tables to be found inside a house, the roof's the limit. Flat-topped trunks make capable coffee tables with the added advantage of all that storage room inside. They also make good bedside tables, doubling as blanket chests. Most old trunks from the attic need cleaning and replacement of lost hardware. Replacement hardware is available in great variety now that trunks have become popular furnishings. One source is Charlette Ford Trunks (Box 536, Spearman, TX 79081). In cleaning, repainting, or refinishing a trunk, it's best to remove the hardware and clean it separately.

Obsolete furnace registers salvaged from old houses are now in demand for casual table tops. These metal grates are taken to a welder or blacksmith who fashions legs for them. Or another register (or two) is cut into graceful arches and then welded to the table top as legs. The latter method costs little, since only cutting and welding are involved, instead of original ironwork.

For a real conversation piece in the dining area, be on the lookout for restaurant booths, especially the Art Deco inlaid-wood booths

from early diners. They can sometimes be had for the hauling and make a very cozy breakfast nook.

Cable Spool Tables

Wooden cable spools discarded by telephone and electric utility workers can quickly and easily be made into end tables, occasional tables, card tables, lamp tables—whatever. Don't be put off by the crude, rough exterior of the wood. *Any* wood sands and finishes to a decent surface or can be painted. Put a lamp on top and use the bottom as a circular bookshelf, and you have a nice reading table. Enterprising souls have arranged spools on lazy Susan bases, resulting in revolving book shelves. Large spools are the right size for tea for two or a card game. For the latter, you might wish to cover the wood with something like Naugahyde. Pull it down over the outside edges and secure with thumbtacks underneath. If the bottom of the spool keeps chairs from sliding up close enough to the table, trim the edge back a few inches with a saber saw.

Once you start working with cable spools, more ideas will occur to you. They make great rocking chairs. Cut out enough core boards to make a seat at a comfortable height, then replace the boards, one crosswise and the other lengthwise, as the seat bottom. You need a piece of plywood, screwed to the sides of the spool, for the back. Nail

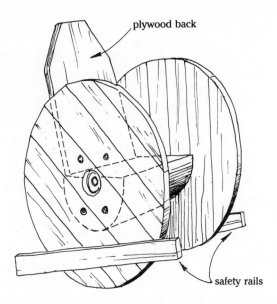

plywood back

safety rails

a board at the bottom on each side extending beyond the spool edges just enough so the rocker can't tip too far forward or backward. Minus the seat bottom and back, the rocker can become a very adequate baby cradle. Small spools can be made into footstools, with or without a padded top.

Slab Wood Tables

Slab wood coffee tables are not as easy to make as they look, but they're practically free if you cut wood for fuel. Slabs may be cross sections of trunk, or longitudinal or diagonal slices of a log. For the longitudinal cuts (with the grain) you need the special ripping chain normally used with chain saw mills. This chain is usually available through chain saw dealers, or you can have your standard blade reshaped to a ripping blade.

Crosscut slices of log will almost always crack through the outer edges no matter how carefully you dry the wood. These cracks are not necessarily a disadvantage in a slab wood table—they add to the natural beauty. Folklore says you can avoid cracking by using slabs from a log that has been dead so long that fungus is growing on it, indicating complete curing and the beginning of rot. That hasn't always been true in my experience, plus the rotted edges have to be cleaned away. Slabs can be treated with PEG-1000 (polyethylene glycol) to resist checking and cracking, but the process is expensive and not necessarily effective in large slab wood slices.

Longitudinal slab cuts involve less radial cracking and result in only minimal checking if the log is already partly dry at the cutting or if it's dried slowly afterward. Let the slab dry a year or two in a barn or unheated garage, then bring it indoors for a few months to dry out to room temperature before working on it. It should be about 3 inches thick, or to your preference. The top of the table should always be the side of the slab that faced the center of the tree, because with that side up, the edge of the slab slants inward, visually diminishing the thickness of the slab. It also hides the roughness of the surface. To sand the end grain smooth, use a belt sander and start with very coarse sandpaper. Even after the surface is smooth, staining might raise the grain again, requiring more sanding and more staining. Finish with wax or whatever you prefer.

Many people buy lathe-turned legs to set their slabs on, but I think this is an expensive mistake. Such legs clash with the natural form and spirit of the slab. Why not continue with your chain saw art? Cut out thick branch sections in imaginative forms for legs, perhaps from the very tree the slab came from. These legs should be more bulky than manufactured legs to maintain proportion with the slab top. You can do some rather artful things with forked branches, or even a single small trunk section from an elm, ironwood, or other tree that tends to flare out at the bottom.

You need nothing elaborate to connect your slab to legs if the legs sit solidly under the slab as they should. Drill ½- to 1-inch holes in the underside of the slab and in the top of the legs and carve some dowels to fit tightly in the holes. Glue will not be necessary. If the legs and slab are not quite dry and the dowel wood is completely dry, the legs and slab should shrink around the dowels enough to keep the joints tight. You can knock the pieces apart later if you need to move the table. You might need more than one dowel per leg for good stability, especially if you try an unusual design relying on only one or two legs. Be creative in your design—twenty years from now, you might see the very same thing in Macy's.

MOUNTINGS AND FRAMINGS

A good way to recycle scrap wood is by making picture frames and shadow boxes. Only small pieces are needed, and variations in form and design are practically endless. To frame a picture or other object, you don't necessarily need a mitre box to cut 45-degree corners. You might use a square or rectangular board covered with fabric scraps as a "frame." You can even get by quite handsomely sometimes with cardboard and tape.

But if you are going to make standard picture frames, a word of caution: Craft books often dismiss the actual cutting of the 45-degree angles without much comment. Some give the impression that the cheapest wood mitre box is adequate for the do-it-yourselfer. Not so. Cheap mitre boxes result in corners that do not fit exactly, and on picture frames, corners that do not fit exactly stand out dreadfully. Invest in a mitre box that at least has saw guides that fasten to the saw blade to help you make a straighter cut. Simple notches in a wooden box and the hopeful steadiness of your hand are not enough. Remember, if you are off only $\frac{1}{32}$ inch, it will show. If both cuts at a joint are off that much, the total is $\frac{1}{16}$ inch, which on a frame will look as wide as the Grand Canyon.

Beginning framers with a table saw at their disposal think their troubles are over. They assume that all they have to do is set the saw guide at 45 degrees, hold the frame moulding against it, and zip it through the blade. Not necessarily. If you think you can work this way, there are two things you have to watch for. First, the moulding is very liable to slip a wee bit as you push it into the blade, or a thin moulding will bend ever so slightly as it encounters the blade. Either way you get a distortion in the angle. Clamp the moulding to the guide, or hold it against a sandpaper-covered block that is clamped to the guide. It will keep the moulding from slipping when held tightly against it. To prevent a fragile piece of moulding from bending before the blade, first cut the piece a hair longer than the correct measurement, then very slowly go through the saw again, shaving off that last $\frac{1}{16}$ inch or so.

Framing underscores the importance of proportion, which is a key to the successful recycling of throwaway materials. The size and width of the frame in proportion to the picture or object being framed; the proportion of length to width of the frame; the size of the margin or mat between frame and picture or between object and edge of display board; the size and shape of the frame to the wall area it hangs on—all these proportions are extremely critical to the overall artistry achieved. There are no set rules for this, but you can acquire an eye and an instinct for it by studying what interior decorators do with framings. The same importance of proportion is evident in other recycling projects. The reason some old, marred, "country" tables look so handsome in the house is that the proportions are right and the pieces were cut and joined accurately. That's why you can get away with bringing some pig feeders into the dining room but not necessarily all pig feeders. If you doubt the value of proportion and harmony within, say, a piece of furniture, procure some of the finest rosewood, planed to the most shimmering finish, and put together an ill-proportioned table with careless joinery. Set beside that table another of good proportions, well cut and joined, made of old, weather-beaten, mouse-gnawed pine. The latter will appeal more every time. This is the reason why one artistic recycler succeeds where another fails.

Fabric-Covered Frames

Fabric-covered frames, for example, can begin with any old wood, even pallet wood. Saw the boards square across on the ends and butt them together. Then glue them together and nail wood joiners across the cracks between the boards. Then paint a thin coat of white glue over the wood and smooth on the fabric. Cut in the fabric at the corners so the material folds down neatly. On the outer corners, the fabric can be folded over as if you were wrapping a package and stapled to the back. This is the best way (especially when batting is used under the fabric) to give the frame a soft, padded look. If you decide to use batting, glue it to the frame and wrap the fabric around and tape, glue, or staple to the backside. The easiest way of all is to glue ribbon (or narrow strips of cloth, if you can cut straight) over the frame, with the lengths of ribbon long enough to lap around at both ends. Let the glue thicken to a good tackiness before smoothing on the fabric.

Board Frames

To display a three-dimensional object in a wall hanging, a frame can be as simple as plywood or any board of appropriate size, covered entirely with a piece of scrap fabric. Burlap makes a good covering, and old burlap bags are usually part of the discard pile of any country place. Corduroy also makes an interesting background fabric. Velvet, felt, and velour are other good choices. Color should complement the object. To mount the object, special clips that look like crooked brads (crooked nails) are available that are hammered into the fabric-covered board. Obviously, you could, in a pinch, use crooked brads. Lighter objects can often be sewn right to the fabric.

The best way to secure the fabric on the back side is to staple it with a staple gun, being sure to stretch the fabric tightly and evenly. First tack down or staple the fabric halfway between corners on one side of the frame. Then, directly across the board from the first tacking down, pull the fabric tight over the edge (don't pull too tight), and staple it. Next move to the adjacent side, pull it straight, and staple. Now go around the frame, pulling tightly and stapling, checking the front of the frame to make sure you aren't pulling the fabric unevenly. Leave the corners till last, and fold the fabric over each corner as if wrapping a gift, and staple. Glue can be substituted for staples or tacks, but you'll need to use masking or cloth tape to hold the fabric until the glue dries. Don't rely on tape alone, because it will eventually loosen.

Another neat way to make a frame without messing with angled corners is by attaching a board to a larger board, and the margin between them becomes the frame. The larger board is usually covered with fabric as described above, and the smaller one has the picture glued to it. Batiks display well this way.

Where the fabric itself is the art work and not background, professional framers use what are called stretcher bars, held together at the corners by slotted tenons but not glued tight. After a fabric is stretched on the frame by hand, little wooden wedges are driven in at the corners to force the frame apart a little more and thus draw the fabric drum tight. Their main purpose is for stretching canvas for a painting. They are easy to use and available from artist supply stores. But you can draw most fabrics up tight enough by hand. Another method is to sew heavy thread through the edges of the fabric back and forth across the back of the frame, pulling opposite edges tight as you sew. This is called latching.

Another way to adorn frames made of nondescript boards is to cover the surface with seeds, pebbles, beads, small shells, or any other small and more or less uniform bits of material you discover. *Picture Framing and Wall Display* (Lane Publishing Co., Menlo Park, Calif., 1980) shows a frame covered with sunflower seeds and black-eyed peas glued on one at a time. It's quite beautiful, and I assume that if you get tired of it as a frame, you can always feed it to the birds.

Lid Frames

A schoolteacher has a cheap and attractive way to display the "art works" of her grade-schoolers. The kids glue their best work onto the top of shoe box lids or any stout cardboard lid. The pictures are cut out at the corners so they can be glued down around the side edges of the boxes neatly, giving the art a three-dimensional look. The lids are then hung on the wall. When such adorned lids are hung inside a standard picture frame, with plenty of mat margin, the result is surprisingly artful. When you run across pictures in magazines that delight you, this is a convenient way to display them attractively on your wall. If you tire of the picture, glue a new one over the old one. Or make a whole stack of cardboard lid pictures and change them as the mood moves you. All you need in the permanent frame is a short slat or two nails to hang the cardboard lid in place.

Cardboard and Tape Frames

If you have a large poster or other picture you'd like to display attractively but cheaply, all you need is plastic tape of the widest size you can find (1½ inches is minimum) and several sheets of corrugated cardboard. Cut the cardboard to the size of the poster, lay down two or three sheets of it with the poster properly positioned on top, and run a length of tape down one side and then the others, sticking it to the front of the poster and folding it over the back to cover the edges of cardboard to hold them together. You need to apply the tape very straight, and cut the outside corner overlap very neatly. When you're done, you'll be surprised at what a nice "frame" you have made.

Shadow Box Frames

Shadow boxes can make dramatic picture frames but are better used to display three-dimensional objects. The simplest shadow boxes might be described as picture frames with added depth. In their more complicated forms, with shelving and glass fronts, they more closely resemble small wall cabinets. Shadow boxes are particularly attractive when used as framing or housing for collections of rather small items—stamps, beads, Indian artifacts, keys, buttons. Let us say you have found several white flint arrowheads or pieces of amethyst quartz crystals in your ramblings (see Chapter 7). A simple shadow box requires only a few pieces of wood scrap plus a decorative background. For white quartz, a box painted black and a background of pale ice blue felt or a wallpaper remnant of mottled grey or silver would be very dramatic. A flint arrowhead, a spoon, or a similarly heavy object is best mounted by drilling two tiny holes and looping a fine wire around the piece, through the holes, and twisting it tightly behind. Lighter objects, like buttons or keys, can be sewn right to a fabric background. All will look stunning. I have even seen a collection of dismantled old watch parts displayed this way to make a *very* nice wall decoration.

Protective Glass

Most people prefer to display collections in frames with glass or acrylic fronts. If you prefer this, you must make some kind of moulding to hold the glass, which means learning to make conventional frames. There's really nothing difficult about that, but I won't describe the methods involved only because there are scores of books and articles on the subject. Clear glass is still one of the few cheap products to buy and every moneysaver worthy of the name has a cache of old windows stored some place on the property or knows someone who has. If not, contact a builder or anyone in the business of replacing windows. Hundreds of old windows get thrown away for lack of use. Nonglare glass is nice for framing pictures, of course, since it won't reflect images, but it is twice the price of regular glass. If you're going to use glass in shadow boxes, make sure the sides are wood— strong enough to hold moulding and glass.

Frames for Mirrors and Clocks

Frames and mountings for mirrors and clocks attract all sorts of recycling ideas. Anything with an appropriate hole in it can, with ingenuity, be made to frame a mirror—porthole windows salvaged from boats, for example. I have seen bathroom mirrors inside horse collars and both mirrors and clocks embraced by fancy old brass horse hames. The latter seemed only slightly less tacky to me, but then, to each his or her own. On the other hand, a clock ensconced in the round hole of an old mandolin or guitar appeals to me almost as much as a beautiful banjo clock, although the guitar alone hanging on the wall is quite decorative enough. A friend once gave me a clock, the shell of which was an old book, the pages glued together and then the housing for the clock works cut out of the middle of the pages. The front and back cover were left intact, except for a hole in the front by which the clock hands were connected to the innards. Clever, but there is something in me that prefers to see old books recycled only by rereading them. But the most grotesque clock-from-something-else I've seen is a manufactured item, which unwittingly parodies the whole trend toward using things for purposes they originally were not intended: a coffee table, the surface of which, under plate glass, is a huge running clock.

DOORS AND WINDOWS

Salvaging doors and windows for reuse rises or falls on a sense of proportion. Windows that are just a little too small for a particular side of a house will look too small however cleverly recycled. A window so small that it is not thought of as a window does not violate good proportion. There is a fine line of distinction but one that is not subservient to hard and fast rules. The difference is that between a pleasing design and one merely awkward. A thick, batten door on a house, reminiscent of barn doors, can be appropriate if the thickness is balanced by a slightly wider dimension than a standard door. But think hard before straying too far from standard door sizes. One problem in restoring old colonial homes is that seventeenth- and eighteenth-century Americans were considerably shorter than their modern counterparts, and their doors are too short for today. A door can, however, be enlarged tastefully by mortise and tenoning a new frame around the old one, although it is a job to be tackled only after you've gained considerable experience in woodworking. The new outside boards are splined along the edges and doweled at the corners to the old frame and the joining must be done with great accuracy in measurements. And the new wood needs to match the old as closely as possible if the door is not to be painted. A tip from experienced salvagers: If possible, buy or beg two of a kind when repair work will need to be done. This applies to doors and windows— particularly damaged stained glass windows. Use parts of one to refurbish the other.

A door can also be cut down in size. In fact, some salvagers have cut doors in half to box in window seats or old freestanding bathtubs, or for small doors to face woodbins in stone fireplace walls. If pleasing proportions are maintained, the results can be marvelously attractive.

Batten Doors

Good panel doors require considerable skill in the making, but batten doors of various designs are easily made and afford great possibilities in using recycled wood. Essentially, a batten door, as on a barn, is composed of vertical boards held together by horizontal battens. Such a door can be weathertight if tongue-and-groove boards are used. A perfect choice for a heavy exterior door are the 2 × 5 tongue-and-groove boards from old wooden silos once common on farms and still standing (or falling down) on a few old farmsteads. Wooden water tanks also contain this kind of wood and were common on midwestern farms just a generation ago. Wooden tanks are still in use atop buildings in older sections of cities. The best wood tanks were made of cypress or redwood, woods practically impervious to the

decaying effects of moisture. Pine and fir were commonly used and will still make good doors if not rotted (see Chapter 5).

Where inch boards are used, the door will be better insulated if the battens extend over the whole door—in other words, a two-layered or laminated door. The boards of one layer run vertically, the other layer (of battens), horizontally. If the vertical boards are not tongue and groove, be sure to clamp them very tightly together before nailing on the battens. Because you're using old recycled lumber, you will not have to worry about shrinkage, which would certainly occur with green lumber. For a more striking door, the battens can be run at an angle rather than horizontal on a two-layer door—or can run at one angle on the top half and an opposite angle on the bottom half, with horizontal battens at top, middle, and bottom.

To maintain authenticity (and also because it is much easier), batten doors are usually nailed together, the nails driven from the exterior door side through the battens on the other side and then bent (clinched) over the battens. The nails should extend through the batten about ½ to ¾ inch for good clinching. Where only three or four battens are used to hold the door boards together (rather than a two-layer door), some people put the battens on the exterior of the door because they like the zigzag design the battens form. This is not authentic as far as good country barn design goes, because water can gather between batten and door, which eventualy leads to rotting. To avoid that, bevel the outside edges of the batten, top and bottom. Better yet, bevel the top and if you have a table saw, notch out a groove in the middle of the bottom edge so the water drips off the batten rather than running back to the door. Drive the nails in a regular pattern so they look like part of the design. Use galvanized nails that don't rust.

Make the door slightly larger than the door opening and measure and check carefully before you make the final fitting cuts. Remember when using tongue and groove that you will want to cut the tongue off one side of the door and the groove off the other, so the edges are solid wood. Allow for this trimming. Even if the door is made of cypress or weathered barn siding that has stood impervious to the weather for years, you will want to protect it with exterior varnish paint or wood preservative, especially the end grain on the edges.

In using salvaged doors and windows, check to make sure they are not warped. Lay the window sash on a level floor. If it doesn't lay flat, it won't slide up and down in the frame. If in trying to twist it flat, you notice in addition that the joints are loose, the window is probably not worth salvaging. Bowed doors won't keep the wind out. If the panel mortises and tenons are loose, throwing the door out of square, you can clamp and reglue. But you may not be able to straighten a tight, warped, or out-of-square door. Don't waste your time on it. If you want to use the old hardware on the door (and who wouldn't?), make sure all the parts are there or else make friends with a clever metalworker who can make a lost part for you. Parts for old door mechanisms are hard to find.

Salvaging Stained Glass

Lead glass transoms or windows in and around old doors are highly prized salvage items and your chances of finding one cheap are almost nil. What you might find cheap is a panel with a few broken or missing pieces of glass. Most people believe that making stained glass is a difficult skill to learn and are afraid to tackle even repair jobs. Actually, leading in stained glass is quite simple—all you need to know is some very basic puttying and soldering skills. If you can solder two pieces of tin together, you can make a stained glass window. Scores of books in your public library are ready to lead you on. (Keep in mind that working with lead too long can be dangerous. Wear gloves.)

If the crack in a piece of stained glass is fairly straight and can be jiggled to a gap of at least $\frac{1}{16}$ inch, you don't have to remove it. Just insert a piece of lead "came," as the lead seam holding the glass pieces is called, to make the piece look as if it were made that way. To do this, cut a piece of H came the right length for the crack. (In cross section, came has the shape of the letter H, or, for around the edges of the window, the letter U.) For inserting into the crack, cut the H came piece in half—lead came cuts very easily by pressing down on it with a sharp knife—then stick one half through the crack and solder the other half back to it. You need solder only on the ends of the repair came to fake a real seam.

If the broken piece of glass must be removed, there are two methods. On wide came, such as that in most old church windows, peel or bend back the came from around the broken piece on one side and lift the glass out. This is the best method if the broken piece is close to the edge. You have to cut the came back at the corners to bend it out. You need bend back the came only on one side—work on the back side, which in stained glass windows is the exterior side. Lift out the broken piece, put in the new piece, bend the lead came back in place, solder any joints and cuts you had to make, and putty.

Finding a piece that matches the original may be difficult, but stained glass comes in myriad colors now. If using textured glass, run your glass cutter on the smooth side. There's always the possibility that if you have all the pieces of the broken piece, you can glue them back together and use it again. In reputtying (repair of an old stained glass window may require reputtying only), an old knife works well to force the putty down into the crack between glass and came. If the came fits tightly, you may have to thin the putty with turpentine and brush it into the seam with a toothbrush.

Where a broken piece of glass is near the center of the window and the lead came is narrow, removing the glass is more difficult and will require the second method. You have to start at the nearest edge and cut joints to remove sections of good glass until you reach the broken piece. Cut the joints by pressing down and wiggling your knife through. Replace the glass and then resolder the cut joints as you replace the good sections in reverse order of that in which you took them out.

It is always safer to work on a stained glass window by first removing it from its sash and laying it on a level table. Removing it from the sash is basically the same as removing any window. It is held by glazing tacks and sealed with putty. When carrying unsashed leaded glass, be very careful to keep it in a vertical position so it doesn't buckle. To lay it on a table, first lower it and gently place the center of the window against the edge of the table and then ease the window onto the table top.

Leaded windows for sale in antique shops or from salvage stores are often bulged out. Flattening them is time-consuming for the typical do-it-yourselfer. Lay the window flat on a level table and begin pressing gently and uniformly, over and over the surface. It may take an hour or so, but the glass will eventually begin to work back into the channels of the came. If a came lip is blocking a piece of glass, bend it back a bit.

When you reputty old windows, you want to make your new putty look old. To do so, mix lampblack with it. To make newly soldered lead look old, apply zinc chloride. In soldering lead, the metal must be shiny clean and well fluxed or the solder won't stick. Sand away joints to a clear shine before soldering. Your iron and your solder must barely touch the lead and move on, else you will melt the lead. Melting a bit of lead won't do any harm, though. Just don't make a habit of it.

A HOUSE—AND MORE—BUILT OF PALLET WOOD

One of the most artful pennypinchers I know makes attractive casual furniture out of throwaway pallets. The woodworking shop he makes it in is built of scrap pallet wood, too. And before you let that impress you too much, he also built the new house nearby out of pallet wood. It is a modest house and not quite finished inside, but so far he has spent only $2,500, most of that going for the vinyl siding.

There has to be a catch, you say. Not really. All it took was the ability to see an opportunity when it arose. This artful pennypincher lives near a factory that receives supplies in extra large, extra strong pallets. Each pallet has several 6-foot-long 2 × 6s of fairly good white or red pine. Artful Pennypincher looked at the pallets, which could be had for next to nothing, and saw a gold mine. With the same kind of farm-boy ingenuity with which he once helped design a rig to raise missiles out of their in-ground silos after Westinghouse engineers had all but given up, he began to devise ways to use the planks productively.

Normally there's not much use for 6-foot planks in building. The shortest unit in a conventional building is the 8-foot stud. Rafters, plates, and joists are much longer. With so much free wood at hand, however, Artful Pennypincher simply spliced planks with other planks, so that every joist, stud, rafter, plate, and so on is double thickness nailed together to attain the desired length. The walls and floor consist of solid 2-inch planking of random lengths.

"Well, if you have free wood, you might as well use it," Artful Pennypincher says, shrugging. As a result, the house is as strong as a boat and could probably ride the waves without breaking. Therefore it doesn't really need a solid footer foundation and, as a matter of fact, it sits on railroad ties laid down on top of the ground! Is Artful Penny-pincher concerned that frost might heave it up and crack something? "Oh, I don't think that will ever happen," he says. "That house is so strong and heavy it will just ride up and down as a unit. We haven't had any problems."

He constructed his workshop the same way, except that he ripped the $2 \times 6s$ in half for the spliced studs and rafters of the small shedlike building. The workshop sits on stone pylons at the corners. Because of its weight, it began to sink on the downhill corner. "It took me a long time to find a jack strong enough to lift it up to add stones to the foundation," the owner says. "I'm thinking about sailing it to Hawaii," he adds, winking. "Fellow out there buys my chairs and wants me to move my shop there."

There's no secret or trick to Artful's simple pallet furniture, either. The back slats for his chairs come from the thinner pallet wood, and arms, legs, and seat come from the heavier planks. The light pine is popular as porch furniture and for other casual uses, and its attractiveness is due to Artful's close attention to basic carpentry. The pieces really fit together, are well-sanded, and are proportioned. But there's no fancy joinery. He uses glue and 2-inch wood screws. He draws the designs himself after studying proportions on existing rockers he likes. He makes the straight cuts with his table saw and makes rockers and curved designs in the chair backs with his band saw. He studies each plank and tries to avoid using the parts with nail holes from the pallet, but if he must use those parts he fills the nail holes with plastic wood that is almost the same color as the pine. He prizes those pieces of red pine, as he calls it, with marked, contrasting red and white grain. Customers especially like rockers and swings made of this wood.

The catch to working with pallets, if there is one, is the hard work and time spent tearing them apart. Even in doing this there are tricks you learn. "You beat them apart with a heavy sledge," says Artful.

"But never strike on the boards you want to save. They'll splinter. You swing against the heavy blocks they are nailed to, and they all come loose at once."

Pallets are often a big nuisance for factories. They can't just open their gates and let everyone "come and get 'em." Factories have tried that and suffered all kinds of mishaps. Others have put employees to work tearing pallets apart, but the labor costs more than hauling them to a landfill and paying to have them buried, which is what often actually happens. But don't be afraid to ask for pallets. Be a bit humble and above all, reasonable, and factory managers can be very nice. You might have to pay perhaps 50¢ each for really large pallets that are in good shape. They're worth it. A tip: You'll have the best luck finding pallets at factories that make or handle large quantities of glass panes.

Artful Pennypincher sands his pallet wood with a portable belt sander he has rigged to use as a stationary sander. The sander is affixed to a post with a toggle bolt on the bottom that adjusts a platform for the wood. This allows him an accurate but independent adjustment method to keep the platform exactly at right angles to the sander. His boards fit together for gluing-up almost as well as if he used a jointer.

His workshop is heated by a woodstove he made from free scraps—the round body of the stove is a discarded electrical transformer. The legs are artistically bent blades from a chisel plow.

There is a fan in the shop to circulate air and an exhaust fan—both found at the dump. "Oh, people throw away everything," he says, shaking his head in wonder. "At the salvage yard, I've seen refrigerators come in with ice still in the freezer compartments."

CHAPTER 2

Gifts from the Recycling Bin

Once upon a time, which is to say in 1984, an 11-year-old girl was walking down the sidewalk near her home, as deep in thought as it is possible for a little girl to be. She was having what her father might call a "cash-flow problem." Here it was a week before Christmas and she had spent her allowance and her baby-sitting money on gifts, and still had nothing for her 4-year-old brother. She stopped to watch workmen building a new house on the block. On the patio, or what would be the patio when the house was finished, a table saw was set up, around which lay scores of pieces of wood that had been trimmed off studs, joists, and rafters: little triangles, squares, and rectangles of wood that reminded her of toy blocks. One of the workmen began cleaning up, sweeping sawdust and wood trimmings into a big pile and scooping the pile into a cardboard box. And that's when the little girl had an idea. If they were just going to throw those pieces of wood away. . . . She summoned up the courage to ask if she might have the blocks of wood. "Help yourself, honey," the man said. "They're just going to get burned up anyhow." She raced home, got her little wagon, and returned to fill it with what became her gift of building blocks for her brother—and, not altogether surprisingly, the gift he played with the most in the days to come.

Out in the country not far away, two little boys faced the same problem and found their own way to solve it. They wanted to give their three aunts something for Christmas in return for all the cookies they had mooched during the year. But they had no money, either, and the prospect of their parents just giving them some was very poor, even for so worthy a cause as pleasing aunts. What to do? While they were feeding their mother's chickens one evening, an idea came to them. The aunts all kept a few hens for fresh eggs. Hens eat corn. Corn costs over $3 a bushel if you have to buy it from the feed store. But they knew where there was free corn. In the harvested corn fields around them, the big mechanical combines always missed a few ears that went to waste if not eaten by birds or wild animals. So for a whole Saturday, the boys trudged gamely up and down the endless rows of their father's corn stubble until they had found three bushels of corn, one for each aunt.

They put the corn in apple boxes and with a sprig of greenery and a red bow on each, delivered their gifts. Not only were the aunts pleased with a very useful gift, but the attractive boxes of corn looked downright beautiful as decorations. (The boxes, incidentally, were originally made from waste wood by the same man who makes rocking chairs from pallet wood, described in Chapter 1. His boxes appeal to home decorators and often show up in a fall or Christmas display.) And the fact that the boys had worked so hard to gather their gifts meant more to the aunts than anything "store bought." I assume the hens were pleased, too, though I did not actually ask them.

None of these children know Robert Rodale, known worldwide for his organic philosophy and ecological pioneering, but they were practicing to perfection what he calls "regeneration," a concept that seeks to revitalize human institutions by, among other things, making more use of abundant resources and less use of scarce ones. I have heard of only one gift as appropriate as these others: a gaily wrapped package of rags given by a sister to her brother who "had everything." They were just the thing for cleaning and shining his new car!

SEASONAL DECORATIONS

A little imagination and expenditure of time can save a heap of money when it comes to seasonal decorations, too. A decade ago (and perhaps still today, for all I know), the town of Russell, Kansas, would go all out for outdoor Christmas decorations. One whole block might sport huge lighted candy canes along the street, while on another block, every front yard held a giant wreath. Close inspection revealed that the candy canes were sections of old stovepipe (or blower pipe or auger pipe from old farm equipment), the crook made from four 45-degree-angle stovepipe fittings bolted together. The "canes," painted white, with red lights attached through holes punched in the sides, were very striking at night. The wreaths were an even bigger surprise. They were old tires painted green or red, completely wrapped with evergreen sprigs and tinsel. The stands to hold them were simple frames of wood or plumbing pipe, two per tire, in the shape of the letter H, stuck into the ground, and painted in holiday colors. The wreath rested in the crossbars of the two.

Tin Christmas Trees

The most dramatic nighttime display of all consisted of Christmas "trees" made of cheap chain and tin can lids. To make one, you drive a tall stake in the ground, with several short stakes (tent stakes work fine) in a circle around it, about 4 feet out from the center and 1 foot apart. Then run a light chain (available from the hardware store) from the top of the center stake down to each short stake. The effect is like a maypole. Next, punch a hole near the rims of tin can lids and attach them all along the chain, about 6 to 8 inches apart. Set two or three spotlights of different colors near the ground so they shine up onto the dangling can lids. Hammer dents in the lids or apply glitter to make them catch more light. Although this sounds tacky, and in truth is not much to look at during the day, at night it is electrifying. The lids shimmer and glow in a kaleidoscope of color.

The average amount of money an American family spends just on Christmas gifts is $300, according to statistics. The typical middle-class family spends much more than that for the entire year, especially when you count in *all* the anniversary remembrances (birthdays, weddings, and so forth) and seasonal decorations you buy. In no other spare-time activity can you save money faster than by using your head and hands instead of your pocketbook. Here are some ideas to get you started.

Corn Trees

A traditional iron seed-corn dryer, loaded with ears of corn (or apples), is a popular decorating item in many country homes. They are made to hang from a ceiling or beam and hold only a few ears—nice for decoration but not very practical for those people who dry popcorn, sweet corn for parching, or field corn for grinding into cornmeal. For these purposes, as well as for an eye-stopping fall decoration, the wooden dryers that look like short hall trees are better.

Authentic "corn trees," as they were called, are very rare, but they are easy to reproduce. All you need is an upright post on which the ears of corn are mounted, some sort of pedestal to hold the post, a metal disk that fits on the post to keep rodents from climbing it, and a few handfuls of 8- or 10-penny finishing nails.

The post should measure about 4 by 4 inches thick. Height is not critical—4 feet is good and will hold about 50 ears of field corn or up to 100 ears of popcorn, sweet corn, or Indian corn, depending on the size of the ears. Since a corn dryer should look its part of an authentic farmyard tool, the wood need not be new or finished perfectly. I've used 4 by 4-inch braces from an old barn for the corn trees I've made, although two 2 × 4s nailed together would be adequate.

After sawing the post to desired length, chamfer (bevel) the four sides down with a drawknife to make an eight-sided post. The chamfers should run from the top of the post to about 16 inches from the bottom. The eight sides allow you to mount the ears of corn in a denser, more pleasing pattern than the original four sides would. In

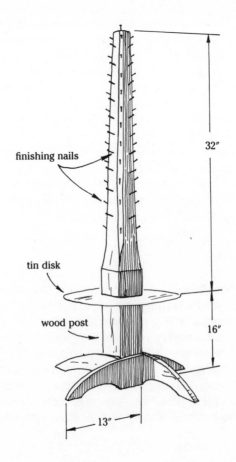

finishing nails

tin disk

wood post

32"

16"

13"

addition, chamfering softens the appearance of a bulky piece of wood. The depth of the chamfer (and therefore its width) should gradually decrease as you approach the bottom to give the post a nice tapered look, as shown in the illustration. It is not necessary that all eight sides of the finished post be exactly the same width, although this would give the best appearance when there was no corn on it. The top of the post ought to be tapered to a flat pyramid or trapezoid shape— whatever strikes your creative fancy. A calculated casualness done by hand and by eye rather than rigorous adherence to precise measurements will work better on a piece like this. More often than not, that's how the farmers made them in the first place.

In the project pictured here, I began cutting the chamfers with a drawknife, then switched to a wide chisel and mallet when the going got tough. The chisel cut much easier and more precisely than the drawknife, especially around knots. You soon learn, with any of these tools, to shave the wood off *with* the grain—that's the direction in which the grain of the wood is slanting up to the surface of the wood. The grain going down *into* the wood away from the surface is the direction against the grain. Once you ascertain the direction of the grain, you can't forget about it because the grain direction will change around knots. And if you chamfer one corner of a block in one direction, you will probably have to cut in the opposite direction on the adjacent corner. Experience will soon teach you this lesson: If you try to pull the drawknife against the grain, it will dig deeply into the wood and tear out chunks rather than peel off shavings, as when cut properly with the grain. The chamfers can be finished off with a plane or by sanding. I use a power belt sander.

The design of the pedestal or legs for your corn tree is again a matter of personal taste. The design I used is simple and easy and some people like the unusual pedestal that results. I just nailed four simple feet to the four sides of the post at the bottom. This makes a strong unit without additional bracing or mortising. Feet mortised into the faces of the four sides of the post may be more visually pleasing. A flat round or square stand nailed to the bottom of the post would be quicker to make but would not be as strong. Follow your impulses— that's half the fun of making anything.

Because I had a band saw available to me, I put curves in my pedestal feet. You could do the same with a saber saw or a bow saw, first clamping the work piece to a bench. I used scrap pieces of red oak because I had it. Pine is easier to work and is appropriate for an Early American piece like this.

The trickiest part of the construction is getting the post on the pedestal so that it is straight and not leaning to one side. The human eye can accurately detect even slight angles out of plumb, so if your corn tree is crooked, everyone will know. The fastest way I've found to assure plumbness is to prop up the post on a level floor by whatever means available and plumb it with a level in all directions. Then carefully place the feet of the pedestal around the post in their proper positions and draw their outlines on the post. Then you can take the post down and nail or screw the pedestal feet in place precisely to the drawn lines. If you do not have a level, tap a large staple into the very center of the top of the post. Put a string through the staple and hang the post just barely off a level floor. The post will hang perfectly plumb or almost so. Then place the pedestal feet solidly on the floor against the hanging post and very gently (so as not to move the post) draw the outlines of the feet on the post as described above. Then take the post down, remove the staple and string, and attach the feet.

Next, you attach the rodent barrier—a tin disk slid down over the post to just below where the chamfers end. The square opening in the tin must be the same size as the post. If you use recycled barn lumber like I do, you will find that with old rough lumber, measurements are neither standard nor necessarily uniform throughout the length and width of any particular board or piece. Measure the post at the bottom where the tin disk will be attached, and cut the hole in the tin accordingly.

I used a piece of tin barn roofing—a scrap 12 inches square—for the disk. This was a shiny new scrap, but you can shine up an old piece by buffing it with a wire brush wheel on a bench grinder. Or leave the old tin with the patina of age on it, as some people prefer. Or if you are making a work of art out of your corn tree with beautiful finished woods, a disk of brass or copper will complement it nicely.

Cut a disk of about 10 to 12 inches in diameter with a tin snips. Then carefully mark where you will cut out the square opening, exactly in the middle of the disk. Mark the post dimensions on the disk; then mark an opening approximately ½ inch smaller all around than the dimensions of the post. Make a starting gash in the tin with a chisel and hammer, then insert the tin snips into the gash and begin enlarging the hole, working in small bits until you have enlarged the hole for greater maneuverability. Then cut to the edges of the smaller square. Next cut a slit from each corner out to the corner of the larger square that represents the dimensions of the post. Now you'll have four flaps. Bend the flaps down to the lines of the post dimensions. The flaps will not bend easily unless you are using aluminum. Start the bend by hand, then set the disk on a firm edge like the top of a vise jaw and with a hammer bang the flap down along the line until it forms a right angle with the disk.

Now slide the disk down over the post, flaps down. After it passes over the chamfered portion, the disk will settle firmly in place if you have measured and cut accurately. A nail through each flap into the post will hold it solidly.

To complete the corn tree, cover the eight sides of the upper post with 8d or 10d nails driven into the wood about ⅝ inch deep and at a 60-degree angle. You can drive in the nails a bit deeper in a softwood such as pine. How close you wish to space the nails is again a matter of your personal inclination. Minimum spacing is about 3 inches apart on a side and the nails should be staggered. Thus the nails in one side of the post should not be directly in line with the nails in the adjacent side. If you don't like the spacing of your nails, you can pull them out and reset them. Nail holes add to the "distressed" look of the wood rather than detract from the finished piece. Don't forget to put a nail directly on top of the post and nails on the facets of the taper so that when you mount the ears of corn, the tree will look filled to the very top.

Some builders use regular nails, then cut off the heads on a slant to make a sharp point to penetrate the cob. But the thin head of a finishing nail is sharp enough. The inner cob is soft and often partially hollow, and with just a bit of pressure you can press the ears down over finishing nail heads. Mount the corn at the butt end of the ear. Be sure you first position the tree where you want it, because once it's loaded with ears, it is heavy and awkward to move.

Corn will dry much faster inside on a corn tree than it will air dry in a crib exposed to humid weather conditions. The corn tree is ideal for drying corn for cornmeal or sweet corn for parching. It is also good for drying a few ears of popcorn quickly. But popcorn *left* in the warm, dry house dries out too much in a month or two and will not pop well. Once it is dry, popcorn should be kept in an unheated garage or similar cool place, where it will maintain just about the right moisture content for good popping. If you don't want your corn tree to become a permanent fixture, you can load it with popcorn and keep it in the garage. (Be sure not to set it too close to walls, however, or mice will climb the wall to get to it.)

A variation of the corn tree is sometimes used as a Christmas tree. Instead of ears of corn, shelled cobs are placed on the nails. The cobs are then decorated with tinsel, glitter, artificial snow, ornaments, and so forth.

If you prefer the smaller hanging corn dryers but can't find or afford the iron ones, you can be just as authentic with a hanging wooden one. One of my uncles made and used them when I was a boy. Instead of a 4 by 4-inch post, he pounded nails into a 2 × 2 that was perhaps 2 feet long. He drove a fence staple or two solidly into the one end of the wood, attached a length of wire, and hung it lengthwise from a hook in a barn beam. The beam was sheathed in tin all around the hook so that mice could not get a foothold to scramble down to the corn. His choicest ears were then stuck on the nails, to dry where no rat or rodent could harm them.

A Wind Chime and Calling Bell from Scrap Plumbing Pipe

Some kinds of metal piping, such as copper and stainless steel and especially brass, have a particularly melodious ring if you dangle a short length of it from a wire and strike it gently with another piece of metal. Different lengths make different notes and I suppose a resourceful musician could rig up a clothesline of pipe sections and play tunes on it. Less gifted individuals put waste pipe to a somewhat more practical use: to make wind chimes that can double as bells to call the kids in from the yard. Even the person on your gift list who has everything won't have a dinner bell made out of old plumbing.

I learned about making "bells" out of old plumbing pipe from The Ragpicker, and I mean nothing scurrilous by using that name. I am as proud of his ability to make money out of what other people throw away as he is, and anyway The Ragpicker won't let me use his real name. The first time I met him, he was collecting beer cans along the road. He picked up one after I said hello and threw it back down again. "Can't make no money with tin," he growled. "Gotta be 'luminum."

"Does it really pay?" I badgered him.

"My good man, it's almost a hunnert percent profit," he answered. But your time, I insisted. "Hah. My *time?*" He took his eyes off the road ditch just long enough to gaze patiently heavenward. "My *time* ain't worth the price of a tin can. And it gainin' none on the antique market either."

The second time we met was behind his ramshackle barn, where he had a big bonfire going, burning insulation off of copper wire so he could sell the copper at a good price. "Hunnert percent profit," he repeated as if half a year had not intervened since we last met. "And I get twice or more than what you kin get, because" (and here he spit into the fire to underline what he was about to say) "I'm a ragpickin' *dealer.*"

Could I become a dealer? He eyed me like a cattle buyer looking over feeder calves. "Doubtful," he finally said. "An' ennyway, you gotta bring stuff in regular before a yard'll give you dealer prices."

And where did he get all that wire? He grinned and winked. "Now if I told you that then we'd both know. How could I make a hunnert percent that way?"

Eventually he decided I was harmless and began telling me about the brass and copper that people throw away "mostly because they're in a hurry." The Ragpicker tended to speak of a landfill the way Moses spoke of the Promised Land. He made his rounds of them regularly, being careful, he said, to park his old truck far enough away so it wouldn't be mistaken for junk and get buried, too. He took me into his barn to show me his treasure—a long row of 55-gallon barrels either full or in the process of being filled with aluminum, copper wire, brass scraps, and old batteries. That's when he picked up a piece of brass pipe and ding-donged it with another piece. "Purty, ain't it?" he said. "You can make yourself sort of like a dinner bell out of these." An idea was born.

To make your own dinner bell or wind chimes, you should use four pieces of piping. Brass is visually, if not musically, the most exciting, although copper or stainless steel will do. A hanger for them can be a piece of scrap wood, 2 inches thick and about 8 inches square. Insert screw eyes at each corner on top of the hanger and attach four short pieces of hardware chain or wire from them to a center ring of wire or chain link that can then slip onto an overhead hook in ceiling or beam. On the underside of the hanger, insert five screw eyes, one about 1 inch in from each corner and one in the very center. Now drill two holes through each pipe at one end and hang the pipes on the corner screw eyes. The pieces of pipe should be of different lengths, if they are all of the same material, to produce different musical notes. From the center screw eye, dangle a length of hardware chain with a metal weight on the end or some other material hard enough to make the pipes chime as the wind blows them against each other. The chimer should be equidistant from all pipes and no more than 1 inch away from them. A metal disk hanging horizontally on the chain works best.

To make a bell out of the chimes, attach another piece of chain below the disk. A bolt through the disk, with nuts tightened on each side, will hold the disk rigidly horizontal and a hole in the ends of the bolt for the chain completes the arrangement. When you want to call someone in from the garden nearby, shake the bottom chain vigorously.

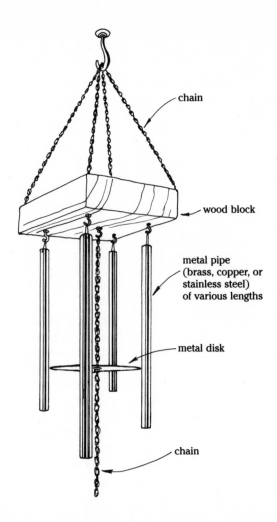

chain

wood block

metal pipe
(brass, copper, or
stainless steel)
of various lengths

metal disk

chain

If the four pipes are of different lengths, you may have to adjust the four top short chains to make the chimes hang straight.

Ornaments from Tin Can Lids

A tin can can be a thing of amazing beauty and utility, whether or not you agree with Andy Warhol that it is a work of art. It takes imagination but not much more. The usual reaction of people who see a tin lid Christmas ornament is to ask what it is made of. When told a tin can lid, they are unbelieving until they examine it closely. The ornament in the illustration is easy to make with a tin snips and a pair of needle-

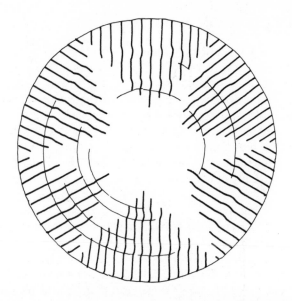

nose pliers. Tin cans cut almost as easily as paper. With a bit of practice you'll have stunning results. You can scratch out the basic design on the can lid with the point of a pencil compass.

All the marked lines will be cut. Cut the longest six lines first, then cut the others, from longest to shortest. Roll a curl into the end of each strip with a needle-nose pliers, and twist each strip slightly to an angle nearly perpendicular to the uncut star. Or some strips can be curled short and some long, spread out to cover space between the uncut star points. The key is consistency. Form the strips of each star point the same way so there is a satisfying balance and wholeness to the finished ornament.

Once you create a standard star, many variations will come to mind. Stars can have any number of points, although six- and eight-point ones are easier to lay out. A much fancier ornament can be made by surrounding the lid ornament with a second ornament cut from the can body. To do this, remove the top and bottom of the can. Then cut the entire can into strips up to the rim, leaving the rim intact. Now begin curling up the strips. Curl every third one up tight to the rim. Now go around and curl every other remaining strip up to a little less than the first ones. Now go around again and curl the remaining strips up a little less still. Now you have a ring of curled rays that you can attach to the can lid ornament at the points of the star by bending the star around the encircling rim. A quart coffee can works fine for this project.

RECYCLED BOXES

If we were to list inventions in their order of usefulness, boxes would no doubt rank close to the top. Besides their utility, boxes have a curious appeal for humans, especially small boxes. There is something in the human psyche that responds with pleasure to any object a human can hold that itself holds space, especially if it has a lid that can be opened with expectant mystery and closed with firm decision. So it happens time and time again that a humble box, especially if made of durable material like wood or tin, finds favor with us when its maker thought only of what was to be put in the box. And as they age, these boxes take on a value the original manufacturer would find totally astounding. The other day in an antique shop I saw a tin Union Leader tobacco can with flip-top lid that "only yesterday" I remember purchasing full of tobacco for 11¢. Its price: $7.50! And it was bent. Cigar boxes, pill boxes, sewing boxes, toolboxes, cheese boxes, fruit and vegetable crates, so-called Shaker boxes, even, for heaven's sake, wooden beer cases are now considered antiques, to be saved, perhaps redecorated, and used again. The commercial marketplace is well aware of this trend and is trying to spoil a lot of fun by reintroducing facsimiles of the old tins and selling specialty foods or tools in beautiful wooden boxes. But this way you pay for the boxes and then some, and moneysavers scoot off to some other possibilities.

Film (and Other) Tins

Are there any neat boxes still being thrown away that you can dress up or use as is? I've mentioned apple boxes and the cute little baskets that you can buy fruit in. You have to pay for these containers but they are still relatively cheap. Another example is the neat little round tin used for photographic film. Professional photographers buy film not by the roll but by the foot and in very short order they have a darkroom full of these tins. An acquaintance of ours who is married to a photographer hand-painted the tins and gave them as Christmas gifts one year. Since she had never before painted much of anything except her kitchen walls, we were all duly impressed by what a little skill and a lot of imagination could accomplish. The tins are perfect, displaying a uniqueness lost on the far fancier decorated tins that proliferate in the stores at Christmastime.

A popular folk art form today is painting landscapes, country scenes, and barnyard animals on bread boxes, cracker tins, grandma's ironing board, defunct crosscut saws, and other junk from Not-

So-Early America. A farmer's wife nearby is so talented at this kind of painting that her work sells as fast as she can finish it. Recently she found an "old" ammunition box, one of those popular collectibles that has nice finger joints at the corners but otherwise strikes me as ugly. She painted a frontier hunter on the lid and sold it immediately for $300.

Decorating the Box

Not many of us are talented enough to paint as well as my neighbor does, but there are other imaginative ways to decorate a box. Sometimes just a few coats of paint will do it. A black enamel surface, overlaid with a stenciled design and airbrushed gold or bronze, can be a conversation starter or stopper. "Airbrushed?" you may ask. Remember in sixth grade when the teacher had you run a paint-laded toothbrush over a piece of window screen held over the stencil? That will give you an airbrushed effect.

I've seen jewelry boxes made of what looks like softly burnished gold that were really dressed-up cigar boxes. To get that look is almost embarrassingly easy. Start with some aluminum foil that's been used and is quite crinkled. Cut it into little pieces that are easy to handle—about 1 by 3 inches—and cut enough to cover the box you are decorating. Now spread a coat of all-purpose white glue on the box, covering about 3 square inches at a time. Glue on the pieces of foil. Cover the whole box. The pieces should overlap every which way and round over the edges rather than end right at the edge.

Now comes the interesting part. Glue small pieces of yellow tissue paper over the aluminum foil, proceeding as you did with the foil. But this time, mix 1 part water with 2 parts glue to make a slightly runnier mixture. After you glue on a piece of tissue paper, daintily paint a very thin coat of the glue solution over it. You may need to paint on a second thin coat, but very lightly. The idea is to saturate the tissue, but not tear or disturb it. When the glue dries, the surface will be translucent gold, or perhaps a little milky. Clearer resin glues make a more transparent gold surface and dry much quicker. But white glue is what we all usually have on hand and it works fine.

Next you can "antique" the finish if you wish. Use a brown wood stain. Dab the stain on with a rag, fluff of cotton, cotton swab, or sponge. An excellent dabber can be made by folding a short rectangle of sponge in two and holding it between the jaws of a spring-clamp clothespin. It's easy to change pieces of sponge that way. Apply the stain more heavily around edges and corners and spread it out thinner in the more open places to achieve the antique look.

Finally, the decorator of this particular cigar box added a small brass hinge nailed on with tiny brads, and glued a small mirror on the lid. Around the mirror she glued a border of brass-colored beaded pull chain from an old light fixture. She glued another border of the chain around the sides of the box near the bottom, just for decoration. She lined the inside of the box with velveteen.

Boxes Out of Cans

You can make tin boxes out of America's most plentiful unnatural resource—tin cans. Books galore and hundreds of adult classes at local schools attest to the fact that toleware, as working with tin is called, is popular and affordable for all. You need a soldering iron, a tin snips, and practice. Japanning tin with black lacquer, then stenciling or free-handing colorful designs, resurrects the lowly tin can.

A Cardboard Box
Turned into a Display Case

All of us at one time or another have found ways to recycle greeting cards, but here's a way to recycle the box!

An imaginative gift-giver caught a beautiful giant silkworm moth fluttering against the porch screen of her suburban home. She saved it in a glass jar for a collector friend of hers. It soon died—these moths live only a few days. She had seen the way her friend kept his insect collection in display boxes or frames on soft beds of cotton with a glass or clear plastic cover over them. She decided to have the cecropia moth so framed and give it to her friend for a birthday present. As she pondered her next move, her eyes fell on a box of greeting cards. The box had a clear plastic lid. About one-third of the space in the box was taken up by a cardboard panel to one side, upon which was printed information about the cards. She realized the box would make a perfect display case for the moth.

She removed the cards and filled the box with cotton, then placed the moth on the cotton. She turned over the cardboard panel to the blank back side and glued to it a piece of paper upon which she had neatly typed the scientific name, a brief description, and short natural history of the moth. Then she put the transparent lid back on the box and taped it tightly behind the box with removable tape. The moth was ready to hang on a wall, put on a shelf, or stack in a drawer.

Wood Boxes from Scrap

Beautiful small wooden boxes can be made out of wood scraps. A commercial woodworker, famous for his boxes, likes to say he makes a good living out of the wood conventional cabinetmakers throw away. A small box can be complex and sophisticated in design—sliding beveled lid, wood hinges, dovetailed joinery, decorated with carvings or inlays. Or it can be a simple, square, butt-joined box with purchased hinges—the kind most of us would make. In either case, the beauty of the wood will provide a charm well worth the time spent in the making.

Copper and brass wire inlays are rather easy to do, compared to most inlay work. After transferring the design onto the wood, I cut the sides of the groove for the wire at a slight inward angle, keeping the groove narrow enough so that it will accept half the diameter of the wire. Without fancy power tools you can't always get the groove that exact, but a hair more or less won't matter because of the wire's round shape and malleability. If the groove is slighty too narrow, the round wire will still fit snugly to the sides, though if it is laid across the grain, the wire may break its glue line if the wood shrinks or swells a bit. But you can always widen the groove slightly and reglue. If you get the groove slightly too wide and deep and the wire sits down in the groove too far, creating a hairline between the inlay and the wood, the cure is easy. Before the glue dries, tap down on the wire with a hammer and some kind of punch—a bolt works fine. The wire will spread a bit to fill in the hairline space.

Once the glue is dried (use an all-purpose white glue), the wire will sand off smooth and flush with the wood. As you get down to the wood, use a finer grit of sandpaper so as not to leave scratches in the wood. A clear varnish or other clear wood finish over the inlay will keep it from tarnishing badly.

Ring Box from Scrap

This heart-shaped box with pivoting drawers began as a solid block of scrap walnut about 2 inches thick, 8 inches wide, and 20 inches long. It was sliced ("resawn," as woodworkers say) into four pieces that eventually would be laminated together again. If you start with four separate pieces of wood, you can do the rest of the sawing with any saw that will cut curves. But a power band saw or fret saw is better if you have access to one. Although the instructions sound complicated, the box is fairly simple to make (even I could do it). The dimensions are not critical. Mine were determined by the scrap board's dimensions, and I drew the heart shape to avoid the defects in the board that had made it scrap in the first place.

Three of the four layers of wood that make up the box should be about ¼ inch thick and the other layer 1 inch thick. They should be laminated together in this order: a ¼-inch piece on top, the 1-inch

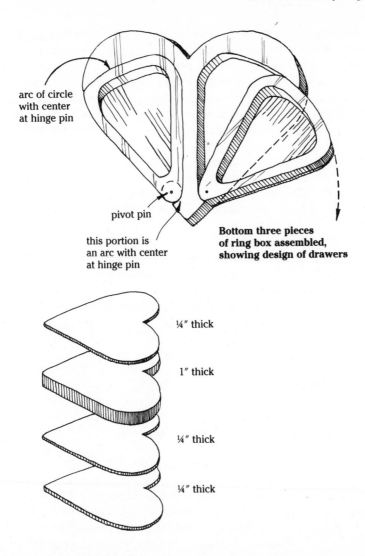

arc of circle
with center
at hinge pin

pivot pin

this portion is
an arc with center
at hinge pin

**Bottom three pieces
of ring box assembled,
showing design of drawers**

¼" thick

1" thick

¼" thick

¼" thick

piece under it, and the other two ¼-inch pieces at the bottom. All four
pieces should be planed or sanded flat so they will fit solidly against
each other. Then place them together in the order given and draw the
heart shape on the top one. To hold the pieces together while you saw
the shape out on all four at the same time, drive nails in the four
corners *outside* the heart form you have drawn. Then cut out the
heart.

Lay aside the top and bottom ¼-inch pieces. You will now need a
compass to draw drawer shapes on the right and left sides on top of

the 1-inch piece. This is the only critical part of the design. Each drawer will be held at the bottom with a wooden pin. The pivoting part of the drawer below the wooden pin must be precisely circular. Place the point of your compass at the spot where one pin will be, then draw an arc where you want the drawers cut. Do the same for the other side of the wood. You must be precise in your markings, otherwise the drawers will not slip in and out of the box smoothly and easily.

After marking drawer outlines, place the 1-inch piece back on top of the ¼-inch piece that fits under it and glue these two layers together. *But do not apply any glue inside the drawer lines.* When the glue dries, cut out the drawers. Lay aside the two ¼-inch drawer bottoms.

On the cut-out 1-inch pieces, draw the inner proportions of the drawer space. Then cut out the inner drawers with a coping saw, after drilling a hole through to accept the coping saw blade. What you have left are the walls of the drawers. Glue each piece on its ¼-inch bottom. When the glue is dry, drill a ³⁄₁₆-inch hole through the drawers at the place where the compass point sat when you drew the arcs.

Next take the other part of the heart shape you have already glued together and glue it to the bottom ¼-inch piece you had set aside and leave it to dry. When the glue is dry, insert the drawers in the box, then carefully drill a hole through the bottom board by coming straight down through the hole already in the drawers with a ⅛-inch bit. The holes must align, and this is a sure way to do it.

Next glue the last ¼-inch board on top and clamp. When the glue is dry, with the drawers again in place, turn the box upside down and drill a ⅛-inch hole in the top by coming up through the hole already in the other three pieces. Carve wooden pins to fit tightly in the ⅛-inch top and bottom holes (but loosely in the ³⁄₁₆-inch hole in the drawers). With drawers in place, put glue on the inner facing of the bottom hole, tap the pin down from the top to the bottom hole, and then apply a little glue around the top of the pin before tapping it in solidly. This sequence of gluing keeps glue from getting into the middle part of the hinge where the drawer must swing freely.

The box is now finished except for finishing the wood and lining the drawers with felt, velvet, or whatever strikes your fancy.

OTHER GIFTS FROM WOOD SCRAPS

A whole book could easily be filled with examples of wood-scrap gifts. With little more than a saw and a sharp pocketknife, one can make rings, belt buckles, bracelets, pendants, combs, spoons, and carvings.

Wood can be sculpted into some shapes with power sanders much easier than it can be whittled or chiseled. I rough-cut a mirror frame with a saber saw, then sanded it to shape on a disk sander. You might find that you have a knack for doing this kind of work even though you can't draw well and have not shown much ability in creating shapes and forms freehand on paper. I did. Working in three-dimensional shapes using only your eye and hand-held wood is different than trying to draw shapes on the flat two-dimensional surface. You study a piece of wood until you can almost see the finished figure in the grain, and then you simply take away the wood that is hiding that figure. Try it.

At most places where wood is worked, there are bins of waste that the carpenters and cabinetmakers will let you go through for likely scraps. Wood scraps are everywhere—pieces of firewood, stumps, fallen tree branches, fenceposts rotted off at ground level, pallets, packing crates. Don't be turned aside by rotten wood, or wood with exposed rotten surfaces. Spalted wood, with its mottled black and white streakings, is highly prized by woodworkers for its unique color and design. Spalted wood is wood that has begun to decay ever so slightly but is still solid. White oak is a good source of it, and larger white oak branches dead and fallen from trees often contain spalted wood—enough to make small carvings and other small items.

The walnut letter opener shown here is just another example of scrap-wood gifts. I made this one with a pocketknife and sandpaper. We've used it almost daily now for ten years. My main purpose was to prove that wood, especially a good, strong hardwood like walnut, can be used for tools we generally think can only be made from metal or plastic. Walnut is a good wood to work by hand because it is much softer than oak or cherry, yet it's strong enough to be carved and sandpapered to a very thin width, as in the blade of this letter opener. The inlay is copper wire, and there's a polyurethane varnish over all to protect the wood and keep the copper from tarnishing.

Another type of inlay that works well for lettering, but when only straight lines are called for, is straw. Rye, oats, or, best of all, wheat stems when mature (but before moisture and decay dull them) have a very nice golden color. You can only use sections between the stem joints, which usually limits you to less than 6 inches per piece. The straws should be soaked in warm water for a few minutes (after the joints are cut out and the husk removed), then very carefully slit open, laid out flat, and allowed to dry again. You may be able to skip that step altogether except when you want the widest possible strip of flattened stem. Cut the stem into desired widths with a razor blade. Very little cutting is necessary, because once a cut is started, the wheat straw will split straight down the stem. These strips are used as "inlay" although they are not really laid in. They are thin enough to be arranged on the wood surface and glued, then coated with varnish or shellac. Straw inlay is traditional in China and some of the eastern European countries, and when very precisely joined together, inlays are quite beautiful, especially against a dark background.

WREATHS

The plant nursery where we buy our Christmas trees did a brisk business in wreaths last year because the juniper boughs they used were loaded with dusky-blue berries to a degree seldom seen. My eye was on the berries for another reason—not to make gin, as friends accused, but because I wanted them for seed. Juniper that will fruit that heavily makes a wonderful winter cover for birds and I had hopes of getting the species started on my place. "Well, if you just want some berries, there's a big pile of discarded trimmings behind the shop," the nurseryman said. "You can have it all for free." Needless to say, the discards were almost as full of blushing-blue berries as the wreaths were, so we made wreaths out of them when we got home and planted the seeds later.

Most everyone knows how to make a conventional wreath. You tie the evergreen sprigs into little bunches, then tie the bunches to a stiff wire hoop (opened coat hangers will do if you have no other wire). Tie on the first bunch, then the second on the other side of the wire right behind the first. The first one will usually want to spin around until you get going. As you tie each bunch to the wire, lay the sprigs in the same direction, with the leafy ends covering the stems and tie of the bunch before it. Garlands are made in the same way.

Bunches of dried weed pods, seed heads, stems, flowers, and so on also make lovely wreaths, although such wreaths may lead to strained relationships in a household with a gardener fanatical about

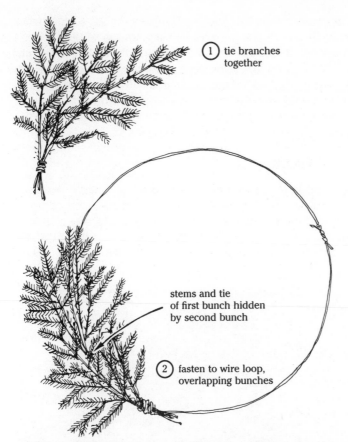

① tie branches together

stems and tie
of first bunch hidden
by second bunch

② fasten to wire loop,
overlapping bunches

weed control. A gardener of that school came into the house one evening, took one look at his wife's new wreath of dried weeds gathered from the roadside and bellowed like a wounded buffalo (or so she described him later to me). "What is that?" he wailed, pointing a quivering finger at the wreath.

"Teasel, darling."

"Darn right it's teasel," he roared. "And right next to it is foxtail and right next to that is sourdock. Do you know how long it's taken me to rid the garden of those things?"

Another, and less controversial, material for a beautiful wreath is the skinny, longish red or yellow hot pepper from the garden. This wreath style, borrowed from Mexico, is practical as well as decorative. The peppers can dry while they are providing visual pleasure.

Quarter-inch mesh hardware cloth cut into a circle or doughnut shape makes a good wreath base. This base is most often used for pinecone wreaths. The cones are tied individually to the mesh with fine wire. My wife covers the back with a piece of felt so that when hung, neither the mesh nor the wire will scratch the wall.

A piece of humble hardware cloth, by the way, makes a stunning background for a dried flower or weed arrangement in a frame. The hardware cloth is tacked to the back of the frame and painted— usually a bright gold or brass color. Then a bouquet of dried flowers, seed pods, seed heads, or a combination of all three is tied to the hardware cloth, leaving about half of it exposed.

Grapevine Wreaths

Grapevine wreaths require no base—the vines are simply wrapped around each other. Wild grapevines are preferred over domestic vines because they're generally more supple and are available in longer lengths. An experienced wreath maker will start with a long length of grapevine and wrap it around itself as if winding up a roll of

wire, tucking the end into the wrap. Then a second length is wrapped around and the end is tucked in. A third piece is added, and so on, until the wreath is of the desired size. With domestic grapevines, pieces are not always long enough and may be too stiff to wrap into a wreath without breaking or at least cracking. Soak them overnight in lukewarm water if that's the case. With shorter pieces, arrange about four into loop shapes and while holding them all together, tuck in all the ends. Then go on to a fifth piece, and so on, until the wreath is complete. You can bind the first four pieces together with string, or wait and tie the completed wreath for greater stability, but that is usually not necessary. Some makers wrap gaily colored ribbon around the completed wreath, or add sachets, or a bird's nest, or whatever strikes their fancy. The photo on the previous page shows a wreath with the dried grapes still attached.

The latest craze is to wrap grapevines around a tall pyramidal shape (usually made from a piece of chicken fence), spray with a white decorative frosting, and add tiny white or red lights. Behold, a Christmas tree. These grapevine trees look dull and uninteresting in the making, but the finished tree is quite remarkable.

Other vines make attractive wreaths, particularly bittersweet gathered in the fall, with its orange berries intact. Of course, some vines should be avoided. One of my sisters, who says she will never speak to me if I tell anyone this story, was out on an autumn walk when she spied some vines sprouting beautifully, with unusual white berries. She made a wreath out of them and shortly thereafter broke out in a rash. She'd made a lovely wreath out of poison ivy!

Corn-Husk Wreaths

I think the most beautiful wreaths are made of corn husks, curled over to resemble flower petals of various shapes and sizes. Many crafts books tell you how to make them, but few tell you how to obtain the husks. If you garden, save them from your sweet corn and popcorn—the inner, soft husks are the ones. You can buy husks, used to make tamales, at Mexican groceries. But if you go for a ride in the country almost any time in late October or November, corn harvest will be in progress and corn husks will be everywhere—skittering across the roads in the wind, clinging to fences, or filling road ditches along the fields. Help yourself. Some gatherers soak the pure white husks in a weak disinfectant solution as protection against a fungus that can spot the husks grey or grey green.

In the South, cotton boll wreaths supplant corn husks. Wheat

straw wreaths and soybean straw wreaths are also popular everywhere. These are bound closely and tightly with tough cord to hold
the straw together in a doughnut shape.

GIFTS FROM PAPIER-MÂCHÉ

Papier-mâché is one of the grandpappies of recycling techniques, but
most of us never think to take it seriously because of our experiences
in grade school. At one time or another, usually about the third grade,
we were all subjected to an afternoon of slopping gooey wet newspapers into ugly shapes. It comes as a surprise that papier-mâché was an
art form hundreds of years before daily newspapers made the raw
material for it almost limitless. The Victorians even made fancy furniture out of the glop—and would no doubt have made a lot more had
newspapers been as bulky as they are now.

I gained some appreciation for the medium by working on stage
sets for our local theater group. With nothing but torn pieces of
newspaper, water, chicken wire, and some reused boards for framing,
we learned to concoct all sorts of stage props—rocks, doors, trees,
storefronts, and backdrops. When painted and lighted skillfully, they
made realistic and even beautiful scenery.

If you add glue to the water, the papier-mâché objects are much
stronger upon drying than if you use only water. But what makes
papier-mâché even more practical today are the new epoxy coatings
that can be applied on the finished objects. With glue in the water and
epoxy coatings added, papier-mâché objects become virtually un-
breakable, waterproof, stain- and acid-resistant, and fireproof. Epoxy,
unlike lacquer, varnish, or shellac, penetrates the newspaper and
makes it stronger.

A good all-around glue mixture to spread on the wet newspaper
consists of ½ cup flour and ¼ cup powdered resin glue for every pint
of water. This mixture is spread thinly over a square of paper, say 1
foot in size. The square is then torn into four strips that are laminated
together. This four-strip piece is the customary building block of
papier-mâché. Many of them are laid over and around the mold until
the built-up "skin" is the proper thickness (an average of three or four
layers of strips, overall).

If, for example, you are making a bowl using one of your kitchen
bowls for a mold, you set the bowl upside down on the table in front of
you, then proceed to lay on strips from one edge over the bowl's
bottom and to the opposite edge. The second strip would go on
perpendicular to the first, and so forth, until the bowl bottom is

completely covered. Then more strips are added diagonally around the sides of the bowl, this way and that, until the required thickness is reached. It is important to continually squeeze from the center to the outer edges of the wet strips to force out air pockets. Be sure to put on the first layers glue side up so they don't stick to the bowl. After the new bowl skin is formed, you can remove the mold. Keep pressing out air bubbles, then place the bowl on a baking sheet and bake in a 250°F oven for five to ten minutes. More strips may be needed in weak spots after baking, especially those strips overlapping the rim of the bowl. Then rebake at the same temperature until completely dry. The bowl will turn brownish, but don't let it burn.

Some procedures call for treating the object with linseed oil before the final baking to increase strength and to achieve a rich brown. At any rate, a coating of linseed oil on the baking sheet will keep the bowl from sticking. Objects too large to fit in the oven can be dried in the sun, of course, or just in the open air.

A second basic way to build papier-mâché objects is to reduce the paper to a mash first rather than use strips. The best way of all is to form your object with strips and then add a coating of mash. Mash is made by boiling small pieces of paper, no more than 1 by 2 inches in size, in water until the paper disintegrates into a pulp. The pulp is then drained in a colander or similar strainer until all the free water is gone. Then only flour is added (no powdered resin), at the rate of 4 cups per gallon of mash. Then the mess is cooked again until the mash is nearly as stiff as mashed potatoes. No water is added. Cook on low heat—flour scorches easily.

Scores of books in the library will give you countless ways to make almost anything from bowls to boxes to bookends to kitchen-ware, furniture, figurines—whatever your imagination is equal to. The main thing to remember is that recycling newspaper this way (other papers with rag in them make even better material for papier-mâché) is not difficult, and the main ingredient is free. The value of your finished pieces will grow as your skill grows. In a world where so many hobbies require expensive supplies and tools, papier-mâché is an exception.

GIFTS FROM SCRAP FABRICS

We are inclined to think of fabric scraps as worthy of gift-giving consideration only if saved up for a long time and then tediously turned into a rug or quilt. While that certainly is a wonderful way to remember a loved one, there are faster, easier ways to turn the contents of your rag bag into a Santa's bag of gifts.

A Satchel from a Pair of Jeans

Denim is American's favorite fabric—the more faded the better. So anything you can sew from the less worn-out parts of jeans will make a welcome gift, particularly for younger people. This satchel uses two matching pieces from the seat of the jeans for the front and back, and two strips cut from the unworn backs of the jean legs for the strap and facings. The two strips form the narrow sides and bottom of the

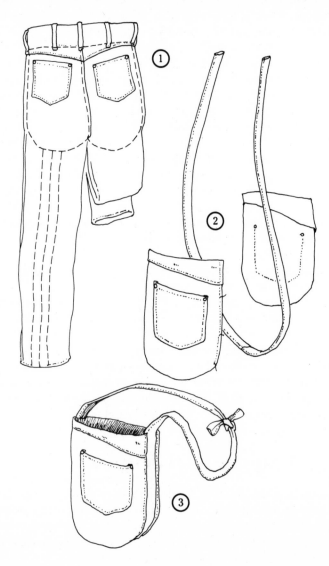

satchel and extend up on both sides for the shoulder strap. Each strip needs to be 3 inches wide and about double the distance from hip to shoulder in length, plus maybe 6 inches more for a knot to tie the ends together.

Center the front seat piece along one strip, placing right sides of the fabric together, and sew. Then do the same for the back seat piece. Fold under the raw edges of the strip along the part that isn't sewn to the seat pieces. For a nice professional appearance, you can sew little strips to the tops of the two seat pieces. Fold these to the inside, giving a neat edge to the top of the satchel.

Next sew the second strip on top of the first, being sure to fold under all raw edges. This strip covers the rough seams of the outer strip inside the satchel and on up the inside of the shoulder strap. Baste it in position and then topstitch it from the outside of the satchel with a zigzag or other decorative stitch. This topstitching will catch the ends of the facing folded inside the satchel opening and hold the facings down. Tie the strap ends together and the satchel is finished. You can add initials on the pockets for a personal touch.

Sacks for Drying Herbs and Seeds

My mother used a sack made of sheet or pillowcase fabric to store apples in after they were partially dry. The material is fine-woven enough to keep out dirt and bugs but will allow in sufficient air.

For drying seeds and herbs, a sack should be made of fabric that is light and can breathe, such as cotton. About a square foot of material is sufficient. Fold the fabric in half with right sides together. Then sew around three sides, leaving one of the short ends open. Turn the sack right side out. On the open end, fold the edge back to make a hem that will hold a drawstring. Sew the hem, but remember to leave an opening to insert the drawstring and bring it back out again. After inserting the drawstring, tie the ends together so it can't pull out. Fill the sack with herbs, pull the drawstring closed, and hang it up to dry.

Burlap makes a good drying sack, too. Although not insect-proof, it is good for things like garlic or seeds that aren't going to be affected by insects. Another way to make a small sack, say 8 by 12 inches, is to start with a piece of fabric that measures 12 by 16 inches. Lay the fabric out flat, and sew a 1-inch-wide strip of cloth about 1 inch from the edge of a 12-inch side, and 1 inch in from the 18-inch sides, to encase the drawstring. Now fold the sack piece in half vertically with the drawstring strip to the inside. Sew the bottom and side shut. Turn inside out, or actually right side out, insert a cord into the drawstring casing, and you are finished. To spruce up the sack, especially for gift-giving, some makers will topstitch around the sides and double over the top edge and stitch it down.

A Nut-Gathering Apron

Gathering hickory nuts is a cherished fall tradition in this part of the country. One woman made her friends what she called nut-gathering aprons for Christmas presents. They're very similar to clothespin bags, only larger. With one of these bags wrapped around one's waist, both hands are free to gather and shuck hickory nuts.

Any scrap remnants would serve the purpose, but my friend used pieces of burlap bags. She took two pieces of burlap about 12 by 20 inches each and sewed them together to form a bag. For the neck strap, she used a strip of burlap about 3 inches wide and long enough to fit comfortably. The ragged edges are turned in and sewn down. On either side of the mouth of the bag she sewed a piece of light rope about 20 inches long to wrap around the waist and tie. She sewed Velcro fasteners along the mouth of the bag to close it and keep nuts from rolling out when one stoops to pick up more. She also added a piece of decorative ribbon across the front.

The sacks not only work fine for gathering nuts but for gathering vegetables such as peas and beans from the garden and for carrying clothespins.

Easy Potholders

Every kitchen can use another potholder. They're especially good gifts for younger people to make. To make one from scraps, choose cotton for the outer pieces, since it will not melt under heat the way some synthetics will. For padding, flannel and corduroy are good, as is wool, such as from a shrunken sweater, if you have no better use for it. Cut the front and back squares to size and the padding about ¼ inch smaller. Sew the padding to the inside of one of the outer squares with a big X to the four corners. This will make the potholder lie flat and keep the padding pieces in place during washing. Then sew the outer pieces together, with the padding inside, leaving one corner open. Turn under the raw edges or cover them with seam binding. If you want a hanger on the potholder, cut a piece of material about 5 inches long and 2 inches wide, fold the raw edges in, and sew them down. Make a loop of the strip, stick the two ends about ½ inch into the open end of the potholder at the corner, and sew up the open end. Sew double or triple across the loop ends so they won't pull out. You can then applique or embroider the potholder to make it a more personal gift.

Mittens

Here's an easy way to make mittens for children. Use an old sweater sleeve for the material. Lay the child's hand on the sleeve just above the cuff to get an idea of size. The cuff of the sweater becomes the cuff of the mitten. The little finger of the hand should be next to the sweater seam, if you are going to cut out a separate thumb. Trace the hand on the sweater with chalk, cut, and sew to fit. Actually, a thumb is not really necessary. If you watch most kids when they are playing in the snow, they have their thumbs tucked up into the main part of their mittens anyway, to keep them warmer.

My wife used to use plastic bread bags to keep the kids' hands and feet drier when they played in the snow. Just slip the bags over the mittens and boots and secure with rubber bands. A bag will last about a day. This may seem an overly motherly practice, but we learned that a bread bag equaled an extra half-hour of play before the kids came to the door crying that they were too cold—a decent enough return from a bread bag.

Throw Pillows

A woman who makes *lots* of pil' __from leftover remnants says that almost any fabric is usable, although she prefers cotton for longer wear, and polished cotton in particular. She stresses that in using scraps one should not be tempted to use any that are already fairly worn, with the possible exception of denim, which she says is popular even for pillows. "Using worn fabric in a new pillow is like putting new wine in old sacks," she says. Better to use new or nearly new remnants. Her latest pillows are made of remnants of the new material left over after her living room chairs were reupholstered.

For stuffing she may use polyester, but mostly, while her supply lasts, she stuffs pillows with old panty hose. "It takes lots of pairs to fill a pillow," she says, "but when you're working a regular office job you can go through two or three pairs a month. To me that's a horrible waste. I *have* to find other uses for them to justify the silly expense."

Nylon panty hose makes good stuffing because it is soft but resilient. Pillows made with it are comparatively easy to wash. The nylon holds the pillow shape and dries out fast. Be sure to cut the waistbands off first. The elastic is too hard and bulky for pillow stuffing.

The two pillow pieces are sewn together inside out on three sides and then turned right side out. Then the stuffing is put in until the pillow is full and firm, the raw edges turned under, and the fourth side sewn shut. Some pillow makers put a zipper on the pillow so the cover can be removed and washed. Some don't. The woman mentioned above says she just cuts the seam open if she wants to remove or change covers.

The real work of making a fancy pillow takes place before it is sewn together. Any decoration desired is worked onto the unsewn pieces—often just the front piece. Decorating offers a good opportunity to use scraps of fabric, too, for applique, piping, or what have you. Lace remnants can add a real decorator touch to a pillow. You can make your own piping if you find none to suit. Just cover old rope or cord with the fabric of your choice and sew it down.

Enamel Art

Probably the most beautiful art form that can make use of pure junk is enameling—pieces and jewelry made from fusing special enamel glass to copper. Enameling is a very ancient art, which is a tip-off that it can be practiced without elaborate or expensive modern tools, although it *is* practiced today with such tools. All you really need, however, is some old copper pipe or (so help me) a refrigerator door or similar junk piece of enameled surface, a blowtorch, a little piece of hardware cloth, and some special powdered enamels from an art supply store. Since these enamels are really glass that is melted and fused to the metal, it once occurred to me that one could grind up colored glass bottles found in junk piles and use that instead of purchased enamels. To find out, I asked Kenneth Bates, world-renowned enamelist, whose work is both breathtakingly beautiful and very expensive. He agreed it was possible to use an old refrigerator door for an enameling base, since you can fuse enamel to enamel even if the base under it is iron, but said that ordinary glass can't be turned into enamel. "I thought when I was a boy that it might work, but learned that it did not," he says in a letter.

In centuries past, the best enameling was done on gold and sometimes silver, and still is, but copper works very well indeed. Normally, enamel coatings are baked on the copper in a kiln, but for small pieces—anything under about 3 inches square—you can get enough heat from a propane torch, or better, two torches, applied directly to the copper. All you need is a makeshift stand and a piece of hardware cloth to hold your copper base.

Start with a piece of copper, such as from a copper pipe, the usual form you find scrap copper in. Cut open a piece of the pipe, flatten it, cut it to shape with a tin snips or metal saw, and buff it sparkling clean and smooth. Apply heat from the blowtorch to the bottom side of it as it lies on the hardware cloth and add an enamel coating to the top side. When the temperature for fusion is reached, the enamel becomes molten and "bakes" onto the metal. The result, even before you know what you are really doing, can be a beautiful blend of forms and colors. Once a coating of enamel has fused, you can add more coats. Refrigerator door enamel works well as a base because the first coat is already in place.

Another form of enameling is in some ways more practical for the home recycler and, in skilled hands, is almost as beautiful. Instead of using copper or a previously enameled surface, the enamel powders are fused onto glass. Almost any recycled glass will do. To bring out the enamel colors, the glass is usually first coated with a gold, silver, or platinum glaze available at art supply stores. The enamels are then sprinkled on, as in conventional enameling, but the fusion takes place in a kiln rather than with a propane torch.

There are scores of books on enameling and at least half a dozen distinct methods of doing it, but strangely enough, outside certain art and craft circles, the skill is not well known. Take a look at masterpieces by Kenneth Bates or Dean Drahos. They, to be sure, do not work on scrap copper or old refrigerator doors, but the beauty of their work might inspire you to try a new hobby.

A good source of information about enameling on glass can be found in *Art from Found Materials, Discarded and Natural* by Mary Lou Stribling (Crown Publishers, New York, 1970). This book will be of interest to any moneysaving recycler with a yen to turn "junk" into art. A major section deals with sculpture made from such castoffs as worn-out automobile parts, nails, bolts, springs, and so forth, which always strike me as ghastly. But artists working in these media have been honored in museums and galleries. Human forms cleverly made out of spark plugs, rocker arms, springs, tin cans, and crankshafts seem to be popular, so who am I to turn up my nose? One rather famous artist creates mobiles cut from plastic bottles. Museums display them, and the critics call them "provocative." A fairly safe adjective, I'd say.

CHAPTER 3

Economizing in the Yard and Garden

I f you stick a copper rod into a potato and a zinc rod into another potato, the acid in the spuds will react with the metals and generate electricity. Most of us have seen this bit of scientific gee-whiz demonstrated on one of those Saturday-morning TV shows. We are dutifully impressed and then go on our way, thinking no more of the matter. After all, who wants to carry a sack of potatoes around to power a flashlight? But where the spirit of Yankee ingenuity burns brightly, such a demonstration can spark ideas. The September 1984 issue of *Countryside* magazine reported that an electronics technician was marketing a clock that ran for four weeks on two potatoes. And a fellow in the West Indies, with the un-Yankee name of Jorge Mirillo-Yepes, carried the idea one step further—he made a battery out of rotting compost. Not many Americans will find it practical to link up twelve or more cartons of compost with electric cable and copper strips just to run a radio and a few light bulbs, but Mirillo-Yepes's "garbage battery," as he calls it, works.

GETTING THE MOST FROM COMPOST

Compost, certainly the grandmother of all recycling endeavors, is still not being fully recycled. Even if its electric power is not (yet) practical, we surely should find more ways to use the heat produced other than just building hotbeds. There are other possibilities.

Robert Rodale, visiting Austria in 1979, found that researchers at the Austrian Academy of Sciences in the village of Donnerskirchen had made a hot-water heater simply by packing ground-up grape seeds around a metal tank of water. (See *Organic Gardening* magazine, December 1979, for the complete report.) They told Rodale that 150 to 180 kilograms (331 to 397 pounds) of grape seed would warm 50 liters (13 gallons) of water a day for about a month. Even more impressive, the Austrians were heating a small greenhouse with the grape seeds—boxes of them under the plant benches and along the walls of the greenhouse. Heat could rise directly to the plants, but most of it collected in perforated pipes inside the composting chambers and was vented to the atmosphere over the plants.

As with so many biological processes, the efficiency did not stop there. The decaying grape seeds also gave off appreciable amounts of carbon dioxide, which plants need an ample supply of, especially in greenhouses. Furthermore, scientists learned that the finished compost was especially rich in certain necessary trace elements not always found in fertilizers. Among other things, the compost improved germination when used as a growing medium.

The ordinary gardener does not usually have a 12-acre vineyard—the acreage deemed practical for the project—from which to heat a greenhouse with waste seed, but moneysavers can find alternatives. For example, weed seeds generate quick, intense heat, too, and every grain elevator across the country collects tons of them in its seed-cleaning operations. Then there are tomato seeds, which are a waste problem for canneries. And apple processing plants, as well as literally thousands of cider mills, have to get rid of tons of apple pomace and seed left over from pressing juice. When a gardener composts waste seeds, even if the heat generated isn't harnessed, the composting process at least kills the seeds so they don't germinate and cause problems in the garden.

Sawdust is another common mulch and compost source the moneysaver should collect. It is everywhere, and it's available for the asking from sawmills, lumberyards, and woodworking shops. Its extra value is not in the heat it generates, which is not much, but in its ability to absorb and mask odors—sometimes a composting problem in urban backyards. Sawdust is ideal to layer with garbage and table scraps. It also makes good mulch for working handily in and around low clusters of plants such as strawberries. Its high-carbon, low-nitrogen ratio has given it a bad reputation as a nitrogen robber as it decays, but you needn't worry if the mulch is left on top of the soil rather than worked into it. The sawdust will then decay slowly at the soil surface and not deplete soil nitrogen. In the compost heap, other nitrogen-rich materials provide the extra nitrogen needed to speed sawdust's decay. If that doesn't convince you, you can always stock-pile the sawdust until it has partially decayed before using it in com-post-making or for mulch.

Fall leaves are, of course, the moneysaver's most provident and abundant source of garden fertility. Their availability will increase in the late 1980s because the Environmental Protection Agency is finally clamping down on leaf burning in small towns and villages. Towns are buying large, mechanical leaf collectors and, rather than haul those leaves to a landfill, will be willing more than ever to bring you a load.

Compost Bins

The ubiquitous wood pallet makes a serviceable compost bin. Lay one on the ground and stand four more around it, wiring the corners together. The spaces between the slats allow for good air circulation, especially under and up through the compost heap. The bottom pallet will deteriorate sooner, of course, so rotate the pallets every year for longer use.

A coil of woven wire fence, steel reinforcing mesh, or chicken wire also makes an adequate bin. Cut a piece that forms a 4- to 6-foot-tall cylinder of about 3 to 5 feet in diameter. The weight of the com-post will keep the wire stable. To turn the compost, unwire the roll, set it up beside the heap, and fork over the material into the wire again.

If you live near livestock farmers, you can often get bales of poor-quality hay at a very reasonable price or even for free. Stack several to form a compartment that will make a temporary bin. After it begins to rot along with the compost, the hay can be used for mulch or added to another heap. Stack the bales so the twine or wire that holds them is not on the inner wall of the bin where they would deteriorate faster.

Old bricks, cement blocks, or flattish rocks can be stacked into compost bins. Leave air spaces between rows. Be aware, though, that the bricks, blocks, or rocks will eventually lean out of plumb and you will have to restack them.

Steel drums make excellent compost bins but, like railroad ties, aren't as free-for-the-asking as they used to be. However, many busi-nesses still give them away if you ask politely. Even if you have to pay $5, drums have so many uses that the money is worth spending. For an upright, stationary compost bin, the bottom of the drum should have holes in it for air circulation and should be set up off the ground. Some composters remove the bottom of the barrel completely and

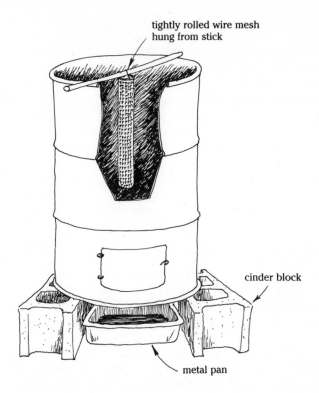

tightly rolled wire mesh
hung from stick

cinder block

metal pan

replace it with some kind of grating or latticework, but you can just punch or drill holes in the bottom. You need a door in the side of the barrel, near the bottom, from which to scoop out finished compost. A perforated tube down the middle of the barrel permits even better air circulation. A tight roll of chicken wire will serve this purpose.

Good compost should not be so juicy that liquid leaks out the bottom, but if you are extracting compost or manure "tea," you will need a pan under the barrel. Another alternative is to set a drum on top of a section from another drum, with a grate of some sort between them. The bottom compartment is used to store and save some finished compost to add as starter when adding new material into the top of the barrel.

A barrel bin allows the composter great control over his compost. By removing or replacing the lid on top, both heat and moisture (rain) can be controlled. The principle is very much like that of a stove: Compost, as it decays, heats up, and air circulation will influence that heat the same way it does a fire in a woodstove.

Compost Tumblers from Steel Drums

Compost tumblers made from steel drums are a bit more complex to build than the stationary drum composters. You can look at a commercial model to see what is involved. The barrel is usually rotated in a horizontal position, although in some homemade models it is rotated at a slant. The reason for this latter, more cumbersome, style is that the drum empties more completely and out of a smaller hole in the end of the barrel than the horizontal models do. Of the several ways to mount this (or any) kind of tumbler, the easiest way is to set two posts in the ground very solidly, with grooves on top of the posts to hold the axle that runs through the drum. The posts have to be tall enough so that the barrel is held above the height of the cart or wheelbarrow or whatever you will use to empty the compost into. In the case of the slanted design, the axle runs straight through both ends of the slanted barrel and the axle—1¼- or 1½-inch pipe is fine—is welded to the barrel. Pipe flanges at each end of the axle keep it from sliding out of the grooves in the tops of the posts. A crank is mounted on the flange at one end (a pair of crossed boards makes an adequate crank). The compost ordinarily needs to be tumbled about five times in the course of bringing it to a finish.

Tumblers in a horizontal position have axles that run straight through the center of the barrel, end to end. A door is cut into the side of the barrel, used for both filling and emptying. The greater the width of the door, the better the barrel will empty, but the weaker it will be.

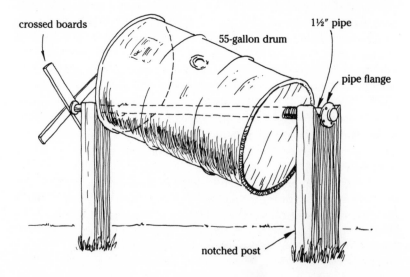

crossed boards   55-gallon drum   1½" pipe   pipe flange   notched post

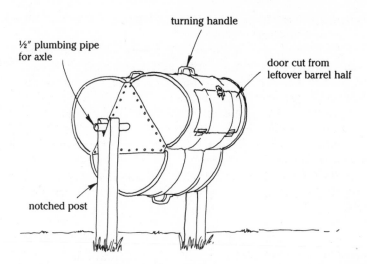

Three small doors between the barrel ribs might serve better, although I've never seen any tumblers made that way.

The drawback of most drum composters is that they don't hold very much. One tumbler I've seen solves that problem. It is made of three halves of drums cut lengthwise and then welded to each other in a cloverleaf pattern.

To make a cloverleaf tumbler, you'll need three barrels, two of which are of the same diameter and rib spacing. Cut one of the matching barrels down its length and through both ends as if you were going to cut it perfectly in half. But don't cut down the other side. Instead, bend the barrel open as if it were a trunk. You will have to cut notches in the ribs at the bend line to make the barrel open up, and perhaps score all along the line of the bend with a dull chisel to make it bend evenly. Next cut the second matching barrel completely in half—making one half of the barrel about 1½ inches deeper than the other. Bend back the 1½-inch edges into flanges. Drill holes in the flanges and matching holes along the edges of the opened barrel and bolt the two together.

From the third barrel, cut two triangular end pieces, which should measure, if you are working with 55-gallon drums, 26 inches per side to lap the end holes sufficiently. You will have to nip off the corners of the triangles so they fit over the ends properly. Drill holes in the edges of the triangles and drill matching holes around the edge of the barrel openings, but before you bolt them together, cut holes in the exact centers of the triangles large enough to accept ¾-inch pipe flanges. Bolt the flanges to the triangular pieces. These will hold a

½-inch axle made from a piece of plumbing pipe. Now bolt the triangles to the barrel end openings.

Cut a door-opening in one side of the tumbler no larger than about 15 by 28 inches. Then, from the leftover barrel half, cut a door that is 2 to 3 inches larger all around than the opening. (You could try using the piece you cut out from the tumbler and attach it with hinges, but it may leak.) Mount the door with door bolts or window latches at either side, or bolt or even wire the cover through holes in the cover and at the edge of the opening. Put handles on all three sections of the tumbler to turn it conveniently.

If the tumbler is to be mounted on a wooden frame instead of on posts, you'll need holes in the frame to house the axle and holes for the bolts or pins that will be inserted on the outside to hold the axle in place.

This and other adaptations of steel drums require cutting and brazing with an acetylene torch. Be sure toxic and volatile residues in the barrel are thoroughly cleaned out before welding. Otherwise, an explosion might result. Some welders will fill a barrel with water before cutting the end out of it, when they are not sure if the barrel is clean.

Cutting an end out of a barrel can be done with a hammer and chisel. Once you have opened a hole, proceed with the chisel at about a 45-degree angle, not straight down, and stay right next to the edge of the barrel.

In cutting holes in the barrel, especially across the body, I use a metal-cutting blade in a saber saw, first starting the cut with a chisel. With a chisel or saw blade, you will leave a very sharp burr on the edge of the cut metal. Be careful you don't cut your hand on it. File the burr off smooth.

You can braze on regular hinges and catches for your doors, but you can get by simply by drilling holes in the door and drum body and passing wires through for hinges. You can use a piece of wire to hold the door closed, too, although you may find it impractical to have to unwire every time you open the door.

CHEAP PLANT PROTECTORS

I've never seen a rosebush dolled up in an old overcoat for the winter, but I expect to someday. When diligent gardeners turn their attention to staving off the effects of adverse nature, their imaginations know no bounds. If a cold snap threatens, prim suburban gardens suddenly take on the appearance of something like a cross between sidewalk sales days downtown and the leading edge of a landfill. To ward off the danger of frost, gardeners will use their whole arsenal of household fabric scraps: old blankets, torn sheets, ragged bedspreads, carpet remnants. One desperate fellow, awakening in the middle of the night to the very real possibility of frosted strawberry blossoms, spread a collapsed camping tent as far as it would go over the bed.

In the autumn this kind of patchwork quilting, ugly as it is, can pay bigger dividends. After a light frost in September that might otherwise kill the tomatoes, there often follows a month of frost-free weather.

In summer the scene may be repeated if wildlife becomes a menace. Then it's cheesecloth and old curtains to the rescue. A blueberry lover from the coast of Rhode Island brought some discarded fishnets to his new home in the Philadelphia area and used them to keep birds off his blueberry bushes. Some gardeners try to get rid of their old newspapers by spreading them around the corn patch in August and dribbling kerosene or creosote (made from steeping chimney soot in water) or mothballs on the papers. This is supposed to keep away raccoons, but I've never found it to do any good.

Even winter gardens provide ways to empty the contents of your rag bag. Tender ornamentals like boxwood will burn to a nice winter-kill brown if exposed to hard winds when the temperature is near zero. They need only minimal protection—a wind barricade of burlap or old carpet. Drive stakes around the bush and tack on a skirt of whatever heavy fabric you have available. A trick that will benefit your

---

HOW TO DRIVE STAKES THE EASY WAY

If you need to drive lots of stakes in your garden, and most gardeners do, heed an idea from fence installers. They use a hollow steel tube with a solid steel end on it to drive steel posts in the ground. It makes the work much easier than pounding with hammer or sledge. You slip the driver over the post, holding on with both hands, and as you repeatedly slam it down against the top of the post, the post sinks into the ground. To drive the smaller, more fragile wood stakes in the garden, use a length of plumbing pipe no more than three-fourths the length of the stake after it is driven the proper distance into the ground. Screw a cap on one end of the pipe. Slip the pipe over the stake, and with repeated up-and-down motions, drive the stake home. You can do it with one hand.

roses is to encircle each bush with a coil of chicken-wire fence and fill the inside space with peat moss or leaves. Buckets that the bottoms have rotted out of will do for this purpose, too. For rhubarb, set a half barrel, metal or wood, painted black, over each plant and it will grow faster and sooner in spring.

But it is in protecting new transplants that the gardener hurls his most sophisticated weaponry of trash into the fray: buckets, jars, cans, baskets, sacks, crocks, garbage containers, window sashes, plastic roofing panels—anything that can be made to cover a plant handily. (I use a fish aquarium to root cuttings or sprout tree seeds in—it hasn't seen a fish in ten years.) In the Midwest, you often see lines of clay field tile standing on end in rows across gardens. They make good plant protectors even though open at the top. The clay absorbs the sun's heat during the day and keeps the space inside warm enough to fight off a light frost at night.

THE LAZY GARDENER—A PARABLE

One of the laziest gardeners I know discovered an amazingly easy way to grow lettuce, melons, and tomatoes, and I suspect his methods would work on other crops. Gardeners brainwashed to the notion that there is an Immutable Right Way to do everything are not going to believe this tale. I didn't until I tried it myself. This gardener, being lazy, as I said, seldom got his garden cleaned up all bare and prim in the fall. Old rotten tomatoes littered the tomato patch and sorry, caved-in cantaloupes awaited the merciful covering of snow. Tall, seeded stalks of Oak Leaf lettuce turned brown, then black, then fell into the mud.

After several years of this, the Lazy Gardener noticed that three of his most troublesome weeds in May and June were volunteer tomatoes, lettuce, and melons. It was not only irritating, but downright humiliating to consider how painstakingly he worked to start melons and tomatoes in seedboxes in the house, transfer them to the cold frame, then set them out in the garden, only to have them turn blue on chilly May nights. Meanwhile, the volunteers came up all by themselves and then proceeded to outgrow his coddled transplants. Although he was lazy, the man was not a fool, so he began to hoe and rake *around* some of the volunteers instead of weeding them out. The lettuce and cherry tomatoes grew fine, but the melons and regular tomatoes, being from hybrids, did not always produce quality fruit. So he switched to growing nonhybrid varieties of tomatoes and melons that come true from seed and after that he quit buying seed, quit planting, and let nature take her course. This worked out just peachy except that the crop came up in the same

Plastic Containers

The easiest and, in my opinion, best plant protectors for transplants are plastic containers that are translucent rather than transparent. Plastic gallon jugs are nearly perfect, although if you can get larger-sized containers made of this kind of plastic, so much the better. The translucency allows in plenty of light for good growth without the full harshness of sunlight, which can be harmful on tender transplants that aren't quite hardened off yet. If you look at the price of commercially available cloches you'll see why junk plastic containers are twice blessed for garden work. Just cut the bottoms out of the jugs and save the lids. Screw on the lids on cold nights and remove them during the day. In warm, sunny weather, remove the entire jug lest the atmosphere inside get too hot. Because they are essentially non-breakable, the plastic jugs are better than glass jugs with the ends cut

place it did the year before and matured a bit later than he'd like. So he initiated Step Two in the height of laziness, a step he continues to adhere to year after year.

He cultivates a farmer friend with a bottle of Boodles gin. In return, the farmer lets him have the bottom layer of straw bales stacked in his dirt-floored pole shed. (The bottom layer usually gets a mite wet and moldy.) It is arguable whether the bales are worth a bottle of good gin, but both the farmer and the gardener believe the other is getting cheated, which is all that matters. The gardener sets the bales in a double row across the garden, just far enough apart for an old window sash to span, to keep the tilled strip of ground between the bales cozy warm in spring. Then he tosses onto that strip of ground some rotten tomatoes, rotten melons, and lettuce seedheads from the past summer's growth, each in its own section of the strip. Then he goes into hibernation until April.

In April he sets the windows over the bales and goes back to sleep again. In May, using the bales as a bench to sit on, he languorously thins out excess volunteer seedlings that have grown between the bales and he pulls weeds at the same time. In June he pulls straw out of the bales as needed for mulch around the melons and tomatoes. Eventually, the plants run rampant all over the bales on either side, and by August the place looks more like a steeplechase hedge than a garden row. The bales (or what's left of them) hold most of the melons and tomatoes off the ground. After harvesting and dutifully salting next year's bale row with seed again, the Lazy Gardener grinds the whole mess up with the lawn mower and tills it in for organic matter. He then manages to loiter at the farmer's house until he gets back half the cost of the Boodles by drinking it himself.

out (and far easier to cut, too). The latter, like the old French bell jar protectors (the original cloches), are fairly fragile. The lightness of the plastic jugs is a disadvantage compared to the glass, but if you scrape a little dirt up around the jug base it will hold in place surprisingly well in the wind—and the dirt will keep cold air out better.

You can cut the plastic with a knife or a tin snips. The cut-off bottoms have a use, too. In some parts of the country, mice will eat holes in cantaloupes from the underside next to the soil. If you set the melons (still growing on the vines) in the plastic jug bottoms, the varmints are deterred. Be sure to punch tiny holes in the bottom so water drains out.

Plants outgrow the gallon jugs in a hurry. Keep a sharp eye out for larger translucent plastic containers, even colored ones if the color is pale enough to allow a fair amount of light to come through.

Old Windows

As homeowners have become more sensitive about heat loss from their homes, they replace old-fashioned windows with the double- and triple-paned kind. The leftovers are stored in cellars, above garages, in outbuildings. No one has the heart to throw away perfectly good windows, so put them to good use in the garden. Hinge them in pairs and set them as inverted Vs over plant rows to add at least two weeks to either end of the gardening season. Old screen doors can be used the same way to shade cool-weather crops or even to blanch celery a bit.

Plastic Panels

Translucent plastic roofing panels make excellent row covers, too. The corrugated ones bend nicely over the row and can be tied or wired to that shape. Don't forget to block the ends on cold nights and to keep birds out. I started using these panels not to get plants out earlier in the garden but to keep birds from eating sprouting corn. Once the corn was about 3 inches tall, the birds wouldn't bother it anymore. I would then move my five panels over and start another row. This method gave me a small amount of fresh corn coming in over a two-month period, rather than most of it maturing at the same time.

I got my used panels off a makeshift greenhouse that was being torn down. Around building sites, particularly at nurseries, you can often pick up discarded panels that the wind has torn loose. The torn nail holes are not big enough to deter the panels' use for row covers. The translucent light green ones work just about as well as the colorless ones. In fact, I've found them to work better over tender transplants.

The cheapest overnight plant protectors are grocery bags. Set three or four stakes around each plant and slip a bag over them. The bags will withstand considerable rain and wind.

Inner Tubes and Tires

The Lazy Gardener would roll his eyes in mock pain at this kind of devotion, but one gardener writes in *Organic Gardening*'s "Reader's Forum" (March 1980) that yet another way to keep a plant warm at night is to encircle it with an old inner tube partially full of water. She cuts a hole in the tube, sticks in the water hose to fill it, then clamps the hole closed with a clothespin. The sun warms the water in the black tube and the water then keeps a nice warm microclimate around the plant at night. Instead of cutting a hole in the tube, you could remove the valve from the tube's stem, immerse the tube underwater in the sink or a tub and fill it partway, then replace the valve. But you'll need a strong back to lift and carry it from filling place to plant.

Another recycled plant protector that (like the row of bales used by the Lazy Gardener) is actually a cold frame in miniature is made from two old tires, one atop the other. Fill the bottom with compost, good soil, manure—whatever you like for a good seedbed in a raised bed. Set a seed or transplant in this soil, water if necessary, set a second tire over the first, and then cover it with a piece of plastic such as the bags dry cleaners use over clothes. Tuck the ends of the plastic between the two tires. On hot days you'll have to roll it back part or all the way. As the plant grows and warm weather comes to stay, remove the plastic and the top tire. Or if you want to keep the plant under cover as it grows taller, add a third tire.

To me, tractor tires around trees make for extremely tacky landscaping, but hidden from view, a cold frame made from a big tractor tire is cheap and enduring. I once spied a tractor tire around a tree, painted red, white, and blue, no less, that happened to be the size my old tractor takes—a size not easy to find anymore. Moreover, it was in better shape than one on my tractor. So I reversed the usual recycling routine. The owner gave me the tire to put on my tractor, improving the looks of his property, if not my tractor.

Standard-size auto tires can be made to look fairly attractive around trees, however, and serve some useful purposes at the same time. Cut the tire in half lengthwise, down the center of the tread. This is not easy to do. (If someone would make a power tool that would turn tires against a fixed knife, the job would be considerably easier.)

First puncture a hole with a heavy butcher knife or hunting knife through the center of the tire *from the inside.* Then use a sawing motion to cut the tire around from the *outside,* starting from the hole you have made. If you have ever tried to push a knife through a tire tread, you'll know why the above procedure is better. The tread will pinch against the knife on the outside, and only great strength or a very sharp stilleto will gain entrance from that side. With the tire halved, turn each half inside out. The smooth surface and bell shape gained by this maneuver improves the looks of the tire around the tree. Slip the tire half over the tree, or if the tree is too large, cut the half tire through, ring it around the tree trunk and then hold it in circular shape with two short stakes. Not only will the rubber border hold mulch around the tree, but it will act as a guard against careless mowing.

Wire Screen Tree Guards

In place of commercial tree guards, wire screening works quite well. Cut a rectangular piece as tall as necessary and wide enough to wrap around the tree trunk and still have some left over. Then bring the edges together and fold them over twice to hold the screen in place. Gardeners in deer country use scrap wire to protect trees. One orchardist claims the only way he can keep deer from nibbling branches is to wrap wire around branch ends near the ground. The deer get discouraged trying to bite through the wire. Another orchardist unrolled old woven wire fence on the ground around the trees, claiming the deer won't stick their feet through it for fear of becoming entangled.

Some orchardists cut lengths of plastic drain tile or sewer tile in half, fit the halves around the trunk, and tie them securely. Sometimes you can push the halves far enough down in the ground around the trunk so they will hold without tying. Some drainage tubing is limber enough so you need cut it down only one side, then bend it back and slip it around the trunk. Use white or light-colored tubing. Dark colors will draw too much heat to the tree trunks on sunny winter days. Sudden drops in nighttime temperatures might then cause the bark to split. This is especially true of cherry, peach, nectarine, and apricot trees.

To keep rodents from tree seeds, some orchardists plant the seeds inside tin soup cans. Cut the top completely off the can and cut two slits in the form of a cross in the bottom. Bend the sharp-pointed tabs, formed by the crossed slits, upward. Fill the can with dirt and a seed, and bury it open side down so that the end with its sharp points

---

RECYCLING TIRES

Because of the zillions of old tires piled up from coast to coast, a great pastime for recyclers is coming up with new and more ingenious ways to use them. You can cut a piece to reheel a shoe satisfactorily. People in Third World countries cut sandals from them that are quite serviceable and even comfortable. I tried on a pair once. A man (in Germany, I believe) made news by using strips of tires in place of shingles to make a very long-lasting roof. A few years ago, *Mother Earth News* excitedly reported a budding business in turning old tires into floormats, but the cottage industry has not been heard from recently to my knowledge. Seems to me, however, that it should be no real trick to cut tires into flat pieces and stitch them together for mats to keep pickup beds from getting scratched during hauling operations. The commercial ones cost $300! (A sheet of Masonite works about as well but has to be replaced occasionally.) And shredded tires appear to be a practical material to use in concrete for road building. Not far from where I live a man with an interesting outlook on life has been stockpiling junk tires for years. He believes his tire mountain might make him rich some day when science discovers a practical way to recycle tires back into great demand.

In the meantime, gardeners do their best to help out. A rubber strip about 16 inches long and 3 inches wide cut from a tire can be looped and the ends bolted to an old shovel handle or stick to make a tamp for pushing materials into your shredder. If the tire-bottomed tamp hits the blades, no harm is done.

---

is just at the soil surface. The tree sprout can grow up between the sharp tabs, but an animal is effectively deterred from digging down to the sprouting seed. The tin can soon rusts away.

SIMPLE PEST CONTROLS

Cardboard rings or rings cut from foam cups make effective cutworm collars, as do toilet paper rolls cut to appropriate widths. The collars don't have to be round. Square ones cut from matchboxes work fine, too. Whatever the shape, if the top lip of the collar is bent outward about 1 inch, slugs will also have a difficult time getting over the barrier. Yogurt cup rims are good for this.

Plastic jugs can be set over hills of cucumbers, melons, and squash to fend off the attacks of cucumber beetles during the plants' vulnerable period of sprouting. The jugs should be set at least 2 inches into the dirt to be effective. Cucumber beetles will burrow a short distance to get to a sprouting plant.

Insect Traps

Those yellow and orange plastic lids that fit over cans after they have been opened make good sticky traps for whiteflies and aphids in greenhouses or around indoor plants, and for apple fruit flies in the orchard. Punch a hole near the edge of the lid, smear Tanglefoot or some other gummy material on both sides, and hang it in the tree or above the plant. The color attracts the bugs, which are then stuck tight.

An effective Japanese beetle trap requires only a bucket, tub, or other large container (a children's wading pool will do fine), a tin can, and a stiff wire. Fill the large container about half full of water. Suspend the small tin can over the water with a stiff wire that runs through two holes in the top of the tin can and stretches from one side of the larger container to the other. The tin can should be just an inch or so above the water. Fill it with molasses water (half molasses and half water), grape juice, rotten grapes, or other fruit that lures beetles. Because they are such clumsy fliers (or just don't give a darn), the beetles will aim for the tin can but more often than not end up in the water and drown.

A tin can half full of molasses water hung in apple trees at blossom time will catch lots of codling moths. They are so greedy for the molasses they go right down into it and drown. To punch holes in the can to attach a handle, use a hammer and nail.

PLANT STARTERS

For practical gardening, you can use most anything to grow transplants in. I like half-gallon cardboard milk cartons for starting tree seeds and the pint or half-pint sizes for garden vegetables. These cartons won't disintegrate in the soil as fast as peat pots, but this can be an advantage. They hold up better as containers for tree seedlings, which I may hold a few months before planting in the ground. At that time, I merely open the bottom of the carton and set it, plant and all, in a hole. If the smaller sizes are used for vegetables that may fall victim to cutworms, open the bottom and set the box in the ground with about 1 inch of the top of the box above soil level. The top of the carton then acts as a cutworm barrier. Yogurt cups also make good seedling pots.

Among the mad theories I entertain myself with is one that says historians can judge the decline of a civilization by the size of its soft drink bottles. If sweetened fizz water is as bad for us as some dietitians say it is, then the now-popular 2-liter bottle symbolizes a steeper rate of decline than the earlier 8-ounce bottle. And a 3-liter bottle is now on the market. I suppose before it's all over we shall have family-size, weekend "refreshment" in handy 40-gallon barrels! But those 2-liter plastic bottles make dandy plant starters, and I imagine the 3-liter ones are even better. The covered plant pot you can make from them is especially well-adapted to rooting cuttings. Many tree and bush species will root from a short branch piece (cutting) if the cutting is stuck into moist soil in an environment that will keep the cutting from drying out before roots form. A glass or plastic cover over the cutting can supply that warm, moist environment. In fact, plastic works so well that often you will find that you must remove the covering part of the time to reduce the chance of harmful molds forming.

If you don't drink soft drinks or have not yet managed to distend your stomach to the point where you can handle 2 liters' worth at one sitting, you may be unfamiliar with the advantages of these plastic bottles. The bodies of the bottles are a clear, flimsy plastic; the bottoms are a stiffer and heavier dark-colored plastic. If you squeeze the body of the bottle near the bottom with one hand, and pull on the bottom with the other, you can pop the body out. The end of the body that pops loose is dome shaped. The dark bottom of the bottle becomes your plant container. Cut the body of the bottle in two just where it begins to narrow toward the neck. Turn the body upside down—dome end up—stick it into the bottom, and you have a rooted-cutting starter, or a terrarium, or a sprouter if you put wet paper towels in the bottom instead of dirt. To slip the body into the bottom, you usually have to cut a slit 1 inch or so up the side of the body.

TRELLISES FROM TRASH

The Lazy Gardener thought he was very clever one year when, instead of raking the garden out smooth by hand, he used an old bedspring as a drag behind his lawn mower. (This works well for dragging a baseball diamond, too.) But his wife was even cleverer, because when he was done with his "drag," she staked it up and used it for a bean trellis.

Almost any kind of woven or welded wire fencing makes good trellis material. Scrap pieces of chain-link fence can be attractive if stretched across one end of your porch and painted to match the porch. Then use it for climbing vines. Check the Yellow Pages for fence company addresses and then stop by to see if they have odd pieces left over from a job. Look for used farm fencing rolled up and rusting away by the ton behind barns and in junk piles. Short sections can be turned into tomato cages. Reinforcing wire (such as that used in concrete) makes good bean trellising, but the mesh is often too small for a tomato cage. A handy way to use any kind of fencing for trellises is to nail 6-foot-long sections of fencing to a rectangular frame of boards. Stiffened this way, the fencing is easy to set over or down a garden row with minimal staking. In fact, two such sections can be tied together on one side and used as an inverted V over the row without any stakes. If the fencing is not framed with boards, it will stand firmer and with less staking if placed in a zigzag or serpentine design down the row.

Some gardeners save Christmas trees for pea vine trellising. By April the tree's needles have fallen off or will shake off, and the skeleton trees are then staked (or simply laid) down the row for the peas to climb on. Fruit tree prunings will work, too. And the gardener with a woodlot can make bean poles out of saplings that he must thin from his tree stand anyway.

A HOMEMADE HOE AND OTHER GARDEN PROJECTS

Every junkyard will yield dozens of garden or farm cultivator disks, from which you can make serviceable hoes. Cut a pie-shaped wedge out of the disk with a cutting torch. This will be your hoe blade. Then

cut a hole near the narrow end large enough to accept a ⅝-inch bolt. Take whatever you choose to use for the handle of your hoe-to-be and drill a hole in the end, slightly smaller than the ⅝-inch bolt you intend to drive into it. Cut the head off the bolt and sharpen the end a bit, then drive it in the hole. It must fit very tightly and go in at least 3 inches. The exposed thread end should be about 1 inch long. Screw on one nut and a lock washer, put on the hoe blade, add a second lock washer and nut, and screw the two nuts as tightly as you can against the blade. They may need retightening occasionally. Your hoe is ready to use. The scoop of the blade edge is at just the right angle to the ground for hoeing, or you can further bevel the edge when you sharpen it. A disk blade also makes a perfect stand for a boot scraper. Weld two uprights and a crossbar in the form of an H onto the convex side of the disk. It won't tip or move when you scrape the mud off your boots.

A Garden Path

A cheap but pretty garden path or sidewalk is easily made by cutting slabs of wood from a log with a chain saw. The slabs should be about 6 inches thick. Treat them with a wood sealant, then lay them in place. The slabs can also be laid in concrete or gravel for a patio floor.

A Recycled Wheelbarrow

What two species of junk are the most prevalent? Tires and steel drums. A reader of *Rodale's Organic Gardening* magazine combined the two into a wheelbarrow. Here's how: He used half a steel drum cut lengthwise for the barrow body and a 12-inch tire for the wheel. Two rods, one from each side of the wheel, run back under the barrow. Two more rods (all from the framing of an old bed) are welded to the top rim of the barrow and run back to become handles at the rear. The maker said the whole thing cost him $2.50. The photo on the previous page shows a similar wheelbarrow made by the folks at the Rodale Research Center.

OUTDOOR PLANT HOLDERS

My mother-in-law once used a stump in her yard as a plant container until it deteriorated. Students at the Fallerones Institute near Occidental, California, once carved a beautiful double sink from a fallen redwood log—an idea appropriate for an outdoor plant container, too. For outdoor use, the best (in my judgment) permanent recycled plant containers are made of used brick mortared into whatever shape desired. Next come old crocks or urns too large for inside the house. There are many possibilities in salvaged pieces of ornamental

masonry—stone lavatories, basins from old garden fountains, ornamental cornices. In the center of our town, the watering trough for
horses still stands in front of the courthouse, with flowers growing in
it.

　　People have always sentimentally recycled the tools of the past
into outdoor plant containers. Along any typical suburban and exur-
ban string of lawns, flowers nod from iron kettles, old wheelbarrows,

wooden barrels, fake wishing wells, railroad carts, Victorian bathtubs, boats, wagons. I have even seen an old car used as a greenhouse, though not exactly as a plant container. Well, there's no accounting for taste. And should the sophisticated think such decorations to be tasteless and tacky, well, if the owner is pleased, isn't it better to honor these objects this way than just heave them in the trash?

REFRIGERATOR ROOT CELLARS

A gardener near Chillecothe, Ohio, recently made the pages of *Ohio Farmer* magazine because of his "refrigerator cemetery." On the hill behind his home he has buried, so far, seven refrigerators. No, he's not crazy. Each refrigerator serves as a miniature root cellar (should we call his graveyard Root Hill?). He lays the refrigerators on their backs, with the door hinge a few inches above ground level so surface water won't run in through the door seal. Junk freezers would, of course, work just as well. Chest freezers would be buried in a normal upright position, but it is not as easy to find junked chest freezers. (There's a lesson there, too. Chest freezers last longer because when you open the door, the cold doesn't all spill out, obliging the freezer to run longer.)

The key to success in this venture is to pick a well-drained location. In summer when the storage vaults are cleaned out, let the sun shine in to kill molds and fungi that might have developed in the moist interior. In the fall, on cold but not freezing nights, leave the lid open an inch to let in cool air. At all times, even winter, a ¼-inch crack in the door for ventilation is a good idea. Some people put a drain hole in the bottom of their buried refrigerators at one end and have the unit tilted slightly toward that hole so excess condensation drains out. In my own experience this would not be a good idea, unless the storage bin were buried on top of a hill with a very decided slope nearby. I bury steel drums rather than refrigerators on a rise of ground in the backyard that normally is very well drained. But this heavy clay becomes temporarily saturated with water in early spring and if I had a hole in the bottom of a barrel, water would seep in, not out. I layer the stored vegetables with straw and leave the lid open a crack for ventilation. Excess condensation is soaked up by the straw. I want my storage area fairly moist anyway, especially for apples, which would wrinkle in dry storage.

It is better to have several mini–root cellars—several smaller junk refrigerators—rather than one large one. Fruits and vegetables should not be stored close together because some vegetables will absorb tastes of another. If you use steel drums, choose the 30-gallon size, because when kneeling beside such a drum buried in the ground, you can reach the bottom. You can't reach the bottom of a 55-gallon drum, unless you play basketball for the Boston Celtics. If you don't have any steel drums lying around, a garbage can makes just as good a root cellar.

If you're using steel drums or cans, cover your storage bins in winter with about a foot of leaves or straw. I've never had anything come close to freezing, even in temperatures of −20°F. A refrigerator, being much better insulated than a drum, would hardly need that much protection. Ventilation is a more important worry. The longer you can keep the door cracked when outside temperatures are 33° to 40°F, the better. I don't really fuss with my barrel lids. I keep a ¼-inch opening all the time, even under the winter bed of leaves. The average temperature is a little too warm, but potatoes and other root crops last till May.

FENCES AND GATES

I wonder what Robert Frost would have written while speculating on the irony of good fences and good neighbors if he were to have contemplated the more imaginative creations people mark their boundaries with. In Nebraska, where old windmills abound, a homeowner made a lovely garden fence out of the blades of dismantled

windmills. The windmill wheels were cut in half and each half became a section of fence. All were painted white.

We make fences out of what lies readily at hand, which is why stone walls run all over New England. In woodland country, the pioneers turned stumps with their spreading roots on edge and made fences out of them. In this way, a spent resource became useful again. In the village of Glandorf, Ohio, in parklike memorial grounds across from the Catholic church, there is a grotto and wall made of old tombstones. Government regulations closed the old pioneer cemetery there in 1900, and by the 1950s the place was in great disarray. The practical German farmers and villagers gathered up the scattered markers and cemented them into a monument commemorating all who lay there beneath the sod, providing at the same time a shrine where the living can go to pray.

A salvage dealer made a handsome gate to his estate by welding together various pieces of junk and obsolete tools. Although the idea appears to be new, it is actually very traditional—examples can be found from nineteenth-century England.

Another interesting wall can be made of red clay field tiles ranked up like a rick of wood, with cement holding them together. The hollow tiles let air through, but the arrangement allows only a slight view for passing motorists, and so makes suitable screening for privacy. Such

a wall would be prohibitively expensive, perhaps, but occasionally a batch of tile at the factory doesn't meet specifications for strength and has to be rejected.

Since house walls have been successfully made out of beer cans cemented together, I suppose a beer can fence is far from being out of the question. And there already are many walls made of bottles embedded in cement.

Recycled planks from old water towers, water tanks on city building roofs, and old farm silos make the best fence boards. The redwood or cypress these planks are made of takes weathering very well, which is why they haven't rotted in 100 years of use.

MAILBOX ARTISTRY

The mailman never knows what awesome creation awaits him at the next turn in the road. Mailboxes might be framed in or supported by almost anything: old cream separators; horse-drawn plows; log

chains welded into stiff, curved braces; old gas station pumps; hammermills; cider presses; cream cans; nail kegs; bunches of gears welded together in a dim resemblance of the human figure; cistern pumps; street-corner light posts; and woodstoves with the stovepipe right-angled toward the road to receive the mail.

Don't let this custom die. It's too much fun. Be the first in your neighborhood to use an obsolete rocket for a mailbox. Seriously, isn't there something creative that could be done with that long forlorn line of mailboxes so often seen at the entrance to subdivisions? Even Army-surplus must have a solution prettier than that. How about empty ammunition canisters welded to the bemedalled chests of a long line of retired generals?

In 1924 a farmer sent an idea to *Farm Journal* magazine that would interest the Lazy Gardener. So as not to have to walk to his mailbox in rainy or cold weather, the farmer had rigged himself an automated model. He tore an old bicycle apart and attached the back wheel, chain, and one pedal to a post on the side of his porch and the other wheel on a post out by the road. (The wheel at the porch was considerably higher than the one at the road.) Then he strung old bailing wire from one wheel to the other like a belt and attached his mailbox to the wire. Using the bicycle pedal as a crank, he could draw the mailbox to the porch, unload the contents, and then let it coast back down to the road again. Or so he said.

HOUSING FOR PETS AND WILDLIFE

Whether you're looking for a way to keep your pet warm and dry or are trying to encourage wildlife into your yard, you don't have to spend a lot of money doing so. The following projects are simple to make and inexpensive, too.

A Doghouse from a Cable Spool

Remember the large wooden spools referred to in Chapter 1 for making neat tables? They can be converted into pet houses, too, with

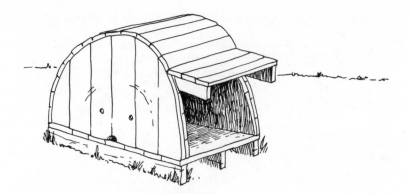

a bit of imagination and some extra scrap wood. First, dismantle the spool. If there are bolts through the axle, remove them. Cut the circles in half and use two of the semicircles for the sides of the doghouse. For a roof, nail on the boards from the axle of the spool. Start on the backside of the semicircular walls and nail the boards edge to edge over the top and partway down the front. Essentially, that's it, though most people will want to set this structure on a wooden platform up off the ground and perhaps extend an overhang on the front of the open doorway. Some of the wood from the dismantled spool can be used, but you will have to scrounge the three or four 2 × 4s needed as joists under the flooring.

A Squirrel Den from a Tire

In older neighborhoods, people complain about too many squirrels; in newer ones, too few. The reason for this is that wild animals, like domesticated humans, have to have a place to live, and for squirrels that usually means hollow trees. Old trees make good squirrel den trees, not young ones, and young ones are about all you can find growing in newly landscaped housing developments.

To encourage a few squirrels where there is no natural housing, wildlife scientists have designed a squirrel den anyone can build from—you guessed it—an old tire. In fact, a tire makes two houses. The tire should not be a steel-belted type because they are too difficult to cut. First cut the two inner rims (beads) out of the tire in two rings with a sharp knife. Then cut the tire in half with a saw. At one end of the half tire, cut the pieces off as shown in the illustration, then cut off pieces measuring about 3 inches per side. About a third of the way from the end you have worked on, cut tabs on each side of the tire as shown, so the tire will bend more easily at this location. Bend the

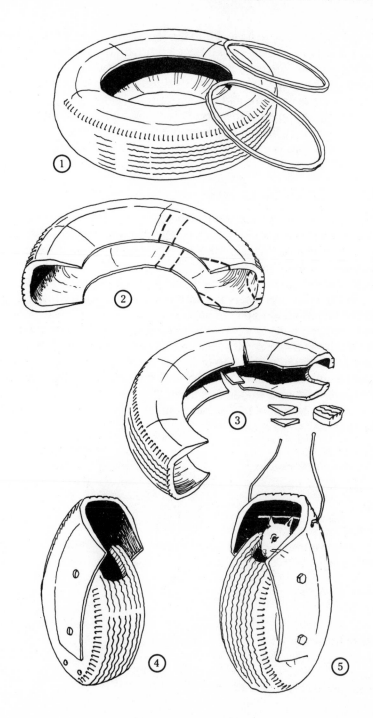

shorter end of the tire up and into the longer end. Punch two or three holes through both layers of the folded tire on both sides and insert galvanized bolts or nails in the holes to hold the tire in the folded position. There will be enough of a hollow formed in the fold to accommodate a squirrel family.

Punch two holes in the top of the house and insert a heavy wire for a hanger. Punch a couple of drain holes at the bottom in case any rain gets inside. Hang the house on a limb 15 to 30 feet from the ground.

A Steel Drum Goose Nest

The Canada goose has decided it much prefers city life to the rigors of the wilderness. A few cities, such as Minneapolis, have been so over-run that officials are not sure this is a blessing. But people love to have the big birds ambling about (or cluttering up, depending upon one's point of view) parks, golf courses, and yards. If you live in a city that has lots of lakes and reservoirs, or if you live near a waterfowl refuge, you might encourage a pair to nest near or on your own small pond or creek. All you need is a nest, say wildlife experts who designed this one, from—you guessed it again—a 55-gallon steel drum. The bottom third of the drum makes the best nest. Be sure any toxic residue is cleaned out of the drum. Punch holes in the bottom for drainage. Bolt the barrel nest to a wooden platform 23 inches wide and 39 inches long, with a deck about 16 inches long for the geese to alight on. On

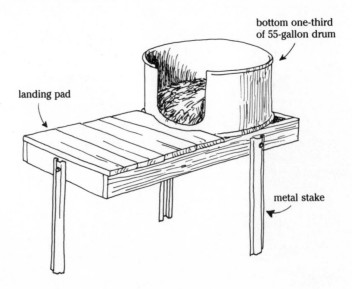

this "gander lander" side of the nest, cut a slot approximately 9 by 9 inches in the side of the nest barrel. The platform and nest can be set out over water or next to it on three stakes.

A Drain Pan Bird Feeder

Outside our kitchen window there are five bird feeders, four of them fairly expensive and attractive. The fifth one is an old plastic drain pan that I pulled out of the trash can years ago and unceremoniously nailed to the balustrade on the deck. Friends would see this ghastly receptacle and at Christmastime we'd receive nice new feeders for gifts, which I do appreciate. But I never quite get around to throwing the plastic drain pan away because that's the feeder the birds prefer. The nuthatches almost have to starve before they will venture to the "nice" feeders. Well, you say, there is no protection for the food in that ugly pan—rains right on the seeds. Yes, and snows, too. But the birds do not seem to mind, so why should I? Less seed by far is wasted out of this "open" container than out of those tricky holes in "all weather" feeders.

Another sure way to attract birds is to hang suet. A piece of hardware cloth works fine as a suet holder. Roll the hardware cloth into a tube, pinch the bottom shut, jam in suet from the top, and tack or tie the bundle to a deck post or tree.

CHAPTER 4

Moneysaving Ways in the Workshop, Garage, and Barn

A t an age when most young men dream of Corvettes and a $50,000-a-year job with a multinational corporation, Danny Downs of Louisville, Kentucky, is building a log cabin by hand, from scratch, in the little woodland retreat his family owns at the edge of the urban development where they live. Danny never was interested in school or much of anything else except working wood and metal by hand. He dreams of being a blacksmith, working quietly by himself at his own pace. Since there is not much call for that kind of workmanship in the suburban society he was born into, Danny can only pursue his goals by adapting an extremely frugal life-style. In another era, another culture, he might have been the equivalent of today's $50,000-a-year executive, and today's $50,000-a-year executive might have starved to death. But so the pendulum swings. He cannot even afford a car of his own yet.

He and his father share the workshop—a pole barn they built beside the garden. His father, Paul, builds furniture on one side and Danny hammers steel and iron on the other side. The shop itself shows many signs of ingenious recycling to keep down costs. The poles in the barn were cut from the same woods Danny is building his cabin in—cedar trees that grow wild and plentiful throughout the Ohio River valley. The wood is one of the best for rot resistance. Shelves for drying lumber were made out of two sets of drag chain from old farm machinery. The shelving hangs from the ceiling, with the boards resting on the crossbars of the chains. Danny made all his blacksmith tools from junk metal and made most of the handles from pieces of ash firewood.

GETTING STARTED
IN BLACKSMITHING

Although he now has a "real" forge, Danny's first one was a brake drum packed with fire clay. All that is really demanded for a forge is a good fire-resistant container with a hole in the bottom and something to blow air up through the hole. A smith in the village of Harpster, Ohio, uses a steel drum with a good-size door cut in the side. An old vacuum cleaner motor pumps air to the fire through a bottom hole and a tube. Some metalworkers build a wooden box, fill it with gravel

and rocks, and top it off with a layer of concrete, dished out like a sink. A pipe from outside the box runs to the hole. For simple projects, take a 5-gallon bucket, cut it down to about half size, and line the bottom with fire clay.

An anvil is not something you can make and a good one is expensive. However, anvils can often be located in salvage yards, secondhand stores, or, if you are very nice and polite, from retiring blacksmiths. If you can't afford an anvil right away, a section of railroad track will work for some projects—it's all you really need for knife-making.

Why go to the trouble of building a forge or scrounging an anvil? As Danny says, there's no kind of recycling that will equal blacksmithing in money saved. Out of readily available junk metal you can make so many useful items: hinges, latches, hooks, hangers, knives, chisels, kitchen utensils, ladles, choppers, strainers, andirons, tongs, pokers, trivets, candle holders, chandeliers, axes, hammers, froes, wedges, rakes, nails, chains, screwdrivers, handles, belt buckles, doorknobs, door knockers, foot scrapers, lawn furniture, kitchen furniture, ashtrays, shovels, and perhaps most important of all, replacements for pieces missing from rare antiques.

"And if you keep a sharp eye out, you can get your raw material free," Danny says. "Another person's junk pile is my gold mine."

Besides ordinary mild steel, the recycler should be on the lookout especially for old wrought iron and for potential tool steel. Wrought iron has little or no carbon in it and so is softer and easier to work at the forge. It is hard to buy today, but old iron fences, decorative furnishings, and implements manufactured before 1910 (particularly farm machinery) are good sources. Wrought iron can be welded at the forge by heating the pieces to a glowing white and then briskly hammering one piece against the other. Wrought iron won't rust much and so is good for outside uses. An ideal place for it is, for example, the legs for the end tables, coffee tables, and plant stands that make use of recycled antique floor registers. These little tables (as shown in Chapter 1) are very popular right now but not difficult for the beginner to make. Danny has made several, designing the leg shapes himself.

The other kind of scrap steel to watch for is tool steel or carbon steel. The leaves from auto and old wagon springs make good tool steel. All kinds of springs and springy steel have good carbon content. Old saw blades are excellent and often available. Those old crosscut saws that sell so cheaply at auctions make wonderful knives. Thicker, circular saw blades are good for meat cleavers and the like.

In addition to the standard blacksmithing equipment, the prudent moneysaver should own a soldering iron and tin snips to take advantage of the abundance of tin, which is more freely available than iron. Add a gas torch of some kind and you are ready to handle brass and copper, too.

Making a Knife from Scrap

This is not the place to teach metalworking processes (there are many good books on the subject; I recommend those by Alexander G. Weygers, especially *The Making of Tools* and *Modern Blacksmith,* published by Van Nostrand Reinhold Co., New York, in 1973 and 1974, respectively), but here's how to make a simple knife that if tempered correctly will be about as good as any you buy. First stick a piece of old crosscut saw into the woodstove when it is very hot and let it heat to a bright orange red. Then cut the draft on the stove, let the fire go out, and let the piece of steel slowly cool overnight. You can do this more easily at your forge, but I want to show just how little in the way of equipment you actually need. The ideal is to get the steel hot and then cool it *slowly.* This is called annealing, and it makes the steel softer and more easily worked.

Next cut your knife blade and tang out of the saw blade with a chisel, saber saw, hacksaw, abrasive wheel on a table saw, or best, an acetylene torch. Cut a blank that is near to final shape—you should do the final shaping on a grinder. Drill the rivet holes in the tang. Bevel the blade to the proper angle (books tell you how in minute detail). After all the shaping and polishing is done, you have to harden the steel—just the blade, not the tang. Heat to an orange red glow. You'll know when the right temperature is reached because at that point, a magnet won't stick to it. You could probably use a stove for this heating process, too, but a forge is better to get the concentrated heat. Actually, when working on a knife blade, an acetylene torch or two of those smaller Mapp gas torches are best of all because they allow you to concentrate the heat on just one part of the knife blade.

After heating the steel, plunge the hot metal in water (some say oil, but watch out for the oil catching fire). This process is called quenching. After quenching, the blade has been hardened. You can tell if you did a good job by scratching a burr on the blade against a piece of glass. It should cut a mark.

The steel will, in fact, be too hard overall and the subsequent brittleness could make the knife blade break easily. So to get it to the proper hard but tough stage, you must temper the blade. You reheat it, but not to as high a temperature as before quenching. This can be done on a hot plate or electric range, although the forge can be fired up cheaper. Press the back of the blade against the red-hot burner after polishing the blade to a high shine. The polishing allows you to see the spectrum of color that heat will cause to flow through the steel down toward the blade edge. The part of the spectrum you look for is pale yellow through bronze, then purple, and then to blue. When the color at the knife edge is dark straw to bronze brown and the back of the knife is purple, that is considered the perfect time to plunge the blade in water or oil, depending on which quench you are using. After the blade cools, sharpen it, put on a handle carved from a good hardwood, and you have an excellent knife—all from scrap, except the rivets that hold the handle on.

Making a Chisel from Scrap

A chisel is even easier to make from scrap than a knife. I watched Mike Bendele, demonstrating at Sauder Museum near Archbold, Ohio, make one in fifteen minutes. He heated the end of a short length of carbon steel rod to cherry red, hammered the tip to a rough chisel shape, reheated and cut the edge off square, reheated and did the finish shaping, then used a file to grind down the proper bevel. Then he hardened the chisel—heating it to its nonmagnetic condition and quenching quickly. But he worked only with the bottom 3 inches of the chisel. The top was left annealed to a softened condition to take the hammer blows. And when he quenched the glowing chisel tip, he only stuck about 1 inch of it into the water. As soon as the glow subsided, he quickly filed the bevel to a shiny surface, then watched for the heat spectrum colors to appear, moving back down out of the hotter steel toward the blade. He waited until the blue part of the spectrum reached the chisel's edge, then quenched it quickly again. The chisel was finished except for final sharpening. Now the edge was hard enough to hold up during metal-cutting work, but not so brittle that it would easily chip. And the metal right above the edge was even tougher, if not quite as hard. Many old chisels thought to be "worn out" need only retempering and resharpening to give years more of work.

SETTING UP A WOODSHOP

After scrap metals, the second most abundant, sometimes free, raw material is wood, and so the moneysaver's shop will eventually include the usual woodworking tools. From a recycling point of view, a power planer or jointer-planer is almost necessary for turning "junk" cratewood and old boards into beautiful wood again. Veterans offer one caution when planing old boards: Remove not only all the nails, which is obvious enough, but also *the rust left around the holes* where you pull the old nails out. That rust can dull planer blades in a hurry.

When planing a board, you can do one side on a jointer that has a wide enough bed to handle it, but you can't plane the other side to make it exactly parallel to the first. That's why most woodworking shops must have both a jointer and a thickness planer. But there is a tricky way to convert a jointer to a thickness planer and save yourself $1,000 or so. On the jointer, you plane one side and both edges true. To make the jointer plane the other side parallel and true, you notch the board down both long edges—put what is called a rabbet into the edge. The top of the rabbet on both sides must be equidistant from the side of the board already planed. This distance must also equal the desired thickness of the finished board. The easiest way to cut the rabbet is on a table saw.

Next cut two strips of wood ½ inch thick and just a bit longer than the infeed table on the jointer. Cover one side of these two strips with magnetic tape. Then when you set them on the steel infeed table they stay where you put them. Set them just wide enough apart on the table so the rabbets on the board fit over them. These two little strips of wood become a track for the board to slide on. Since the tops of the

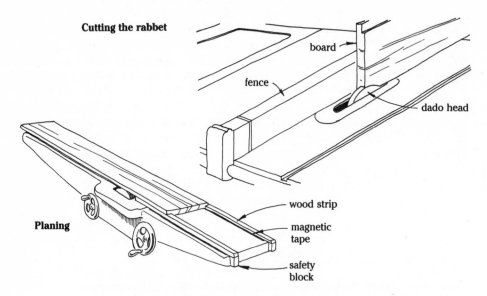

Cutting the rabbet

board

fence

dado head

wood strip

Planing

magnetic tape

safety block

rabbets (where the board slides) are equidistant from the top of the board already planed, the board will slide over the cutter knives parallel to the top of the board, regardless of the cant or warp in the bottom side, which is then planed true after several passes. Plane until the rabbeted edge has disappeared. To make sure the track strips don't creep, glue two little blocks of wood to the outer bottom ends, where they overhang the edge of the infeed table. The blocks press against the table edge and strips can't creep. It's more bothersome and not quite as accurate as a thickness planer, but it saves lots of money until you can really afford one.

A STOVE FROM A WATER TANK

With scrap metal to work with and scrap wood to burn, the first project a recycler ought to undertake is a stove to keep the place warm. A forge helps, but not enough. Adequate stoves can be built from steel drums, but old hot-water tanks and water pressure tanks are better, and they make considerably handsomer stoves. Of the two, water pressure tanks are preferable. Old hot-water tanks are often rusted nearly through, but water pressure tanks are usually built of thicker metal and are better galvanized. Check salvage yards or landfills; there, you're apt to find some in prime shape for a stove.

Converting a tank to a stove requires welding equipment, but even if you have to hire the welding, consider that you will end up with the near equivalent of an $800 airtight stove. (That might even be all the excuse you've been waiting for to buy welding equipment.)

Stan Eusey made the stove in the photo. Although only about a yard long and maybe 20 inches in diameter, the stove heats a fairly large shop at the landfill where Eusey works and where bulldozers and other equipment are serviced. He cut a rectangular hole in the top of the tank and welded a hatch on it with a lid that fits tight and flush. Notice the handle has an extended spring around it to stay cooler to the touch. At the bottom front of the tank he cut a 4-inch-diameter hole and slid a perforated 4-inch-diameter steel pipe into it the full length of the stove box. This allows draft to draw in under the entire fire. He made a sliding draft control over the pipe opening, held tight against the pipe by a spring-loaded bolt right above it. He next cut a hole in the top, behind the hatch door, for the flue, using a collar from a drum stove kit to connect the flue pipe to the hole. The flue connects to a chimney, which is a salvaged grain pipe from a farm grain elevator and storage system.

Some tank stoves are made with the door in the front, as on a drum stove. This means stooping over more often when feeding wood to the fire, but a top hatch may mean a puff of smoke in the room occasionally when the hatch door is opened. However, Eusey says this is rarely the case when the draft is strong. Legs on the stove come

from old spring-tooth cultivator blades but could be made out of any heavy strap metal.

TOOLS FROM RECYCLED MATERIALS

Making do by reusing old, obsolete, or supposedly worn-out material is a way of life in all home workshops, where the need for more tools always outruns the available cash. Unlike Uncle Sam, the shop owner cannot artificially increase his money supply. For example, he doesn't (or shouldn't) throw away broken band saw blades. Smaller sizes can be cut to proper length and width with a tin snips and used for jigsaw blades in a pinch. The wider ones (1 inch or more) make handy wood scrapers after the teeth have been ground off. They are especially useful in scraping a rounded surface like a table leg. Power hacksaw blades can be used as scrapers, too, after the teeth are removed.

In addition to splitting and carving out handles for tools from chunks of ash or hickory firewood, you can use mop, broom, shovel, hoe, and pick handles that usually get thrown away when they break or when the business end wears out. Broken baseball bats are excellent sources of handle material. You can cut any of these materials to an appropriate length and whittle a handle shape, or better, clamp the wood in a vise and use a drawknife.

Where a ferrule is desirable, as on carving tools, you can use the metal rim of a spent shotgun shell or the end caps from copper tubing, available at your local hardware store. To get the metal rim off the empty shell, drill a ¼-inch hole in the end (you have to drill a hole there anyway to accept the tang of the tool). Then you can easily pull the shell cylinder and padding out of the rim. File the hole to the shape and size of the tang. Do the same if using copper end caps. Next reduce the handle diameter so the ferrule fits snugly on it. Then drive the handle on the tang and the job is finished, unless you want to coat the handle with linseed oil.

After you've taken the time to make your own tools, take a few extra minutes to fashion protective holders for them. Short lengths of hose fastened with a nail or two to a wall or bench edge make good holders for screwdrivers, awls, small chisels, and carving knives. The hose won't harm the blades.

Clamping and Gluing

How often have you faced the situation where your C-clamp does not have a deep enough throat for the job at hand? You mutter deep in *your* throat and swear once more to buy some of those expensive

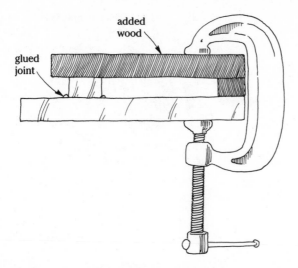

clamps that solve this problem. But all you need are two blocks of wood to extend the jaws of your C-clamp as shown in the drawing. This setup won't give you as much pressure as a deep-throated clamp in the same situation but is good enough for most ordinary gluings.

Here's a tip for gluing veneers (or whatever) on an uneven, rounded surface. Instead of using scores of clamps to get uniform pressure, use sacks of sand. If you don't have any cloth sacks handy, pillowcases will do.

Speaking of gluing, the plastic gallon jug strikes again. It makes a good glue pot for white and yellow glues. Cut the jug off at the shoulder and jam the neck upside down into the bottom part. It now serves as a funnel to direct loose glue back into the jug. What glue does remain on the funnel will peel off after drying.

An Unusual Carving Bench and Other Tools

An old croquet ball or even a bowling ball makes an excellent carving "bench." Simply build a four-legged stoollike stand, with the top of the four legs concave on the inside to accept the ball. The ball moves inside the legs like a universal joint. Two threaded rods run diagonally from opposite legs of the stand to form an X right below the ball and, when tightened by wing nuts, draw the legs against the ball, holding it solid. The wood block to be carved is mounted on the ball (usually with a long lag screw though the ball), and the carver can move it to any angle or position he desires by loosening the wing nuts, repositioning the ball, and then tightening them again.

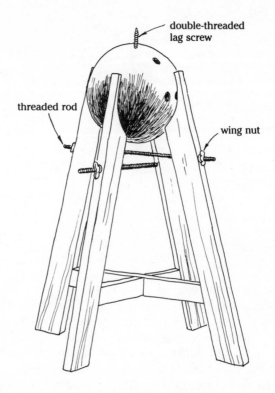

Another ingenious woodworker has learned that the wheels from skateboards make good idler or tightener pulleys for homemade vertical belt sanders. Another veteran of the make-do-or-do-without school says he made his first shaper out of two brake drums. An article in *Fine Woodworking* magazine (September/October 1984) tells how to make a horizontal power tool sharpener out of a garbage disposal unit. And if you have one of those little aquarium air pumps left over from the days the kids suddenly got interested in fish (and just as suddenly got disinterested), you can tape a plastic tube to your saber saw or jigsaw, hitch it to the motor, and use it to blow the sawdust away as fast as the saw blade makes it. Some other clever recycling ideas include using a lathe as a drum sander. Turn out a 4 by 4-inch board, about 18 inches long, to a cylinder with just the right circumference to accept a standard piece of sandpaper. Glue the sheet of sandpaper on the wood cylinder and wrap cord around it tightly to hold until the glue dries. Use hide glue so you can get the paper off when it's worn out.

Here's a tip on storing paints, varnishes, and other finishes: Photographers use collapsible bottles for their darkroom chemicals.

If they have only half a bottle of developer left, for example, they can squeeze the bottle, like an accordion, to half its original size, thus eliminating the air that can degrade the liquid. These bottles serve well in home workshops, too.

A Stump Bench

Blacksmiths can mount their anvils cheaply but effectively on a thick section of log, stood on end. Sometimes they bury the bottom part of the log in the ground for extra stability, but a good heavy chunk of oak is usually stable enough sitting on the floor and can be moved outside or to a craft fair for demonstration work. Such a "stump" makes a good outdoor movable bench, too, for woodworking purposes. You can use a solid log 33 to 35 inches high or, to reduce weight, use one about 12 inches high and put legs on it, like a giant three-legged stool. All it needs is a vise, but standard vises can hardly be fitted to a log chunk. The situation calls for a "hold-down" or "hold-fast," the original types used for centuries in blacksmithing.

A hold-down clamp is a simple piece of iron in roughly an upside-down L shape, with the short arm of the L curving down a bit. When the long arm is inserted into a hole in the bench or anvil, and the short arm comes into contact with the piece to be held, a sharp blow will drive the long arm farther into the hole and cause a pinching tension that clamps the piece firmly and rigidly to the bench. On your stump bench, all you need to do is drill a few holes for the hold-down, some on top to hold a board horizontally, and some on a side that's

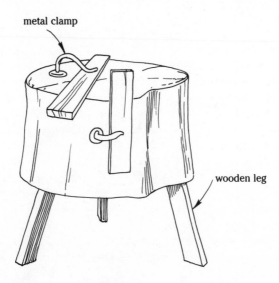

metal clamp

wooden leg

been flattened to hold boards vertically. For woodworking, you can buy a somewhat more sophisticated hold-down that relies on threaded adjustments for clamping, not just the tension between the two arms. With this hold-down come little metal collars that are inserted in the drilled holes to hold the clamp. The tool is as cheap as $10 and can be bought from most mail-order supply houses.

A Pedestal Stand from "Junk"

When you buy a metalworking or woodworking tool, you can usually figure on adding another $100 or more to the price tag for a stand. But a trip to the junkyard will yield the materials for a better stand than you can buy or build out of wood. You need a truck wheel, without the tire; a brake drum; a length of iron pipe 4 to 6 inches in diameter (one smaller or larger could work, too); and a piece of flat metal large enough to accommodate the tool.

The truck wheel is the base of the pedestal stand. Next comes the brake drum, then the pipe, then the flat piece of metal on top of the

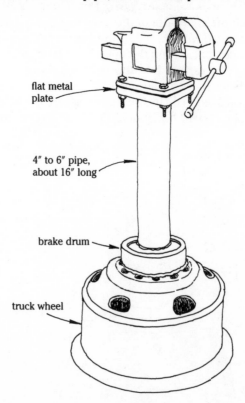

flat metal plate

4″ to 6″ pipe, about 16″ long

brake drum

truck wheel

pipe. Weld everything together. Drill holes to accommodate the tool and/or its motor if needed, and you have a very stable, solid stand. Having gone that far, you will think of other uses for this basic structure. It could be fitted on top with a roller and used as an extension of a table saw table, when ripping long boards. Made of lighter material—a smaller wheel and smaller-diameter pipe—it could serve as a stand for music, a drawing board, or a raccoon-proof bluebird nest. Painted, the stand looks quite attractive, not like the collection of junk it really is.

More Uses for Old Wheels

An auto or truck wheel makes a handy reel to wind wire on. You need to mount it on a horizontal axle—a pipe—and add a handle out toward the rim to turn it with. Attach the axle ends to the three-point hitch behind your garden tractor and you can then wind (or unwind) a whole roll of electric fence, or as much as you need when you make your corn patch raccoon-proof. Use the reel to roll up barbed wire, too.

Another use for an old wheel is as a post puller. Set the wheel on a board that slants upward from the base of the post, with a rock or

chunk of wood at the other end to create a ramp. Tie a log chain or cable around the bottom of the post, then run it over the top of the wheel and onto the drawbar of the tractor. As the tractor pulls, the wheel directs the force of the pull upward, like a pulley, and the post pulls out. The chain or cable should be long enough so that the tractor driver is out of harm's way, should the post come up in a hurry.

Using Used Oil

Save used oil to smear on plows, disk blades, cultivators, and sickle bar mower blades between work seasons. Douse hoes, shovels, and spades in it, too. Used oil can be burnt as fuel in shop stoves of the right design. In the September 1970 issue of *Mother Earth News,* an article reprinted from *Popular Mechanics* shows how to build just such a stove. The design of the burner is critical and ought not to be tried without expert help. But one shopowner I know drilled a hole in the top of his homemade woodstove, to which he finagled a feeder line from a drum of used oil. When he had a good bed of coals in the stove, he'd turn a spigot that allowed the used oil to *drip slowly* into the fire. (Fuel oil of any kind needs to work up a hot temperature before it burns well.) This method extended the burn time of a load of wood considerably but could be a bit dangerous. Get expert help before you try it. Another use for used oil is as a quench bath for tempering steel—but watch out for flashback fire.

RECYCLING AROUND THE BARN

Around the backyard barn or farmyard, recyclers are in their glory. The barn itself can easily be moved from another location or built from reused material (see Chapter 5). The windows of my chicken coop come from a torn-down house. The waterers I use in winter are the bottom halves of plastic antifreeze and bleach bottles. If water freezes in them, a sharp rap against something solid sends the ice flying. This particular kind of plastic holds up fairly well, even under this kind of treatment. The bottom corners are rounded, so the ice slips out easily, too. And if the waterers do finally crack, there's always more available. (For an indestructible livestock waterer, use an old bathtub. Old lard kettles work fine, too, although they are now desirable antiques.)

For hens' nests, I have used nothing more than old 5-gallon buckets, laid on their sides on supports and nailed securely to the wall. I tilt the bucket up slightly so the eggs don't roll out.

My "cistern" for emergency livestock water is composed of two steel drums buried in the ground up to the rims. Water drains into them from one side of the roof. That's all the storage water I need because, except in muddy and extremely cold weather, the livestock go to the creek for water.

I know of a schoolbus body that was converted into a pighouse, but it looks so ugly (even worse than a bathtub waterer) that I hesitate to mention it. On the other hand, a farmer near New Reigel, Ohio, converted four round-topped steel freight car covers into very satisfactory hoghouses, each big enough to hold twenty-two dry sows. He paid only $100 apiece for the "hog huts." They look attractive and are virtually indestructible.

Around my farmyard, flattened tin cans cover anchor post tops so they don't rot so fast. Baling wire from hay bales holds gates to posts all over the place—and holds half my ancient machinery together. The world might starve to death if farmers didn't have baling wire to make repairs with. I once held up a pair of pants with it, but twine from twine-tied bales works better. The twine will also make a decent pair of suspenders in a pinch. Farm wives of yesteryear wove doormats out of it. I once watched a sheep shearer hog-tie a belligerent old buck with baler twine so he could shear it in peace. My mother used it to tie all kinds of plants to all kinds of trellises.

Uses for Old Machinery

Bob Frey, just down the road from us, drove for thirty years what looked like an old Ford 9N tractor. Actually, he had revamped it (in the '50s) with a nearly new 100-horsepower Ford V-8 engine and two truck transmissions—all from wrecked vehicles. The tractor has twenty-six gears—twenty-two forward, four reverse.

We are not all master mechanics like Frey, to be sure, but recycling old machinery on small acreages can still pay even if you have to have major repair work done by someone else. In every community there are mechanics with small shops who will repair cars and tractors for somewhat less than the going rate. Even if they charge the going rate, economies are still possible over buying new. I'm pretty klutzy about the finer points of engine repair, so when I bought an old tractor with a cracked block for $300 I had the engine restored like new for $800, which sounds like a lot until you remember that an equivalent to this 30-horsepower tractor would cost nearly $10,000 new. I found a replacement block cheaply in a tractor graveyard.

My disk and harrow were so old when I got them that the farmer charged me nothing. But they've worked fine for ten years. My old plow cost me $20 and a load of wood.

Water Tanks and Telephone Poles

The discarded hot-water heaters and pressure tanks mentioned earlier will serve as cheap culverts and will hold up under traffic when buried in the ground. Just cut both ends out. When you do this to a gas water heater, the bottom should slip out with the gas flue intact, and this can make a small version of the pedestal stand described on page 128.

Old telephone and electric poles are most valuable recycling materials. Utility companies generally give them to adjacent landowners at the time of replacement if the landowner will haul or drag them away. If you are not the direct beneficiary of this largesse, you can often ask the farmer who is if you may have a pole or two. What often happens is that a farmer ends up with a pile of poles behind the barn—thinking he will use them some day but never doing so. You can usually buy these for a very reasonable price. The heavily creosoted butt ends (or whatever preservative was used) make excellent cornerposts for fences, lasting much longer than any post you can buy. Usually the used poles are in good condition even though they may no longer measure up to the high standards the utility companies must maintain. I have used them with good results to build a pole

shed and as pillars in my livestock barn. I even placed two nice long
ones over the creek and planked them to make a bridge stout enough
to cross with my Gravely tractor.

Speaking of bridges, they are another kind of "wrack" available
along country roads. Old country road bridges are being replaced in

large numbers right now, and farmers find uses for them. I occasionally pass a farm where an old bridge is being reused as a ramp up into the second story of a hay barn! The owner of a local stone quarry bought a rather large steel bridge very cheaply when it was replaced. He cut up the framing and braces and used the pieces for the structural supports of his stone-crushing and conveying machinery, saving many thousands of dollars in the process.

RECYCLING WINDMILLS

So-called obsolete windmills still in good condition dot the country landscape and can sometimes be had for little more than the cost of moving them. Moving can be dangerous work if you are inexperienced. In every Amish community there is usually someone who makes a business of it; this is another way these frugal people recycle to save money. You might be able to hire someone to do the job at much less expense than buying a new windmill.

A windmill's four legs usually are solidly embedded 4 to 6 feet deep in cement and it is not practical to try to dig them out. Instead, they must be unbolted at their bases. But first the wheel and vane are taken down. An Amishman tells me the usual way is to erect a 10-foot, 4×4 post on the mill tower, lashing and chaining it solidly so that it extends above the wheel. A block and tackle is fastened to the top of the post and the other end to the wheel, after removing the vane or tail. The wheel is lifted out of the socket it swivels on and then is lowered carefully to the ground. Workers on the tower should wear safety belts so if they get bopped or pushed off by the dangling wheel or if the post breaks, they won't fall.

Once the wheel is down, the rest of the pump machinery and then the tower itself can be dismantled or it can be lowered in one piece by a hefty work crew with ropes and poles and a tractor forklift. Most crews use a power boom that works off a tractor's hydraulic lift system. At the new site, the whole process takes place again, in reverse.

A friend of mine moved a windmill to his yard, where he uses it for emergencies should the electric power go off. He hacksawed two of the four legs completely through and the other two halfway (this mill did not have bolts holding it at the base of the concrete). As he lowered the tower, the two partially sawed legs bent but provided stability so the tower didn't twist.

He used a tractor with forklift and a work crew to lower the windmill to the the ground. But then the hydraulic hose on the tractor

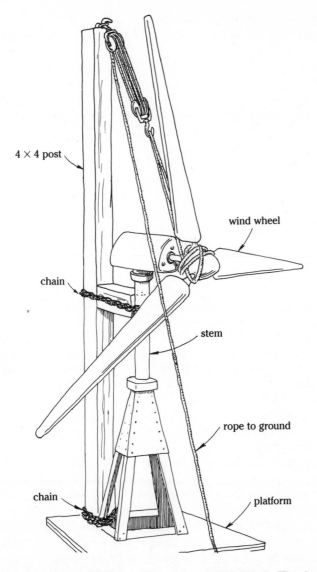

4 × 4 post

wind wheel

chain

stem

rope to ground

chain

platform

broke as the forklift carried the mill to the waiting truck. The fork fell
and the tower, which has little strength on its side, collapsed. My
friend was undeterred, however, and built a wooden tower to hold the
windmill wheel. He thinks it is stronger than the original metal one,
easier to set up, and easier to work on while installing the wheel. His
advice is to tackle only windmills of 30 feet and shorter. He thinks the
taller 50-footers should be handled with a power boom.

CHAPTER 5

Recycling Buildings of All Kinds

Y ears ago, the Wisconsin Historical Society used a large, enclosed metal trailer for traveling historical exhibits. When that project came to an end, a farmer bought the trailer cheaply and used it to haul and store hay in. Then a second farmer purchased it to mount his sawmill on, thereby making it easily portable from woodlot to woodlot.

The second farmer and his family then learned of a small country church that was to be burned just to get rid of it. The family was in the process of building a house and bakery shop. They tore down the church and used the dimensional lumber in their building and the decorative inner wallboards as paneling in their new home. (The full story is in the February 1978 issue of *Countryside* magazine.)

All kinds of buildings stand around empty today, begging to be recycled. The village of Carey, Ohio, after interminable haggling with the railroad that owned the depot in town, finally secured the abandoned building and turned it into an attractive senior citizens' center.

In Minnesota, an enterprising homesteader bought an old township hall building for next to nothing, moved part of it intact to become his garage, and tore down the rest for enough household and backyard uses to last a lifetime.

The most dramatic recycling feat that I've seen in recent years is now a tourist attraction in Akron, Ohio. A large cluster of grain silos,

where the Quaker Oats Company used to store its grain, was converted into a luxury hotel and convention center—the Quaker Square Hilton.

IS IT PRACTICAL?

How practical is using one's labor and salvaged materials to build with? A visit to your local lumberyard will answer that question quickly. New wood is high priced and often of lower quality compared to the best that you can salvage. *If you are willing to borrow your time rather than borrow money,* savings in terms of actual out-of-pocket costs can be considerable. Even in building a house, which is probably the least practical way to use salvaged lumber (see page 139), savings can be monumental if you can substitute labor for borrowed capital. Here's why. Let us say you borrow $80,000 to build a house today—which isn't all that much house anymore. Depending on interest rates and the length of the mortgage, you will end up paying something like $300,000 before you own your home free and clear. In that light, taking a year off other work to build a house, or building it in spare time over several years, while keeping borrowed money for work and materials at a minimum, would probably represent some of the most lucrative hours you will spend working in your lifetime.

If you say you don't know how to build a house, my first answer is that it is not that difficult to learn and one good way to start learning is to tear an old building down. Do not worry about expertise. Once you start building, your friends will be only too glad to stand around and give you more advice than you thought you needed. But if the idea of building a house overwhelms you, build confidence by building a shed first. The principles of building—foundations, walls, and roofs— are about the same no matter what the structure. Or buy an abandoned house that looks bad but is still structurally sound. Then you don't have to worry about building—just repair and replace what's needed.

A man and woman I know well bought just such a wreck when they were first married. They paid little more than the cost of the country acre it stood on. No one had lived in the house for years. The exterior was never painted so far as you could tell. The windows were broken out, the inside more or less gutted. But the roof did not have leaks in it and so the structural framework, built of virgin oak, was solid as the Rock of Gibraltar. Husband and wife, of very modest means, eventually both worked in factories and in their spare time repaired the exterior of the house and renovated a couple of rooms so they could move in. They were not so proud or delicate that they could not live awhile in less-than-average housing rather than borrow a lot of money. To make a long story short, their house today is very nice indeed. If still on the modest side, it has everything they need and want. A wealthier home could have only more of the same: more space, more expensive furniture, a bigger television set, and so on. The couple have been content—or rather made themselves content—with their factory jobs, turning their home life into their "career." Together they make around $50,000 a year now, have twice that much money saved, mostly thanks to no big mortgage payments, and are indeed in better shape to weather the financial shakeup that is sure to come in this country than some doctors I know who live in $300,000 homes. A word to the wise, they say, is sufficient.

TEARING DOWN FOR SALVAGE

There are three ways to recycle a building: (1) tear it down and reuse the salvaged material; (2) move it to a desired site; or (3) renovate it where it stands. The first way usually requires the least up-front cash but the most labor and time. Tearing down buildings is tedious, hard work—don't kid yourself—and on large buildings it can be dangerous. And there are drawbacks to salvaged lumber. For example, if the framing is oak or a similar hardwood, it will be difficult to drive nails in it. I know a determined fellow who framed his new house with salvaged lumber and drilled holes for the nails. Others use 10-penny ring shank nails. They won't bend, but they will break in hardwood if you don't hit them squarely, so wear some protection for your eyes. Once such a nail is driven into hardwood, it is virtually impossible to take it out again. Rough-sawn lumber salvaged from old barns or sheds will vary slightly in dimension and so is not practical for wall studding, floors, or ceilings. Planing takes care of this problem, but few commercial shops will plane salvaged wood for fear an unnoticed nail will tear up the expensive blades in their machines.

A few other caveats are in order. First, tearing down houses that have plastered walls is generally not practical. All that plaster and lathe is nasty to get rid of. Second, try to work out an agreement with the owner so you can burn the worthless wood on site (where allowed). In fact, first try to get an agreement whereby you take only what you want. This may cost you a little money, since the owner's motivation is to get rid of the building completely, at no cost to himself. He may insist that everything be removed. He may go along with burying concrete and so forth on the site, but that means you will need a bulldozer. Most important, if the owner insists you have the building removed by a certain date, make that date three times longer than you think it will take you, because it will take you three times longer than you think! (I'm assuming you'll be working in your spare time, like I do.) If the owner won't agree to an extended time, forget it.

Stay away from very large barns and similar buildings until you gain experience. Let the professionals take them while you stick to the small and mid-size buildings.

In sizing up a building to salvage, always carry a pocketknife with you. If you can poke into a plank almost as easily as into Styrofoam, you're dealing with dry rot. If it is extensive, you may not want to waste your time—depending on what you are after. If the weathered siding is what you desire, dry-rotted dimensional wood is of less importance.

With the popularity of the "country look" in home decor, even old *painted* barn siding is becoming desirable as "antique." This kind of siding often has intrinsic value. On old barns and henhouses it is usually high-quality yellow pine that you just can't buy for siding anymore. Yellow pine is very resistant to the weather and makes fine recycled wood for garage and shed exteriors, gates, and board fences.

And splintered boards of yellow pine make excellent kindling for starting fires—the oil in the wood makes it reach kindling temperature quickly and burn hotly.

Beams and other structural lumber in midwestern barns are sometimes made of walnut, but with old wood you can't tell by looking. I always shave a tiny sliver off beams. If the freshly exposed wood underneath is chocolate brown, you have a valuable piece of wood to salvage. Hand-hewn beams of any wood have antique value, especially if they're about 8 inches square or larger.

Tools of the Trade

Wear heavy workshoes when salvaging a building—if you step on a nail, it won't go through as easily as it would if you were wearing sneakers. Better yet, consider buying steel-toed shoes. Other essential equipment includes a hard hat and a tool belt, a couple of crowbars to pry boards and pull spikes, and a claw hammer. A flat iron pry called a "wonder bar" is most useful in prying up boards. When considering ladders, use a wooden one, please. Aluminum ladders are not nearly as stable, and they could be dangerous. From time to time you hear of people who brush an aluminum ladder against a bare electrical wire and are electrocuted. A wooden ladder is really not that much heavier, anyway. To round out your list, you will need some heavy rope or a strong cable with good hooks at either end. And, of course, you'll need a truck or trailer to haul away your loot. You will also find it well worthwhile to take along a chain saw to cut through boards and beams when they can't otherwise be taken apart easily. For example, old mortised, tenoned, and pinned barn beams were put together so tightly in the old days that even after 100 years it is almost impossible to take them apart. Use the chain saw.

If you have shingles to take off the roof, use a square-edged shovel to push under and pry up, salvaging the shingles. You can use old shingles to shim up new kitchen base cabinets on an uneven floor, as wedges for knockdown furniture, to shore up an uneven floor, or for quick-starting kindling.

The Razing

In the actual razing, there are no hard-and-fast rules other than common sense. On barns and sheds, one generally tears down in the reverse of the way the building went up; that is, work from the top down by starting with the roof. But with houses or old public buildings like a school or town hall, you will want to take out the inside lumber first, so it doesn't get wet. Hardwood flooring, especially, should come out before tearing off the roof, as should stairs, door framing, stair railings, and paneling. Before starting any work, be sure electricity, gas, water, and oil are *cut off permanently* from the structure. After all the interior that can be safely removed is out of the house, take out the windows so they are not broken when you start throwing things off the roof.

Once you start on the exterior of the building, you essentially undress it. The roofing comes off first. If it is slate and the slate is not rotten yet, it is quite valuable. Standing-seam tin roofing is even more practical for recycling. It does not have exposed nail holes like corrugated metal roofing has. Tin roofing is loosened a strip at a time, then each strip is rolled up, or rather rolled *down*, to the eave and gently lowered to the ground. Standing-seam tin roofing is the longest lasting for the money, but it is out of fashion. Some people are removing it from their houses even though it is still in excellent condition—all the better for the recycler.

Corrugated metal roofing can be used again, too, if you pull the nails out carefully so you don't tear the holes bigger or flatten the corrugations too much. Set a little piece of wood in the channel between the corrugations next to the nail, so your hammer pries against the wood, not the corrugation. Or use a professional nail-puller. In reusing the metal, put the nails in the same holes, and daub generously with roofing tar. The metal panels are also great for covering stacks of firewood or lumber to keep the rain off.

Once you remove the roofing, the roof sheathing boards and the siding come next. You may want to remove the rafters before the siding. But always remember: Every board you take off reduces the stability of the building, especially in stud construction. At some point, the building will become too shaky to support you. I prefer getting all the siding off first before working on the structural framework, because by the time the building is getting unstable, you should be working down on the ground pulling off siding boards. On very large old buildings where there is more than one story, such as a big barn, be very careful. On such a building, when it gets dangerously shaky, pull the walls over, one at a time. When possible, pull a wall over to the inside. The reason is that when a wall falls to the outside, the framing (studs, posts, beams, plates, and so forth) is on top and must be pried away from the siding, which is twice as difficult as prying the siding boards away from the framing.

On smaller buildings it is usually possible to take off all the exterior siding, a board at a time, while the building still stands. This will seem slower to you than yanking the whole wall down, but it is a much better way since you will not splinter as many boards—every board saved adds to your hourly rate of income. Do a board at a time and remove the nails as you go—don't wait until the end, when you'll have a whole pile of boards with nails to contend with. Set up two sawhorses or the equivalent to lay the boards on while pulling nails. If you can work over a floor, you can let the nails drop and later scoop them up. Otherwise, have several big buckets or pans handy to toss the pulled nails into. Some people save nails, straighten them, and use them again, but if the nails are partially rusted through, this doesn't pay.

In taking down the structural framing of a building whose rafters and joists went up as trusses, loosen the joists at the top plate and pull down each truss in one piece. Use ropes to do the lowering and a ladder to get up there to tie the ropes on. The less scrambling around on the shaky skeleton of the building, the better.

Once the building has been dismantled, the wood should be stacked and stored as carefully as you would treat newly sawn lumber. Stack straight and solid, with strips of wood for spacers between each layer for good air circulation. You need a spacer about every 4 feet. Even if you are storing the wood inside, it is best to space it for air circulation.

Salvaging a Silo

An easy and practical building to salvage is the wooden silo, now obsolete, but still standing on many old farmsteads. The wood of these silos, like that of old water tanks on farms, along railroads, or on city roofs, is redwood, cypress, pine, or fir. All are resistant to moisture decay, especially redwood and cypress. Redwood silos are real prizes to find and are not uncommon west of the Mississippi. Unlike salvaged hardwoods, these woods are easy to pound nails into, are tongue-and-grooved, and will serve very well for walls, flooring, or exterior sheathing. Wooden silos often measure 8 feet in diameter and are about 24 feet tall. One of them provides the makings of four very nice hot tubs.

Even if you have to pay $50 or $100 for a silo, the price is right. Redwood would be worth more, but most owners of these decrepit old Leaning Towers of Pisa are often glad to get rid of them and neither know nor care what kind of wood is involved. Test the wood of a prospective silo with your trusty pocketknife. Lower boards, especially if pine or fir, are likely to be dry-rotted, but the rest should be okay. If there is much dry rot, salvage is probably not worthwhile.

Some silo builders spiked the 5 by 2-inch staves together through the edges, and these silos generally take too much time to tear apart to be practical. But ordinarily, the silo staves are held together only by their tongue-and-groove design and the steel hoops around the silo. When wet, the wood swells tight and waterproof against the hoops. To dismantle, first disconnect the silo from the barn to which it is invariably attached by 2 × 4s, guy wires, or cables. Disconnect lightning rod cables if there are any. Soak the threaded fastenings that hold the hoops together with Liquid Wrench or a similar rust solvent so that, with some hammer tapping, you should be able to get the rusted burrs loose again. Loosen the hoops as far as you can or remove them entirely, except for the bottom and top ones. Remove all the silo doors. Hook a cable to the top hoop. If there are anchor bolts around the bottom of the silo, unscrew them. Hitch the other end of the cable to your truck or tractor, making sure, of course, that the cable is long enough so you don't pull the silo over on yourself. Slowly ease the cable taut and then, without jerking, keep on going until the silo falls over. A few staves will no doubt break, but the majority will come apart into a loose pile as the silo hits the ground. If you can do the job in the dry part of the summer when the tongues and grooves are looser, all the better.

Building with Old Logs

Perhaps the easiest kind of building to tear down and move is one made of logs. Mel Sanford, who happens to be the police chief in our town, and his wife, Joyce, first decided to build a log home from a commercial kit, but when they added up the total cost of such a house, they found it was quite expensive. So they did what they really wanted to do all along—build a house with logs from old houses and cabins.

It took them two years of spare time just to gather the materials. Counting some reused cedar shakes on the porch roof and reused concrete blocks in the foundation, their "new" house has parts from *nine* older structures! The house is T-shaped, with the walls on the east section mostly from a log cabin, and the west side mostly of barn beams, when they could not find enough logs from log houses to do the whole thing. The Sanfords devised their own code to mark the logs so they could use them in the same position at the new house site. N-1, for example, indicated the bottom log on the north wall of the original house. "We tacked aluminum tags to the log ends and then stamped the code letter and number in the soft aluminum," Sanford says. "Chalk will fade and wash away if the logs are left out in the weather for a year or so before building."

Some of the logs and beams had to be cut to fit. "Sawing through an oak barn beam is not fun," notes Sanford. "I once dulled two blades on just one beam."

But the hardest part of the job was putting the insulation between the logs before chinking them. They used scrap Styrofoam they got free from a factory that makes sound speakers, then cut it to fit, piece by piece, in the varying spaces between the logs. Each piece had to be nailed into place. Then, inside and out, hardware cloth had to be nailed to the logs over the insulation to anchor the concrete chinking. They used a special cement for the chinking, known in the trade as Type M, which dries three times stronger and harder than ordinary concrete. "There's 7 *tons* of concrete in the chinking," says Sanford, glancing proudly at his wife. "I think Joyce handled 5 tons of it herself."

The Sanfords did most of the work themselves in their spare time and moved in the summer of 1985. "We can hang wallpaper together," says Joyce with a smile. "Our friends said if that were the case, building a house together would be a snap." But when they got 9 feet high with the walls, they did hire some help. Even with a friend's hydraulically powered hoist that could raise the logs 28 feet if necessary, they couldn't handle the job alone. "We were fortunate to find some Amish carpenters. They were terrific. They work for less and work harder than any carpenter I've ever known," says Sanford. "And when they notched a log end on the ground, it always fit up on the wall."

Proceeding up a wall, the Sanfords would cut a log for window or door space only when it was in place, not down on the ground beforehand. Either way will work, but their way means less chance for a beginner's mistake. They faced the openings with 2 × 10s and then with proper moulding so the windows and doors fit tightly. "But there will always be air seepage in these areas," says Sanford, "at least in my case. I just couldn't cut the logs off square with my chain saw." To seal up all such cracks and crannies, they found a spray foam (called Insula-Tec) that comes in a pressurized can. Sprayed into cracks, it expands as it dries. "Ten pounds did the whole house," says Sanford.

In exploring for logs and other recyclable materials, the Sanfords met all kinds of interesting people. "Some wanted more than we could pay for logs and barn beams, but others were glad to give them to us if we cleaned up the building. Some even helped with the work. A few would not part with an old building, for sentiment, not money. And we can understand that," says Sanford. "We love old things. I hate to see an old barn torn down or be allowed to fall down."

Despite the hard work, the Sanfords look back on their project as an adventure. "Actually," says Joyce, "the hardest part was keeping up two places. We'd go out to the new house in the evening and work maybe till midnight, but there was still the regular housekeeping to do, too."

"What I hated most," says Sanford, "was cleaning out the cooler when we got home after a long evening or day of work."

He's already planning an addition to the new-old house. "Yes, I enjoy the work. I wish I had more time. I know I could find all the materials to build a house for nothing, from scraps and waste, except maybe the plumbing and the wiring—though I bet I could find them, too."

Building with Railroad Ties

Railroad ties are used in house construction much the same way as logs are, although instead of notching them on the corners, builders usually lay them up as if they were long cement blocks. Because ties are heavy, spacers are usually put between them, then concrete is worked into the crack—much the same as chinking logs. Be sure to

use ties that are at least 10 years old, by which time the odor of creosote has dissipated.

At his experimental research farm near Salina, Kansas, Wes Jackson found an even cleverer way to use a hoard of railroad ties he got for free. He had them sawn into boards to make siding for his big pole barn. Anyone who knows old railroad ties immediately raises an eyebrow or two. Ties get stones imbedded in them or in the tar that often coats them, and no sawyer in his right mind will risk dulling his saw on them. But Jackson is an original thinker and he had an idea to circumvent that problem. He noticed that the ties were affected by tar and stones on only *three* sides—the fourth was clean. He discovered that in cold weather, the tar coating became brittle and if he rapped the clean side of the tie sharply with a hammer or sledge, the caked tar on the opposite side flaked off cleanly, taking the occasional stone with it. Soon he and his helpers were busy hammering off the tar. The other two sides became the outer "slabs," as on a log, when the tie was run through the saw. These outer slab boards were used, tar coating and all, for fences and gates that will never rot.

The inner boards became siding for the barn. They will not rot because they're soaked through with creosote. And moreover, brown-stained as they are, they make an attractive exterior wall—with knots and marks from the railroad spikes adding to the beauty.

MOVING BUILDINGS INTACT

The idea of moving a building conjures up a big house being slowly hauled down a street from which utility lines have been cleared at great expense, and traffic rerouted at great inconvenience. Moving even a big house that way can be cost-saving, but that kind of project should be down toward the bottom of the list of moneysaving techniques, since it requires professional movers. *Small* buildings are the ones more practical to move—say 15 by 30 feet and smaller. For example, the smaller metal grain storage bins, now obsolete on large farms, make good storage buildings and are not hard to move. Wes Jackson, the ingenious director of the Land Institute at Salina, Kansas, has moved several of these from farms to his research headquarters. Small metal ear corncribs, round like the storage bins but with wire walls, are also easy to move and are available at little or no cost, because they're obsolete on larger farms. They can be put to good use on small homestead farms for corn. I've also seen them used as dog kennels.

Any small building can be turned into a summer kitchen for canning if you want to save on air conditioning or don't have any. An 8 by 10-foot structure will hold a stove, table, shelves, and tubs. And you can do a good job of drying fruit in there with a good hot fire. A small shed can make a nice suburban woodshed. I've even seen cute old privies painted and used for garden and lawn tool storage or converted into huts for fishing on the ice.

When the new basketball court was installed at our high school, a local farmer got the old gym floor for free. He put the old floor down in his barn and for years it has been the scene of neighborhood basketball games all winter long. Where there is imagination, all things are possible.

The round, old-fashioned brooder house, in which chicks were kept warm during their first month or two, can be moved easily. One family tipped up their brooder house with the hydraulically powered manure fork on a tractor, ran a hay wagon under the tipped up side, lowered the house to the wagon, then went around to the other side and lifted and slid the rest of it onto the wagon. Then the little building was transported to a wooded glade where it became an all-season vacation cabin.

From Caboose to Cabin

Another family recycled a railroad caboose into a cabin beside a rural pond, where they spend weekends away from town in cheap luxury.

To find a caboose, they badgered railroad representatives and inquired of other caboose owners. They learned of a company in Kenton, Ohio, no longer in operation, that installed new cabooses for the railroad and took the old ones in exchange. Inquiries brought the answer that to get an old caboose one had to see so-and-so, who had a contract with the company to sell and move the cabooses to private individuals. The caboose they bought was disconnected from the running gear, lifted onto a big low-boy (a heavy trailer with a bed built very low to the ground), and hauled right to the pond site. There the new owners jacked it up and built a cement-block foundation under it. The porch had been removed because it wouldn't fit on the low-boy, so they built a new porch. Inside they tore out everything—coal bin, coal stove, the benches up in the crow's nest (or cupola) where the trainmen usually ride, and the lower benches. Other than the fact that the caboose was very dirty from years of coal dust and smoke, the refurbishing job was not too difficult. An area at one end was enclosed for a tiny bathroom and the rest of the car was divided roughly in half between kitchen—with stove, refrigerator, and heater—and living room area. Couches along both sides doubled as bunks, and two more bunks were installed up in the crow's nest in place of the benches there. Had they wished, the owners might have kept the coal stove or installed a woodstove, since the chimney flue was already in place.

Some folks want a caboose that is track-worthy so they can have the railroad haul them from place to place. Finding a caboose in that good a shape is difficult and perhaps expensive since, obviously, the railroad only gets rid of them when they are just about worn out. Other caboose lovers don't want to ride the rails but want to set their "cabin" on a short stretch of track and thus avoid building a foundation. This can easily be arranged, but the track won't come free. Cost of the caboose might be as high as $2,000 or more if in good enough condition to ride the rails, or much less for an old caboose without running gear. The caboose in the photo cost its owner only $150 delivered, but that was some years ago and the cost might be considerably higher today.

Making the Move

Moving wooden buildings, other than the smallest, requires mostly patience, says our local shed mover, Dave Pahl. He got his first experience moving a building onto his own property. He wanted a combination butcher and harness shop—something about 15 by 30 feet. He chanced by a bulldozer one day, busy pushing down an old house and burying it. Next to it was a building of about the right size. "Yep," said the bulldozer operator, "she goes down tomorrow."

Could Pahl have it for the moving? "Yep," was the reply, "but don't wait too long." So Pahl jacked it up, first a little bit on one side, then a little on the other, blocking up with pallets as he went, until it was far enough off the foundation that he could back a low-boy under it. Then he set the building back down on the bed with a couple of beams between so he could jack it back up again easily when he got home. Other than making sure the building on the low-boy was not taller than any telephone or electrical wires he had to pass under, and perhaps having the police on hand to direct traffic if necessary, there wasn't really much more to it.

If a building has a floor in it, you have to raise from underneath. One way to do this is to knock holes in the foundation and slide in heavy beams that extend out both sides to put the jacks under. Don't forget to cut the bolts that hold the plates to the foundation.

If there is no floor, you can go inside and nail or bolt heavy 2 × 8s across the studs and raise from them, putting the cribbing or blocking out of the way of the low-boy. It is always a good idea to install extra bracing in the form of 2 × 4s at various angles up to the upper joists and rafters from each point where the jack lifts. This distributes the stress of the jack to many points of the building rather than just the four or six lifting stations, and also holds the building rigid during the jolts of moving.

The bell jack or screw jack is the traditional tool for lifting a building. One costs about $50 new but is often sold at auctions for less—and it's a good buy since these jacks are virtually indestructible. For most jobs the bell jack is fine, but in very heavy work it is hard to turn. A hydraulic jack in the 12- to 20-ton range is better, but more expensive, at about $150. It's a good tool to rent.

Lifting under the plates or sills is best, but of course you can't do this until you get the plates far enough off the foundation. Never lift under just one joist, but place a heavy plank under at least three and then jack under that. Have plenty of material on hand for blocking or cribbing. Keep the cribbing plumb.

Although farmsteads may be the best place to look for unwanted small buildings (Wes Jackson even found a good privy that he turned into a composting toilet), town and village backyards are good places to look, too, for chicken coops, garden houses, small barns, smoke-houses, and summer kitchens that might be had for the asking. If you have no "practical" use for them, think what a wonderful child's playhouse one might be turned into.

I once moved a 10 by 15-foot chicken coop about 200 feet with nothing more than three husky sets of human muscles and the power of gravity. The moving happened to be all slightly downhill, so I laid out two parallel board "tracks" about 30 feet ahead of the coop toward the place I wanted to take it. Then we jacked up the coop and slid some more "track" under it, plus three lengths of 3-inch-diameter steel pipe to serve as rollers. We could roll the coop over its board track with pryes, picking up the rollers as the coop passed over them and putting them down in front again—and doing the same with the board track. Slick as a whistle. Our only problem was keeping the building from rolling *too* fast and coming completely off its rollers and track.

Moving larger houses is not for amateurs, but it can still save money. According to statistics, a moved house finished and ready to live in costs on a nationwide average half to two-thirds of what the same type and size of house built new would cost. Small houses purchased for little or nothing and moved in rural areas or small villages would cost less because of fewer obstacles and less traffic. The biggest job you are responsible for as the owner of a house to be moved is to find a good mover and make sure you (and the mover) are properly insured against liabilities. Also agree upon who shall pay for what in the case of minor (or major) damage or for necessary alterations in the building to get it moved. It is a good idea to take pictures of the house—especially if the walls are masonry—so that you have proof of new cracks and the like to show the insurance company after the move. A good mover, however, can move a brick house and never crack a seam, so they say. The new foundation should be ready for the house ahead of time, of course, and rather than being perfectly level, it may have to match some settling of conformation in the base of the old house being moved. Contractors and house movers should be well aware of these details.

Both of the houses across the road from us were moved to their present locations years ago—with horses. One of them was not only moved a mile but several years later it was turned around on its foundation! Moving a house was more or less a common skill when money was dearer than it is now, and no one would think of wasting anything. These houses were modest in size when moved, which of course helps. Since then they have been added to and few people even remember them being moved. Today, when we rip up the landscape at every whim for airports, highways, commercial development, rezoning, and housing projects, many houses are moved, but unfortunately many more are simply demolished. Young people who believe they can't afford their own home should keep their eyes open. Get your land or your lot, and be ready when opportunity knocks.

RECYCLING AN EXISTING STRUCTURE IN PLACE

Renovating an old house, barn, schoolhouse, mill, train station, livery stable, garage, town hall, library, church, or whatever into a home is the handiest way to quit renting. You don't need to be an architect to do so, unless your renovation is going to be extensive. Many young couples believe that a way to save money is to buy a huge old house on the market cheap and then work on it a room at a time until death do they part. If you have a passion for that kind of antique restoration, plus patience and enduring energy, fine. But don't expect to save much money in the reconstruction or in heating and maintaining the old monster ever after. Big houses are a pain, and I say so from experience. The only way I see people *saving* money on one is if they tear half of it down and use the material to refurbish the other half. (I hear the lovers of old Victorian houses screaming in protest.) Fixing up a monster may prove to be a good investment in the long run, however, if you finish before you die—you can usually find an innocent buyer who will relieve you of it so that at least in retirement you can have some leisure.

What to Look For

In buying an old structure, outward appearance is of least significance. Unpainted or decaying siding, leaky roofs, broken windows, and yawning doors are more or less easily repaired or replaced. These are only skin blemishes. What you should be concerned with are the bones—the framework and foundation. Straight rooflines and plumb walls may indicate a solid structure no matter how sordid the skin blemishes, but you must look deeper into the building to be sure. Check the foundation first. Stone foundations of old houses, barns, and so forth don't rot, but they can buckle, usually inward into the cellar. This condition usually means that drainage around the foundation is poor—moisture has caused severe frost heaving, disturbing the walls until they began to sag. If the buckling is not too severe, you can dig a ditch around the outer wall, install drain tile to take away moisture collecting there, and then repair the wall. The most common way to do this is to build a new concrete block wall just *inside* the old wall and fill the intervening space with concrete. Where deterioration is severe, the house must be raised and a new foundation poured or laid—expensive and not a job for an amateur. The moneysaver should look for another building unless this particular one has other moneysaving features.

The sills that rest on the foundation are most likely to be rotted if anything in the framing is rotten. You can jack up the building, almost as if you were preparing to move it, and replace the rotted sill. In any kind of jacking to replace sills or other framing, the trick is not to raise the building but just to ease the weight of it off the part to be repaired. The jack, topped with a pressure plate (a piece of flat steel about 8 inches square used so the jack doesn't dig into the wood), is inserted under a temporary header to do the raising. The header might be a 6 by 6-inch timber spanning several or all the joists above the rotten sill, or in the case of lifting a post or pillar, the header(s) might be placed under block(s) bolted to the side of the post. To hold a floor up from the room (or cellar) below while you move jacks to a second position, post jacks are used. A post jack is set under a header and the top screwed up tight against it. Then the hydraulic or screw jacks used to do the actual raising are slowly lowered until the header rests solidly on the post jacks. Post jacks cost about $25 and can be rented cheaply. In all cases, all jacks should sit firmly on a solid level surface, otherwise they might kick out under pressure, becoming very hazardous to your health. When possible, jack from outside the building, with the other end of the header resting on cribbing. Remember, you won't have to lift the header very much—just enough to take the

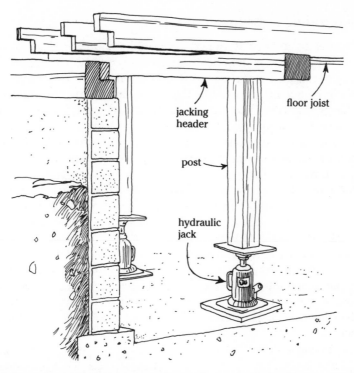

jacking header

floor joist

post

hydraulic jack

weight off the old sill so you can knock it out. In the unlikely event that you must jack up rafters to remove or repair a top plate, nail extra braces across the angled rafters so they remain rigid and do not spread from the upward force of the jack.

The upper parts of the building will in all likelihood be sound *if* the roof has not developed leaks. So especially check those parts of the building under areas where roofing has come loose or in those places where leaks are most likely to occur: around chimneys, at sagging corners, in roof valleys.

Dry rot is not so easily spotted—you'll have to poke structural wood with a knife. If attic areas have not been properly ventilated, roof sheathing and even rafters may be rotted. Our first house had mushrooms growing on the rafters when we bought it. They were moneysaving mushrooms, however. It cost me $700 to fix the roof, but I used the mushrooms to bargain $3,000 off the price of the house.

Once the "bones" of your building are structurally sound again, you are free to add (or subtract) inside walls and redo the outside "skin." In fact, your work with the bones will teach you which walls can be safely knocked out and which are load-bearing, as you go about turning the shell of your structure into a home.

A Schoolhouse Becomes a Home

A good example of what imagination and hard work can produce is the old schoolhouse Jeff and Betsy Bell turned into a home in our county. In this part of the country, one-room schoolhouses, often built of red brick, dot the rural areas. When they were in use, no child had to walk more than a mile to school. Most of these picturesque little buildings are falling into disrepair or are used for grain or machinery storage, but a few have been converted into houses by people like the Bells, who want something unique in a home and know that the chances are good that such buildings are very solidly constructed.

The one the Bells found appeared, indeed, to be in good shape. But to make sure, they hired a building contractor to take a look at it and pronounce judgment. The contractor pointed out that although the building was erected in 1895, the plaster on the inside walls had not cracked—an excellent indication of a solid foundation. (Subsequently, they would find out that the footers were 5 feet deep!) The walls were three bricks thick, and at the corners and intervening pillars, they were four bricks thick. The masonry joints between the bricks were all solid, so tuck-pointing would not be necessary. The

interior gussets, bracings, and rafters under the roof were all built much more solidly than usual to support the heavy slate roof. The roof was not in good shape, but the Bells planned to reroof with shingles anyway.

So they bought it, after the owner was convinced they would take good care of the treasured landmark. The price, with nearly an acre of ground, was a very economical $4,000. The Bells stripped the inside, saving the unusual wainscoting, which alternated white oak and black walnut vertical boards around the room, for reuse later. They dug a basement under the school and arranged the rooms above on three levels, taking advantage of the 14-foot ceiling. In fact, for the top level, they raised the ceiling up higher. Thus in a room that originally was only about 25 by 35 feet, they have squeezed in a fairly large basement, a bathroom and guest room on the second level, living-dining area on a third level, and a master bedroom on the fourth. With an adroit use of railings rather than walls for separating every area from the other, there is even a feeling of spaciousness in the house.

To guarantee no trouble with water in the basement—a problem in the level, sandy soil of the area—they built the basement wall inside the deep footer and put drain tile *between* the wall and the footer. More drain tile went *under* the basement floor. With a sump pump working, they have had no problems, even during bad flooding a few years ago. Digging the basement was no fun. They used a conveyor to transport the dirt up out of the hole to a truck. "But we ran into a bunch of rocks that we learned came from the *previous* school on the site," recalls Betsy. "They wouldn't fit on the conveyor belt. It got to be my job to carry them out by hand."

The Bells moved into their schoolhouse in 1979, when it was barely livable. "Yes, it is probably better not to move into a house until it's finished," says Jeff, "but ours was a very long-term commitment. We still aren't finished.

"Moving in early has its advantages. We pay as we go and have very low payments on the money we did borrow in the beginning. And I think we have avoided mistakes this way. When you live with your work, like we do, you learn as you go along. Some things that I might have done five years ago, I know better than to try now."

The Bells found another advantage to saving money by not spending it before earning it—they are able to afford high-quality material on the interior, and super insulation. They have a regular insulated stud wall inside the extra-wide brick wall, and the woodstove in the basement will heat the entire house with no trouble. "I suppose by the time we are finished, we will have spent about as much money as we would have on a new house of this size, but that house would not be as interesting, unique, or as well built as this one," says Jeff.

Much of the interior decorating is recycled, too. On one wall, Betsy displays antique children's clothing on old wall hooks—a favorite "country look" idea. But Betsy does it with a special twist. An old photograph in an antique oval frame nearby depicts one of her aunts as a baby, wearing the same gown that hangs on the wall. In their bathroom, the Bells have an old pedestal sink that they tracked down through a local want-ad publication. The folks with the pedestal sink also had an old freestanding tub they wanted to get rid of, but the Bells had already found one for their bathroom.

The hardest problem they had to solve was finding new windows for the unusual-sized, tall, top-curved window frames. They hunted and inquired for someone who would make custom windows at a reasonable cost, and that led to another interesting story. As it turned out, the curved windows at the top were not practical, but the company that helped them through this problem to an eye-pleasing alternative was an unusual lumberyard in New Knoxville, Ohio. The lumberyard does a lot of work from scratch—takes in logs and goes on from there, using bark from debarked logs, sawdust, and scraps to generate its own electricity. Money saved is money-savings passed on to their clients. "The cost was very reasonable," says Jeff. "And I was amazed. The fellow who came up here and took measurements and attended personally to our windows was also working on a bowling alley destined for Japan!"

Part of the little schoolhouse's charm is the unusual entrance porch, not found on other examples in the region. One of the steel pillars holding up the porch roof is bent (see photo). Why? "Well," says Betsy, grinning, "there are two stories. One says that years ago a team of horses backed a wagon into it. The other version says it was a tractor. Either way, we decided the bent pillar had been there so long it was part of the building's character. So we left it bent."

CHAPTER 6

The Moneysaver Goes Shopping

The American shopper, *Homo shoppiens,* is a rather new species, evolving in the middle of the twentieth century from earlier strains of *Homo horse-traderiens.* This species differs from ordinary humans in that buying has become an essential function of its daily life, almost like eating. *Homo shoppiens* must shop for well-being. There need be no special goal or purpose other than pleasure, like art for art's sake. *Homo shoppiens* stalks up and down the rows of merchandise on sale until the lust to buy can no longer be denied. Then whatever happens to come next into the line of vision is pounced on, carried triumphantly to the cash register, and money exchanged for it. Back home, the Great Bargain Hunter lays the fruits of the hunt on the table and receives the adulation of family and friends. To be the Hero in the mid-twentieth century, one must capture the biggest bargain.

Homo shoppiens believes firmly that he or she is smarter than the merchants whose stores he hunts. But it is the merchant's turf. The merchant thought up the idea of bargains and grows rich selling them. *Homo shoppiens* never admits that, as long as he is buying, money is going out of his pocket, not in, no matter what the price tag suggests. A case in point: My wife and I were in a K Mart recently, tagging along with friends. In the first place, entering a K Mart is for *Homo shoppiens* tantamount to an alcoholic entering a bar. I thought we were going to escape unscathed, but at the very last minute here comes my wife brandishing two jars of peanuts that were marked down about 20¢ below normal price. A good buy? Not really. We had a jar of those same kind of peanuts at home, half full, stale from not being eaten. They had not been eaten because peanuts, much as I love them, do foul things to my digestive tract. Even if that were not true, one jar of the bargain peanuts would have been plenty for us until we ran afoul of another peanut bargain. What we did in purchasing two jars, whether we eat them or not before they go stale, is buy at least one jar's worth we would never have considered buying had my wife not seen the marked-down price. We did not save 20¢, we lost $2.26. The merchant knows. The funniest thing about the situation, in a pathetic sort of a way, is that with the peanuts weighing on my mind, I of course ate some, and then thinking about stale peanuts, I ate some more, and spent the whole next day with a stomachache.

SOME MONETARY PHILOSOPHY

I do not mean to say that one cannot "save" money while buying, but only that it takes a very disciplined mind to do so. Before discussing that, however, there are considerations about the definition of money that bear mightily on the subject of saving it. There are two basic views of the function of money. (A) Money is a medium of exchange, a substitute for real goods that makes buying much more convenient than bartering. Who wants to carry 5,000 bushels of corn to town to trade for an automobile?

If mankind stuck to this simple function of money and no more, we would probably have fewer financial problems in the world than we do. Money has another definition. (B) Money has intrinsic value. It represents wealth and *becomes* wealth because you can put it in a bank and it will "grow." We have made money function as if it were something biologically real. This is not the place to discuss the rightness or wrongness of that function, but it is most important in measuring how much money a moneysaver saves or does not save.

The person for whom money is simply a medium of exchange would take $10,000 won in a lottery and buy a new car, or some such item. He's "saved" his money in a vehicle that will cost more money if purchased next year, most likely, and that will not need repairs like his old one does. He finds security in that view even though he knows the car will rapidly lose value. The person who believes in money as having intrinsic value will probably invest or put his $10,000 in the bank to "grow" unless or until he is in dire need of it. He gets satisfaction knowing he is $10,000 richer, with the amount increasing every day. Consumption is the way to happiness for A; financial independence and therefore social independence is the way to happiness for B. Both probably pursue mythical goals. Security is an elusive prize that neither spending nor saving can guarantee. The spendthrift's $10,000 car may turn out to be a collector's favorite, worth more in 30 years than it is now. The $10,000 in the bank may "grow" more slowly than inflation, and so lose value.

Nevertheless, the true moneysaver will lean toward B, not that he will necessarily hoard money to watch it "grow," but to *protect himself or herself from having to borrow money* and so suffer the negative effects of money growth. Money only grows because someone is paying the interest on it. If you buy a car on installment loans, you pay for it thrice; if you buy a car with saved money, you pay for it once. That, in a nutshell, is the secret to *real* moneysaving.

TAKING ADVANTAGE OF SALES

In the ordinary and necessary purchases of a lifetime, the moneysaver takes advantages of discount sales but is aware of their limitations. When you buy on sale, your timing is of the merchants' choosing, not yours. Tons of money can be saved buying Christmas gifts in January when the prices are marked down from December. But you buy what is left over from Christmas, not necessarily the choicest goods. And

since prices are marked up in December, the markdowns in January might yet be higher than the normal price in July.

The way to benefit much more from any sale, if indeed you know that the price *is* a significant reduction from normal (furniture in some stores is always on sale, which means it is never on sale), is to buy in quantity. Or so some moneysavers believe. Certain wealthy persons follow this formula, and when they die, they have storage rooms full of cases of canned goods, crates of toilet paper, and so forth. Buying ahead with money that could be "growing" in the bank or invested in a growing business is not necessarily saving, even in an inflationary economy where the price of toilet paper is "growing," too.

The Amish, great moneysavers, operate under a contrary philosophy. They buy only what they need at the very moment, so that every penny possible is working for them until it must be spent. This kind of moneysaving works when you do not have much to buy. As an old piece of financial advice puts it: "Every farmer will understand me when I say that he ought to pay for nothing in money which he can pay for in anything but money."

Nevertheless, there may be advantages to either ploy, if no money is borrowed in the process. I would like to see two imaginative economists debate which of the following buyers saves the most money, all things considered: One person buys three new Fords at the same time and drives each of them for ten years. Another person buys a new Ford every ten years. At the end of thirty years, which person has saved the most money?

Taking advantage of sales may be an art, but success is based on strict science. To be on sale, an item must be priced lower than that same item normally is. That is much trickier to ascertain than it sounds. The "normal" price changes. What *Homo shoppiens* deems to be a sale price might just be a reflection of current supply and demand. One must know what the price of an item is today in several stores and then make sure that the item being priced is indeed exactly the same. A photographic memory helps, as does a free tank of gas to go scouting on. When food stores offer a loss leader, which represents true savings to the buyer, the merchant is betting his money that you will buy something else you might have bought in his competitor's store or might not have bought at all. How many shoppers buy a gallon of milk at a savings of 42¢ and then feel so righteous that they also take home a couple of 3-gallon jugs of sugar water from the soft drink rack, too? The sugar water represents a double loss: money value and nutritional value. The merchant makes back more on the soft drinks than he "lost" on the milk.

THE GREAT COUPON DEBATE

My sisters have had a raging, running argument with me that has lasted twenty years (with no sign of pulling back on either side) over the merits of comparative shopping, saving coupons, buying only on sale, and so forth. They insist that if a shopper works hard at it, savings of over $300 a year, minimum, are possible on groceries. I do not exactly disagree with their figures. (How can you disagree while being backed into a corner by seven pointed fingers operated by seven angry sisters?) I'm just not sure that the money represents a real savings. Supermarkets and food companies, not shoppers, put out coupons, so they obviously make money on them. Whose money do they make? The shoppers', of course. Let us say, in addition, that the shopper spends four hours a week pursuing coupon phantoms

through the streets and stores. If you save $300 a year, that's a wage of only $1.50 an hour and you haven't counted your gasoline, mileage, and those tidbits you buy that you don't need and are fattening besides, while cashing in your coupons. Add to that (this is what infuriates my sisters) the $300 extra weekend vacation you take because you "earned" it piddling with all those coupons. You are now considerably more in the hole than if you'd just gone to the grocery every week and bought what you customarily needed. And now your family is sick and tired of all those specials and sale-priced food— some of which is getting stale, which is why it was on sale. And one of the kids is liable to be so inconsiderate as to wonder out loud if the time spent shopping for bargains might not have saved more money if spent cooking something good. *The place to save money on food is in the garden, not in the store.* Having said that, I must also admit that taking advantage of coupons *sensibly* can save money. There are certain items you know you are going to use every month. Saving coupons for them, waiting until they go on sale, or buying them in quantity can save a little. Buying clothes and other seasonal items in the off season saves significantly, although choices may be limited. And while you are chasing down the bargains, you can at least pump your own gas and save that way, too.

DEBUNKING THE AUCTION MYTH

Another myth of *Homo shoppiens* is that great bargains await the bidders at country and suburban household auctions. The chances of finding real bargains are very slim, actually, since each bidder is betting he is not only smarter than the auctioneer, but smarter than the other bidders as well. He or she may be and occasionally may buy something for considerably less than its value, but for every great story you've heard, remember the thousands of people who attend auctions every week who have no great (true) stories to tell, but perhaps a garage full of junk to show for hours of standing around.

You will get very few bargains in antiques and collectibles at auctions. I've worked auctions and attended them regularly for forty years. There is always someone else there, usually a dealer, who knows the legitimate prices. Dealers can make mistakes, but if you know what mistakes they can make, you don't need to read this. You are already far more expert than I am. Guns, coins, stamps, antique furniture and dishware, dolls, toys, Indian artifacts, pottery, primitives, antique tools, and quilts will invariably go at current prices and in fact will often go higher than their normal value. Reason? When the dealers quit bidding, people with money who have waited all

afternoon are peeved or excited enough to go even higher. Or two family members or neighbors, suddenly finding themselves in competition, bid higher than they intended just to save face. An auction is very much a stage, and all the bidders are actors on it. Realtors and auctioneers like to sell land and houses at auctions. The auction not only forces people interested in the property to act, but forces them to act emotionally. At a farm sale I recently attended, two rival (and wealthy) farmers bid a tract of land $500 per acre higher than current prices and $300 per acre higher than they intended to bid. They both admitted it afterward. As one of them put it: "I was a little perturbed, and decided if he wanted to take it away from me, by God, he was going to pay for the privilege." (These are, by the way, the kind of farmers the government subsidizes so heavily with your tax money.)

Finding the Bargains

The only collectibles I have seen as bargains at household and farm auctions are books and sometimes certain kinds of so-called folk art. Even some dealers are not always savvy about these items. Quite often $5 will buy all the books you can carry under both arms. Quite often that's all they are worth, too. Most people know about McGuffey Readers, or think they do, and most of the time these sell higher than they are worth. But really rare books often do not look rare or auspicious in any way.

At a sale in the Philadelphia suburbs (I have had much better luck getting "bargains" at big city and suburban sales than way out in the country where folks think the bargains are best) there were two volumes of some value in one of many boxes of books for sale. I put them in another box with old, interesting books of little value, thinking I'd buy them all in one lot rather than having to lug home two big boxes full. Then, of course, I kept my eye on the box. Another book collector went through them, took one out I had chosen, and put it back in the box I had taken it out of. All right, fair enough, I thought. I'll bid on his but not too terribly high and maybe he'll let me have the other. But he was smarter than I was. He put his book back in with a bunch of Reader's Digest abridged books and other junk. My book, a slim little history of the Black Hawk War (all old Indian history is usually valuable stuff), was now buried under an imposing, thick 1865 History of the Civil War. I bid my competitor's box of books to $39 and let it go to save my meager resources for the Black Hawk War. But by this time the bidders were alerted—suddenly a box of books for $39 after whole wheelbarrows had gone for 50¢. Their eyes fell on the 1865 history. A book over 100 years old! At that time it might have been worth $15 but the bidding soared quickly to $50. After that, it was just myself and one other young man with more money than brains and a very bug-eyed auctioneer. I quit at $75, which was all the money I dared spend in those days even if I could sell Black Hawk for $100, which I was not sure I could do. I watched the successful bidder paw proudly through his 1865 history. I sidled up, friendly like, congratulating him on his great conquest and asking, as casually as I could, if he cared to sell that little-bitty old weird book there in the bottom of his box. But he was suspicious right away. The moral of the story: If you are going to hide a golden egg, don't put it under a silver tray.

It is, however, often lucrative to try to buy something out of a lot that a successful bidder has just purchased. He or she may want just one thing in the box and care little about the rest of the contents. I have bought interesting old bottles that way, and many books.

A final word on moneysaving and collectibles: Don't try to compete with dealers on popular antiques if you want to save money. Find something *you* like even though it is not the latest heartthrob on the antiques market. That was my mother's way. She would buy pieces of

Wellerware pottery when it was so cheap it often got thrown away. She thought it was pretty. Eventually so did everyone else, of course, and so her collection, nickled and dimed together, became quite valuable.

What you *can* save money on at auctions is the everyday stuff: furniture, pots and pans, outdoor furniture, and tools and gadgets more or less obsolete but not yet old enough to be collectibles. Pots and pans, of finer quality than what we can now buy reasonably, usually sell cheaply. We bought our pressure cooker at a suburban house auction in 1967. It was old then. We put a new rubber seal in it, and it's still going strong. A good hoe, axe, shovel, sledge, or rake might sell for $1. Log chains, belts for power take-off (PTO) pulleys, grease guns, jacks, fence-stretchers, fence posts, fence wire, stacks of boards, and gates will all sell well below their value. In cases of multiples of the same tool, the first will usually sell higher than the last. At the last sale I went to, there were three big PTO belts. I needed one to power my cut-off saw. These belts cost over $100 new. The first sold for $42, the second for $38, and the last, which I bought, for $32. If an auctioneer is on the ball he will try to sell them together—high bid takes one or more at the same price. At an auction in the country, you want to be listening so you know precisely what's being sold.

An honest auctioneer sells flawed items "as is" or makes a big show of pointing out the flaw, like a chip in a piece of china, so that everyone knows how honest and aboveboard he is. If you buy a chipped dish unknowingly and unwarned, don't be bashful. Present it to the auctioneer and if he missed the flaw or did not make a big point of it in his spiel, he will usually take it back and auction it over again.

It is risky to buy motorized machines at auction unless you know the machine has been well cared for. If you do bid, make sure the machine is started and runs for a while first. Most auctioneers insist on this practice and it is a good one. Pull the oil stick out and look at the color of the oil. If it is milky grey, there is water in the oil and so, no doubt, the block is cracked. Cheap lawn mowers and rotary tillers that you have no history on are especially risky to buy at auction. If you are a good mechanic and can tell by the sound of the motor that it is not worn out, fine. Everyone else should buy a used lawn mower from a reputable dealer who supposedly has repaired the machine before selling it or who will have to listen to you gripe and complain later on.

Heavy-duty motors on mowers, sometimes called industrial motors, are better used buys than just standard motors. Age is not necessarily a criterion to go by. A 20-year-old Gravely, with the original high-quality Studebaker engine, may be a better value than a

5-year-old discount store special of the same horsepower. Even if the
Gravely is not running, it normally can be repaired better, and its new
life last longer, than if you expended the same amount of time and
money on an El Cheapo. For the same reason, a 1950 farm tractor of
around 20 to 30 horsepower, valued at $1,000 to $2,000, and in reasonably good condition, may be a better quality tractor than a 1985 20- to
30-horsepower one selling for $8,000 new. I've driven both, and the
latter just doesn't have the same kind of guts (easily demonstrated by
operating a hydraulic forklift on one, then the other).

The Art of Bidding

Once you get over beginner's bashfulness at auctions, you can enjoy
bidding. Don't be too eager. When the bidding gets close to your limit,
put on a show of agony. Mutter. Start walking away, just in case the
auctioneer is pulling bids out of the air, or the owner is bidding you
up. Such an act also can psych out a competing bidder who may have
gotten caught up in the rhythm of the bidding. When he sees you balk,
he may become shy himself, thinking either the price is too high or
that if he bids again, he'll end up owning something, when in reality
he just wanted everyone to see him throw out bids in a bold manner.

If you use your hands a lot when you talk, better not carry on
conversations within eyesight of the auctioneer or you may end up
with an $8,000 tractor that will barely fit on your garden plot. Actually,
that can hardly happen. The most your gesticulating hands will do is
act as a foil for the auctioneer to jump the bid himself. If he gets
caught, he will simply say, "Hey, you waving your hands there—are
you bidding or not?"

Public auctions encourage strange displays of human eccentric-
ity and inconsistency. If all the world is mad, and it surely is, the
madness tends to concentrate at big city train depots and public
auctions. Many times an item of rather recent vintage, like an electric
welder that still looks fairly new, will sell higher than the catalog price
of a new one. Go to a sale knowing what you want, how much a new
version costs, and how high you will go. If the weather is perfect or the
auction site famous for some reason or another, or a lot of sentimental
family members are bidding on Papa's lifelong belongings, you might
as well stay home. There'll be no bargains that day. Nice weather
makes a crowd want to buy, as does notoriety. There once was a farm
sale in our county after a man had murdered his wife, which was why
the auction was being held. Nearly half the county turned out, bidding
everything above market price and carrying away half the cow stable
where the foul deed was done.

A NOTE ON FLEA MARKETS

Flea markets are the worst places in the world to buy only what you came looking for. If you can spend an afternoon at one and not buy something foolish, you already know how to save so much money that you don't need to read this book.

At most auctions nowadays, you are required to register your name with the cashier and be given a number. When you bid, the purchase price and your number are entered on a sheet of paper that is being tabulated by the person who sits next to the auctioneer. Save time by keeping your number in view in hatband, vest pocket, or your hand, so the auctioneer doesn't have to stop everything and ask you for your number. Don't lose your number or someone may run up a handsome bill on you. The tabulations eventually make their way to the cashier, who usually has a table set up in the only warm room in the house in winter, or on the porch in summer. You pay when you leave. Once you have purchased something, it is your responsibility to see that no one steals it or picks it up accidentally with his or her own purchases, which can happen easier than you think in a crowd. If you have lost your head and bought something too big to fit on your truck or in your car, you can often find someone at the sale willing to haul it for you if you're not going too far out of his or her way. A $5 bill works wonders in this regard. By the way, if a local church group is providing the food for the sale, you are in luck. This is one of the few places where *real* homemade pie is still available to the public.

THE ALL-AMERICAN GARAGE SALE

Just when the old-time market day, the local fair, and Saturday night in town seem to have disappeared into history, up pops their reincarnation: the garage sale. Garage sales have become America's most popular form of recycling—and the most profitable in terms of local economy. They flourish because of our craving for bargains. Even the inventory for garage sales comes from this craving—it's the extravagance of junk that *Homo shoppiens* drags home from his hunts. But what makes these front yard market fairs an intrinsic part of local tradition today is that they are social functions as well as economic ones, which is precisely as it should be. People come to understand each other better. More important, they begin to understand the economic need to rely on each other. The relationship is circular; the goods and money moving around and around in the local area, encouraging a sense of community. I've watched the same baby crib filter through a dozen garage sales. Each time money changes hands for that crib it recirculates in the community. It does not drain off to some faraway national or international corporation. It does not end up finally in the coffers of a large city bank. Mark Twain said that people can't get rich taking in each other's washing, but on the other hand, they can't lose money that way, either. And if more business were conducted this way, there would be real profits. For example, there was a bakery truck drivers' strike in Ohio a short while ago, resulting in a shortage of bread. There was a great clamor over this "problem." But if bread were unavailable from the few large bakeries left in the state, half a dozen or more little bakeries would spring up in every town. Not only would this keep most of the money spent on bread circulating locally, but we'd eat better bread and save on the cost of bread distribution, which the strikers hope to add to.

Pricing Your Goods

Whether you buy or sell at garage sales (and if you do one, you will probably do the other eventually), what is involved is a highly complex form of barter. You exchange your unwanted possessions for someone else's, using money as a way to keep score of the game. The main idea is to get rid of the merchandise so you can go out and buy some more, so you should not price items very high—err on the side of cheapness. Experts—if there be such on the subject of garage sales—believe that clothes should be priced at about one-eighth of the current store price. Tools, furniture, kitchenware, and so forth should be priced at one-third to one-half current prices or lower, depending on wear. Antiques and like-new items are difficult to price. If a piece is like new and you price it accordingly, the buyer will reason correctly that he or she might as well buy it really new from the store. Antiques require expert knowledge to price, and even then you never know. Something you consider elegant or dear may be just your sentimental value showing. Something you don't like out of the attic and would just as soon give away may be worth considerably more to someone else. You end up pricing your goods mostly by guess. That's half the fun of it. Everyone in the world would like to be a storekeeper, at least for a day.

It's best, when possible, to write the price on the object with chalk or other marker that is fairly easy to remove. Tags will be necessary for some items, but tags can be exchanged. At any rate, put a price on every piece. A good idea is to run your sale both Saturday and Sunday, or Friday and Saturday, and advertise that on the last afternoon prices will be lowered on what's left. Lower them 10 percent every hour if you want to make sure nothing is left to haul to the dump. Decide ahead of time if you are going to accept checks. It is almost always worth the risk to do so, especially in a smaller community where people know each other.

Be sure to have plenty of money on hand to make change—$50 to $100 in coins and small bills is not too much. But don't necessarily keep it all in your cash box, and keep taking money into the house to some safe place as it mounts up. There's no use in tempting your customers. Someone should be in charge of the cash box at all times. Some garage sale entrepreneurs use special pockets in their clothes for a cash box.

You will learn much about people at garage sales. You will be surprised (the first time) to find that poorer people buy more freely than wealthier ones and without haggling. The rich want to haggle. If dealers come to your sale because of antiques you offer, they will haggle, too. Keep your cool. Your antiques must be worth something or they wouldn't go to the trouble. If a dealer wants a percentage cut on everything he or she buys beforehand, look thoughtful and allow as how you will consider that on a piece-by-piece basis.

If you are a buyer, you need to know what the items being sold are generally worth. Then you can haggle if you wish, but garage sale prices are usually low to begin with, and to me there's something a bit gauche about haggling over $3 on Saturday. Maybe on Sunday, when the sale is winding down. . . . If the garage sale is one of those semi-businesses that open every weekend, haggle. You are dealing with pros now, and a victory will mean something.

Whatever, be assured that a garage sale can be a good place to save money—yours and your neighbors'. If you get carried away, you will just have to have your own sale later on. Start being extra nice to your friends—you'll need them later to help you out.

SHOPPING THE THRIFT SHOPS

Many people who otherwise wish to save money are too proud to shop at places such as Goodwill. A friend who has a good bit more money than I do told me that such stores were excellent places to buy old books because hardly any collectors think to look there. I started checking. Occasionally, a little gem (at least to me) did turn up. Years ago I was amazed to learn that another friend, whose family was quite wealthy, occasionally bought her clothes at Goodwill. She tailored them to fit and she always looked as nice as any girl on the block, and a good deal better than the fashionable models in *Vogue* today with all those drape-shaped, wrinkled rags that appear to be hiding not flesh and blood but a saggy skin of silkily tanned leather. I admired her disdain of style, her cool parsimony. And I understood why her family was rich.

At a spot in the road called Edison, Pennsylvania, north of Phila-delphia, there used to be a marvelous secondhand store. It may be there yet. In a big old barn, you could find, if you hunted, just about anything imaginable in the way of furniture and household goods. It was dirty and cold in there, with barely enough room to walk between the jumbles of furniture. I loved it. The mahogany desk I work on came from there. The mahogany secretary in my daughter's room also came from there. We paid a total of $42, if I remember correctly, for both of them. I've no idea what their true worth is today, but they were fairly good pieces of furniture to be found in a secondhand store. Such are the fruits of assiduous treasure hunting. I prefer going to stores like that over going to an auction, because you don't have to stand around all day waiting for something to sell, and you can haggle over price. Furniture purchased in such places invariably has scratches in it but the challenge of polishing, waxing, tinting, or stain-ing them to the vanishing point is easier to endure if you are several hundred dollars ahead of the game. And besides, you don't worry much about the kids scratching furniture that is already scratched.

BARGAINS FROM SALVAGE COMPANIES

An acquaintance of mine owns a hardware store. Around Christmas-time he bids on truckloads of what is called "stressed" merchandise and cheap imports. He sells these goods in his store as loss leaders, although he still makes a little money on them. There's nothing shady about the operation. He shows the people the dents, scratches, and scrapes on the items, which is why they are selling for less than half price. He even tells customers that the socket wrench sets, or what-ever, from Taiwan are quite inferior to his regular lines and may break the first time they're used. But at $3.89 a set, you can't lose, especially when the profits from the sale go to help the starving Ethiopians, as they did during the winter of 1985. People love these sales—a dent in a window fan that doesn't interfere with the blade is not going to affect the operation of the motor, and a mailbox with a dent in it will last as long as one without.

Some people get on mailing lists from all kinds of salvage companies. This can lead to big savings. Companies that deal in motel and restaurant salvage sometimes sell kitchen supplies, furniture, and the like by the pound. This may mean you have to buy in large lots that you don't need. And if you buy by mail, you will wait a few months for delivery. But it's a market the ordinary consumer knows little about. A cattle feeder told me he once cheaply bought a train carload of burnt Tootsie Rolls, which he fed to his cattle along with a regular feed, and made money. There are far-out surplus dealers, like the well-publicized Jerryco in Evanston, Illinois. Owned by Jerry Luebbers, it warehouses and sells by mail all sorts of weird merchandise for which there is no apparent market. In *American Way* magazine, Luebbers tells of a big load of World War I grenade belts that he sold to fishermen and carpenters for tool belts.

Some salvage companies move around the country holding sales of tools and appliances at terrific prices, or so the advance advertising says. I have checked with a number of veterans of these sales and all tell the same story: Either the tools are inferior imports or only a few actually sell cheaply to draw a crowd. The standard good stuff sells just as high as anywhere else.

There is, however, much controversy among cabinetmakers over the woodworking tools imported from areas of cheap labor, such as Taiwan. As little as ten years ago, most of these tools were crude replicas of American table saws, planers, and so on, and even at less than half the price, were not really a good buy. But now some of this machinery is being designed, tooled, and built better, say its users, and is not bad for the money. The May-June 1984 issue of *Fine Woodworking* ran a long article on Taiwanese power tools and concluded that some are okay and some aren't, which isn't too helpful.

A PIECE OF ADVICE
ON DISCOUNT STORES

In our village hardware store one day, a *Homo shoppiens* picked up a hammer for sale and hooted loudly: "Twelve dollars! Why I can buy a hammer at K Mart for four!" This statement is indicative of why America loves discount stores. *Homo shoppiens* thinks great bargains lie waiting there and refuses to believe that when you walk into a store, "you gets what you pays for," just like the old saying goes. Discount stores can and do offer discounts that average below what the corner hardware store charges, but the difference is seldom significant, especially if you count the small hardware store's personal service, handier location, and sometimes more responsible concern for your problems.

Let us take the case of hammers. Out of curiosity, I made a study of hammers in various marketplaces. The $4 hammer is so poor a tool that it is beneath the dignity of a true hardware man to sell. However, also at the discount stores were a number of other hammers of various brands and models, priced according to quality. I found *exactly* the same hammer in K Mart that day that I found at the corner hardware. At K Mart it cost 79¢ less—a savings still, but not a real ring-a-ding bargain. At the same time, in Garrett-Wade's catalog, there were hammers priced from about $12 on up to $24, which made the corner hardware look like a discount store. Exactly the same brand of hickory-handled hammer was priced from $13 to $23, depending on weight, with the models ranging from 10 ounces to 24 ounces. The important point to note is that to the typical *Homo shoppiens,* a hammer is a hammer, whereas in truth, there are not only many kinds of hammers but many different variations within any particular kind, and many different variations in quality between hammers of a particular kind. Merchants know how to use this variability to becloud the issue of price. Before you think you are saving money, make sure you are comparing not apples with oranges, not apples with apples, not even the same variety of apple, but the same variety, size, and condition of apples. Or hammers, or lawn mowers, or anything. Two 5-horsepower Briggs & Stratton motors might look exactly the same mounted on a tiller. But look closely. If one is an industrial (heavy-duty) motor and the other is a standard, the difference is considerable.

BUYING USED MERCHANDISE FROM NEW-MODEL DEALERS

As previously stated, buying used power machines secondhand at sales or auctions is fraught with risk unless you know how the machine was cared for. It's better to buy such merchandise from dealers who are selling the same thing new. Cars, trucks, lawn mowers, garden tractors, farm tractors, rotary tillers, anything with a gasoline or diesel motor falls into this category. I would include large appliances, too, although these are less risky at auction. If you buy from a reputable dealer, the machine should be in good running condition considering its age. Contrary to the stereotype, most used car dealers are honest or could not stay in business. The dealer will be quicker to repair a machine if it needs repair, not only because you bought it from him but because he is hoping you will buy from him again when you want a new model. The machine will cost you more, perhaps, than buying it at an auction, but the extra cost is worth it.

Two of the biggest possibilities for savings in life are your home and your automobile(s). Saving $300 a year on groceries is piddling compared to what you can save starting out with a very modest home and improving it on your own, as discussed earlier. The same is true of cars. Buying a new car is an extravagance we all sooner or later fall prey to, but the moneysaver is thousands of dollars ahead dealing in 1-, 2-, or 3-year-old cars, especially if he is satisfied with less expensive models of a given line. Remember, the motors in any given line all have about the same quality materials in them. There's just more of the bigger models, and more accessories. If you do buy a new car, however, buying stripped down is not necessarily a savings. If you order a car with your own selected accessories, it may cost you more than one that comes from the factory with more accessories than you are ordering. You buy less and pay more if you want a combination the computers have not considered popular among buyers.

"New" Cars

If you buy a new car, it pays to buy the old model year just after the new models have come out. On paper your new car is a year old, and if you haggle you can get the price down to reflect that. But in reality, your car is brand new and will last as long as any brand new car no matter what its book value. If you then take excellent care of the car so that it lasts even longer without repairs, you save again.

If you sell the car in three years (for another new but year-old car) you will continue to save, but the greater saver will be the fellow who buys your old one, runs it for three years and trades it for another good 3-year-old car. Such cars should be undercoated when new. As soon as it is yours, go around the bottom, especially under the door panels and behind the tires, and clean out all those little holes that drain water out of the bottom edge of the body. Water collecting behind this edge is what causes the first rust problems. With the drain holes clear, squirt a coating of used oil all along the inside bottom edge of the body, wherever undercoating has not covered well. Then keep the car serviced like you're supposed to.

When buying a used car or truck, check the grease zircs. If the grease protruding from the zircs is hard, the vehicle probably has not been serviced for a long time. Jack up the car or truck so you can wiggle the tires back and forth on the axle. (If you can put the vehicle up on a rack in a service station, all the better.) If there is more than just a very slight play, say ⅛ inch, you may need a new kingpin in the near future. Spin the wheels, too, with the vehicle out of gear. If there is a grating, scraping noise, your brakes are badly worn or need adjustment.

Experts have much advice on what to beware of in buying a used vehicle, all of it good. But I wonder sometimes if much of it is not futile. A used truck is going to have worn parts in it, and the older it is, the more the wear. You might spot trouble ahead of time by expertise such as that given below, or you might not, but in either case you have to be prepared to make repairs. The more mechanically minded or skilled you are in doing it yourself, the more money you will save. Or if you know an honest skilled mechanic, he will also save you money, because in any case I have experienced, it is cheaper to repair well than to buy new, no matter what the salesperson says. Milky grey oil indicated water in the oil of my old tractor, which indicated a cracked block. But the tractor cost me only $300 "as is" and with the engine completely done over with a healthy block, plus a new radiator and

A USED-CAR BUYER'S CHECKLIST

Here's a checklist of conditions and the problems they may indicate in used cars or trucks:

1. Oil in water or water in oil. Cracked block. Big trouble.
2. Play in wheels. Kingpin worn badly.
3. Streaks of hydraulic fluid on inside of wheels. Leak in brake cylinder.
4. Corroded muffler and tailpipe. Replacement will be needed soon. If excess noise indicates holes already in exhaust system, replacement will be even sooner.
5. Lots of *white* smoke out exhaust when engine is raced. Probably needs new rings—a rather major overhaul.
6. With motor idling and out of gear, let out on clutch. If there is a faint jingling sound that disappears when you push in on the clutch again, it may be a worn ring gear, which means sometime down the road, hopefully not literally, the clutch will need work done on it.
7. Body rust—easily seen unless the vehicle has been painted recently. Paint can cover a multitude of sins. Check the body closely. Rough, bubbly areas under new paint indicate rust. A knife blade

other more minor repairs, I still had less than $1,500 in a tractor that now was the equal of an $8,000 new one.

When buying a used truck, make sure you end up with the right kind of vehicle for the jobs you have in mind. A ½-ton pickup is okay for light hauling and good for road travel. Serious hauling calls for a ¾-ton job, with at least heavy-duty 6-ply tires on 15-inch wheels (16-inch are even better). Six-cylinder engines are easier to work on than eights and are hefty enough for serious hauling. Whether you choose standard transmission or automatic is a matter of preference, so the experts tell me. Newer automatics are almost as tough and durable as standards, they say. I still prefer standards. Four-wheel drive is very nice, and expensive, but it's worth it if you know you will have to drive in snowstorms. Two-wheel-drive pickups gain considerable traction from a load, however, and I get by most of the time. Empty, though, they are as helpless as a hog on ice.

Most of the above opinions and advice apply to farm and garden tractors, too. Old tractors converted to lawnmowers with belly mowers slung underneath, or converted to garden tractors, last even longer than pickups—much longer, in fact, because they don't often

will push right through if the rust is bad. Don't necessarily reject a truck because of rust, since rust will be with us always, sooner or later. Use it as a lever to beat down price.

8. Engine idle—it should be smooth. The way to really listen to a motor is to put your ear right on it or some extension of it—like the radiator cap—which will get your ear burned if the motor's been running very long. Some mechanics hold one end of a yardstick against the block or valve cover and their ear against the other end. Such close contact allows you to hear worn main and rod bearings, valve rattle, tappet poppings, and a whole lot of other noises that will mean nothing to you but might to a good mechanic if you can persuade one to help you out. The easiest way to tell if a motor is running well is to take the truck or car out on a level road and see how smoothly it will move ahead with the motor only idling. If it bucks and jumps and dies, not good. But then all it may need is a carburetor adjustment.

9. Drive down a fairly steep hill and take your foot off the accelerator. If the truck does not slow down at all, compression is low, indicating you'll need a new ring job soon. If you turn the ignition off and it takes a comparatively long time for the motor to come to a stop, that's another sign of low compression.

rust out. The main thing is to deal in brands you can still get parts for: Ford, John Deere, Allis Chalmers, Massey-Furgeson, Case-International, and sometimes Olivers and Minneapolis-Molines through White dealerships. You can find used tractor and farm equipment parts in graveyards that dot the country—best located by checking the classified ads in state and regional farm magazines. There is a new, computerized locating service for hard-to-find parts from Joe Goodman Tractor Parts Co., P.O. Box 80957, Lincoln, NE 68501. Its catalog is free.

Although you can still save money (over a new tractor) by fixing up an oldie with new parts, the new parts are expensive. Finding what you need in machinery graveyards saves—and can be an adventure. I will never forget encountering the proprietor of a tractor graveyard near Willard, Ohio. He was standing in the midst of literally acres and acres of dead tractors, as far as the eye could see. I asked him if he had a usable block for a 1950 WD Allis Chalmers. He thought a little bit, scratched his head, and snapped his fingers. "Yeah, I believe I do." And he led me through that maze of junked machinery unerringly to a corner where, under a piece of tin, sat the motor I was looking for.

CHAPTER 7

Foraging and Other Money-Making Ventures

W hen we want to save money, we normally think of the direct approach—we go to the store and buy when prices are reduced. This can be an excellent moneysaving ploy, as I learned while shopping for summer clothes in August with my wife. She bought a nice pair of slacks, knocked down from $68 to $32. In a few more days it might have been further reduced to make way for the fall clothes. Hundreds of items of clothing were marked at half price. It amazes me that anyone in the low- to middle-income bracket who values financial independence would ever buy *any* clothes until late in the season. Who cares if you don't get the pick of the new season's offerings? Buying on the off season can save literally *thousands* of dollars in a lifetime. Of course, what too often happens is that, carried away by half-price sales, we buy twice what we need.

There are indirect ways of saving money that people seldom think of as moneysavers, and they are certainly more pleasant activities than fighting crowds at sales. For example, a vacation is usually considered as a time for spending money, but some people enjoy vacations that are extremely economical. And if their trip includes some time foraging for pharmaceuticals (see page 178), it might even pay back money. Regular leisure activities can be expensive (golf), cheap (watching TV), or profitable (gardening). Thus life-style itself can be an effective form of moneysaving. Walking, jogging, and bicycling can all be cheap yet satisfying and healthful exercises—exercises that may also save money another way: in medical care. The following activities are examples of moneysaving leisure-time pursuits, and even if they don't make you any extra money, they can make your life intellectually and emotionally richer, which may be the best extra income you'll ever make.

FORAGING FOR PHARMACEUTICALS

In southern Oregon a remarkable man by the name of Richard Miller has organized a cooperative to gather and market wild herbs to the pharmaceutical industry. Those of us who have done the Euell Gibbons trip may cast a jaundiced eye, but the venture appears to be both practical and profitable. First of all, contrary to popular belief, pharmaceutical companies sometimes would rather extract drugs and medicines from the real plants than synthesize them—mostly because it is often cheaper to pay foragers than chemists. Secondly, according to the Department of Commerce, drug sales will double by 1990 and double again by 2000. Miller, head of what he calls the Organization for the Advancement of Knowledge, or OAK (1305 Vista Drive, Grants Pass, OR 97527), has written a booklet called "The Potential of Herbs as a Cash Crop," and puts out a newsletter, "The Herb Market Report for the Herb Farmer and Forager."

Southern Oregon is an area of great natural beauty, OAK associate Carol Danz explained to me, and it lures people there who have had it with crowded city areas. But as with most such regions of natural beauty and low population, unemployment is a problem. Miller sees pharmaceutical herbs as a form of supplemental income for spare-time workers or retirees. "One of our retired couples, working slowly, made $10 an hour together," says Danz. "More vigorous people can make more if they want to work hard."

The market is obviously limited compared to that of wheat or corn, but foraging for herbs is small scale by its very nature, requiring lots of hand work. Knowledgeable people, rather than stupid machines, are the main ingredient, and therefore the door is open for more enterprises like Miller's. In its first three months, his cooperative reported gross sales of $34,000, and that was before they got interested in eucalyptus leaves. About $1.5 million worth of eucalyptus oil is imported into the United States every year, according to Miller, and it could be produced here. With about 100 members, the cooperative (The Southern Oregon Herb Gatherer's Association) has been concentrating on several herbs: aspen leaves, which are used in cough medicines; the root of Oregon grape, used in liver medicine; horsetail, used in special lubricants; and Prince's pine, which has replaced sassafras in root beer. But some of their other accomplishments intrigue me even more. Members cleared one farm of Canadian thistle and sold it—a bitters extract from this cursed weed is used in vermouth! (If we could get the world to increase its consumption of martinis significantly, I know some Ohio farmers who could get rich and never have to plow or plant again.) Another time, members cut mullein, also marketable, out of a stand of young trees in a reforestation program. The weed was interfering with tree growth. "Forty people made $120 each, saved the foresters an herbicide bill, and actually made the Forest Service money because they had to buy brush permits," says Miller.

Obviously, what we are talking about is recycling free weeds into valuable pharmaceuticals, and it seems to me that its significance is not so much as a serious business, though it can be that, but as an interesting leisure-time activity—one that not only saves money by its very nature but offers the possibility of making a little, too. I think immediately of enthusiastic walkers I know who double up the time by picking up litter along the way. Several I know get satisfaction from saving the aluminum cans so gathered and selling them, though they need the money hardly any more than a Rockefeller would. One man, who happens to be a master mechanic, even has built a little motor-driven machine to flatten the cans into more easily manageable disks.

People so motivated need to know more about projects like OAK. For example, along those same roads where the aluminum cans sprout so luxuriously grows chicory. OAK says that the United States imports thousands of dollars of chicory from Bulgaria for making chicory root coffee—called Louisiana coffee in fancy restaurants. Enough chicory grows along midwestern roads to supply the market for 10,000 years at least.

Ginseng

Currently one of the most lucrative pharmaceuticals to gather is ginseng, which collectors are selling for $175 a pound! Because of its value, wild ginseng is threatened with extinction, or thought to be threatened, and some states are moving to restrict or ban gathering it. Needless to say, you can't gather ginseng where the law forbids it, although this is an unnecessary prohibition where good ginseng hunters are concerned. They don't overhunt their supplies but, like any commonsense farmers, leave enough for future harvests. They even plant more themselves. Ralph Aling, a weaver and herbalist in eastern Ohio, has his own patch in his woods, which he tends like a garden. He uses and sells surplus plants, seeds, and roots, plus other herbal remedies. I went foraging with him when he was in his 80s and could barely keep up as he plowed ahead up and down steep hills. So if he thinks ginseng adds vigor to old age, I'm not going to argue. Science argues, but recent studies done in China and Russia seem to indicate beneficial results, however slight, from using the plant.

It's been a year since I've seen Ralph, but at that time he was still working vigorously in the little woolen mill he owned for years between Berlin and Millersburg, Ohio, and which he sold to his grandson. He sells dried ginseng root for $5 an ounce. Need I say more?

Goldenseal

Another plant in fairly good demand is goldenseal, or yellow root. Tommie Bass, an herbalist in Leesburg, Alabama, who was recently profiled in the *Wall Street Journal* (which ought to tell us something, too), is quoted as saying: "Yellow root is absolutely real stuff; now that ain't no joke."

Goldenseal, rightly or wrongly, has enjoyed that kind of reputation in folk medicine for centuries. Buyers of ginseng almost always buy goldenseal, too. F. C. Taylor Fur Company, 227 East Market Street, Louisville, KY 40202, and S. B. Penick & Company, 100 Church Street, NY 10007, are two old standby markets. Regional and local fur buyers also buy ginseng and goldenseal and sometimes other plants, like burdock and mayapple. You can find their advertisements in country newspapers, local farm magazines, and hunting and trapping magazines. In Ohio, for example, Little Beaver Furs, 14301 Ellsworth Road, Berlin Center, OH 44401, and Ohio River Fur Company, P.O. Box 2347, Route 267, East Liverpool, OH 43920, buy ginseng and goldenseal. Richard Miller's book (see page 178) and his newsletter are good sources for markets. For both identification and markets *A Guide to the Medicinal Plants of the United States,* by Arnold and Connie Krochmal (Quadrangle, The New York Times Book Co., 1973), is helpful.

GATHERING GOURMET MUSHROOMS AND DYE PLANTS

The pharmaceuticals industry is not the only plant market for the casual hiker who knows a little botany. Gourmet restaurants pay well for various types of wild mushrooms, and professional plant hunters make a living that way. When I was young, I could always sell all the morels I could find to people in town who loved them enough to pay 75¢ a quart for them, a good price then. They are worth more than that now. Some mushroom hunters I know take a week's vacation to hunt morels in Michigan every spring and often bring home several bushels' worth.

Wool spinners and weavers are always on the lookout for unusual materials to dye their fabrics with. Fungi, especially those that give a reddish or bluish hue, are most desirable, but even common wild plants like pokeberry are in demand. I have a standing order from a spinner in Cleveland for pokeberries. Whenever I have time and know where some plants are fruiting, I freeze up a pound or two for her. All you need to do to start tapping into these possibilities is spend time in the library studying the appropriate books and magazines, such as *Spindle, Shuttle, and Dyepot.* Once you're armed with this knowledge, any walk might become a treasure hunt.

SALVAGING FUR

In addition to collecting aluminum cans, there is another profitable bit of recycling you can do along the highways and byways. Cars and trucks kill thousands of fur-bearing animals every year and from November to March valuable furs are thereby wasted. Actually, few are wasted since trappers and other people in the know will cruise the highways and pick up any animals that may be still valuable. If the hide of the animal has not been cut through and the animal has not started to decay, the fur is still good. Pull on a few hairs. If they come out easily, too much decay has set in. If not, put the carcass in a plastic bag and freeze it if you can't get it to a fur buyer soon. The carcass may be frozen already. Foxes and raccoons are the two most profitable animals and the two most likely to be found. Red and grey foxes were selling in 1984 for up to $30 each and raccoon for $28. Don't worry about skinning the hide out unless you know how—fur buyers will take the whole carcass at a slight reduction in price and often prefer to do so because improper skinning can ruin the fur.

IN SEARCH OF INDIAN ARTIFACTS

My favorite form of "landcombing" is hunting Indian artifacts. No vacation or leisure-time activity has provided me with more pleasant exercise, more excitement, or more financial return. An unbroken flint arrowhead may be worth $5 or $25 depending on the type, and larger stone knives and spearheads are worth much more. A large, perfect, dovetail spearhead can in fact be worth several thousand dollars, and polished slate figurines and other artifacts of artistic design associated with the moundbuilding cultures are worth even more. Although the chance of finding rarer pieces is limited, it is still possible.

The rise in value of Indian artifacts doesn't gladden my heart particularly, since it means more people are tromping the fields. Landowners become nervous and may refuse permission to artifact hunters, not because they begrudge them the finds they make, but because they trample crops, leave gates open, and break down fences. So if you want to take up this most pleasant of hobbies, be sure to get permission, and limit hunting time to either early spring before crop cultivation begins or late fall after it is over.

Fall-plowed soil is the best place to hunt in the spring, because rains will have washed the bare soil surface over winter. Any bare land in late fall, winter, or spring holds the possibility of an artifact find. A low hill above a stream or river is a good place to concentrate on because it's likely that Indians may have camped there.

I have found arrowheads in all kinds of locations—in creeks, on river shores, and sticking out of cliff banks. (Searching in such places does not incur the risk of arousing a farmer's wrath, because you're not walking on his cropland.) I've also found arrowheads in the bare ground around recently erected buildings, in gardens, and along paths laid bare by sheep. I've even found them around the ruins of old houses, where I think a collection of arrowheads may have been kept and forgotten, to be scattered by time back over the soil, along with the bricks of the chimney. A friend of mine found a flint arrowhead embedded in the sidewalk in downtown St. Louis. It had been mixed into the stone used in the concrete mixture—not too surprising since part of St. Louis is built on Indian mounds. In areas where there are Indian mounds there will always be Indian relics.

When I hunt new territory I follow a set procedure. I look on hills where erosion has carried topsoil away, not in lowlands where erosion has deposited topsoil. If examination of the soil surface reveals flint chips, I keep hunting, because flint is not native to most areas. Its presence, especially in the form of numerous thin chips, is a telltale sign of early Indian habitation. Then I walk back and forth across the area systematically or aimlessly, as fits my mood.

ROCK HUNTING

Searching for rare minerals and semiprecious stones—rock hunting—provides treasure-hunting excitement and is a way to make a vacation pay for itself. Panning for gold or prospecting for uranium come quickest to mind, but while some people do these on their vacations, there are possibilities closer to where most of us live. Rubies and sapphires can be found near Franklin, North Carolina, and the area caters to rock hounds. Rock hounds still flock to Murfreesboro, Arkansas, to hunt diamonds. In 1956 one woman's $2 admission reportedly bought her a $75,000 find. Near Prineville, Oregon, you can hunt agate, jasper, and opal. Idaho and Utah boast good opals and other semiprecious gems. Mason County, Texas, is known for topaz, the shores of Lake Superior and the north Pacific coast for agates. Agates can be found in many places—even Iowa, not thought of as a gem-collecting state. New York is home to garnets.

There is value in any good rock collection, whether it contains precious gems or not. Rose quartz and blue quartz are valuable enough to sell and you may find them anywhere from South Dakota to Pennsylvania. Petrified wood and fossils of all kinds have value. Specimens of the latter can be found in many areas. Meteorites are worth money and can turn up anywhere. A very solid, heavy, brown or black rock like none other in your area could be a meteorite, especially if it attracts a magnet. Then there are geodes—dull-colored, roundish, bumpy rocks. The creek beds of southern Indiana are littered with them. When broken open, they are partially hollow, but chock full of glistening crystals that are extremely attractive, especially when polished. When we lived in that part of the country, children often sold geodes along the road for $5 each. (We have a set of bookends of cut and polished geodes that cost considerably more than that.)

A trip to the library will acquaint you with many good books on rock hunting, a very romantic and exciting kind of recycling. Wherever man or nature has cut deeply into the earth, leaving exposed vertical or horizontal surfaces, the hunting can be rewarding: Road cuts, especially the deep ones along superhighways, and stone quarries all bear investigation. Due to the popularity of rock hunting, some stone quarries don't allow hunting anymore because they are not able to handle weekend crowds. Others cater to rock hounds and require a fee and safety gear—hard hats and hard-toed shoes. Sometimes you must sign a paper releasing the quarry from any liability if injuries are incurred. Scaling the walls of a stone quarry can be dangerous business—I can vouch from experience.

Though I have hunted for semiprecious gems in quarries (without luck), my main purpose has been a much more humdrum type of landcombing. Two very nice quarry owners gave me permission to haul out rocks for free if I did the work of loading and hauling myself. I secured the stones for my fireplace in this manner, as well as for some terracing outside. One of the most desirably shaped slabs of stone was perched high on the wall of the quarry and in getting it down I created a minor avalanche that might have injured someone below. So if you're going to start climbing quarry walls, be conscious of your own safety as well as that of others.

Painted Rocks

While your rock hunting may not turn up any semiprecious stones, you can still benefit from your nondescript finds—paint them to look like animals or other objects. This requires a keen imagination. Look for a rock that looks vaguely (to you anyway) like something else. A frog, perhaps. Or a kitten. Then paint it to bring out the imagined form so well that even a clod like me can see it. Painted rocks sell fast at garage sales if the price is kept under $5.

BROWSING FOR BONE AND HORN

Knowledgeable woodland strollers always have their eyes peeled for antlers, which hunters collect avidly. Finding them is rare because rodents usually eat them soon after the bucks shed them. In addition, deer and antelope horn is collected in the West for Oriental markets, where powdered horn is thought to be an aphrodisiac. An old buffalo skull in good shape may be worth $50 or more to collectors of western Americana. A longhorn skull, horns attached, sells for more. Almost any bleached bone or skull, particularly of a small animal, is now popular with artists, who use them in necklaces, pendants, and collages.

THE WONDERS OF WEATHERED WOOD

Weathered wood is the term preferred over driftwood because the seashore is by far not the only place you can find good specimens. Pieces of beautifully weathered wood occur in forests, too. Extraordinary pieces are used in restaurants for decor, in clothing stores as backdrop or to hang clothes on display, and by artists (or the artist in all of us) for floral arrangements, table settings, or as sculpture. My doctor tells the story of a piece of driftwood he brought at great expenditure of energy from the shores of Lake Erie to his garden 60 miles away. About a year later, he hired a handyman to saw up and remove a dead tree in his yard. The job was done while the doctor was at work and the tree remover called him there. Said the yardman to the doctor: "I got rid of that old stump in your rock garden, too, while I was at it."

That story underlines the principle by which a landcombing recycler operates. Beauty may be in the eye of the beholder, but more than likely it is applied to something that is not normally in the eye of the beholder. The forester, farmer, and fisherman may never notice anything unusual, let alone pretty, about the weathered wood that is a part of their daily lives. But if your daily surroundings are more contrived, that is, made up of products built by man and machine, you may find a naturally decaying stump arresting and, therefore, beautiful. *If orchids were as common as dandelions, we would not tolerate them in our yards.*

Bits of weathered wood, alone or with pebbles, bones, or seashells, can be used to make wonderful mosaics. No one can tell you how. Look at examples in craft shops and books and then let your imagination run wild. All you need is a plywood backboard and glue.

COLLECTING BOTTLES, COINS, AND STAMPS

Other exciting leisure-time activities that can be quite profitable are hunting old bottles (especially in old dumps), seeking coins wherever crowds have gathered over the years, and collecting stamps.

Old Bottles

Years ago trash collection was unknown. People dumped their junk back in the woods or over the nearest hill and there it still lies, awaiting the treasure-loving recycler. Bottle collectors have driven the price on old bottles up high enough that every one of these old dumps is a potential treasure trove. You won't collect bottles worth big money unless you are very, very lucky, but you'll earn enough to satisfy any moneysaver who likes the idea of getting paid for having fun.

About twenty years ago when we were living in the suburbs north of Philadelphia, we used to walk along the Reading Railroad tracks. It provided a nice country walk without traversing private property. One day we found a pile of old glass, mostly bottles, at the foot of the railroad embankment, which was quite high at that particular point. It was apparent that more was buried beneath the soil surface. The railroad had been in operation as far back as the Civil War and it seemed that the debris must have been dumped off a train at some time, since there were no roads or dwellings that could account for the junk pile's location. Most of the bottles we found were circa 1920 as far as I could tell and nothing much of significant value. But what fun we had, digging them up.

After that, we started looking for old trash heaps. To our surprise, the many wooded areas in the neighborhood—second growth mostly over what had once been farmland—held quite a few old dumping sites. You could tell the old ones because only glass and pottery remained. Tin and iron had mostly rusted away. Poking in these sites was how we found the old bottles now on the shelves that divide our living and dining rooms. None of these bottles are old or rare enough to be highly valuable, the oldest being about 1880, but they aren't worthless, either, and I like them. They remind me of some very happy hours that cost us nothing in money.

Being aware of the possibilities of landcombing makes life always interesting, never dull. I know carpenters who were working on a building uptown and found several dozen old inkwells in a crawl space up under the roof. No one has any idea how they got there. When I'm in old barns, I have a habit of looking up on beams and shelves where great-grandfather might have hid his whiskey from great-grandmother. Old whiskey bottles are valuable. Backhoe operators digging sewer, water, or cable lines, especially in cities and villages, often unearth old glassware and pottery worth money. Keep your eyes open.

Lost Coins

Recently I visited Put-in-Bay Island in Lake Erie, which has been a tourist spot for well over a century. There were crowds of people milling about, some getting soused on the wine for which the area is famous, most just lolling around, bored, eyeing each other's suntans. The only person I saw really having an exciting time was a man with a metal detector, hunting coins over areas where tourists have been dropping change since at least 1860, and where once the largest hotel in the world stood. He was finding some, too. Nothing spectacular, he said. "Just enough to pay for the trip over from the mainland." But there was always the possibility of a big find every time his detector sang out.

Where's the best place to hunt? Wherever crowds gathered before about 1933, since most coins before then are worth much more than their face value. In fact, almost all coins made before 1965, when the government debased our currency, are worth a good deal more than their face value.

Collecting as a hobby is a good example of moneysaving recycling, although we rarely think of collecting in that way. A collection of almost anything, built up slowly and shrewdly, has increasing value greater than money in the bank, especially in those collecting categories that become very popular. Every moneysaver should be collecting something. Or perhaps do as I do and try to maintain just enough knowledge in several categories to be able to identify, or at least suspect, items of value, should you happen upon them. Thus, the 1950 nickel with the D imprint (for Denver Mint) is unusually valuable relative to its age. Chances of finding one now are poor, but ten years ago moneysavers developed a habit of glancing at any nickel that came their way, just in case. Coins may not be a good category for the jack-of-all-trades moneysaver to monitor, however, because so many people are aware of coin value increases. In fact, there is a tendency to overvalue. There is a virtual hoard of pre-1965 common, high-silver coins being held by individuals and dealers that probably will never be worth much more than the silver in them. Stamp collecting may be a better alternative, though postage stamps suffer from the same overcollected situation.

Stamps

It is no trouble to study a U.S. stamp catalog and memorize a few rules of evaluation. Not all old stamps are valuable. Stamps on envelopes are almost always worth more than individual stamps, so don't tear them off if you suspect value. High denominations of older stamps are almost always valuable. Uncanceled stamps are almost always more valuable than canceled. Older commemorative stamps (the rectangular ones depicting historical scenes or occurrences) are always worth saving. And, of course, if you find a U.S. stamp with the Graf Zeppelin on it, you've just made yourself about $300 or more.

I once helped a church group that ran a little stamp business. People would donate boxes and sacks full of stamps, sometimes even old albums with stamps in them, and the church would sort and resell them to dealers or individuals. The treasure hunter and moneysaver in me never had a more exciting time. We would winnow through the mounds of loose stamps, separating out the commemoratives, which sold higher per pound to stamp marts than common stamps did. Quite often there were rarer stamps jumbled into the mixture. It was like finding golden needles in a haystack. Then one day in a box of loose stamps there was a nineteenth-century album. In the excitement of pricing those stamps I learned all about invisible watermarks, different perforation sizes and slight differences or imperfections that often make a common old stamp into an uncommon old stamp. But you have to be careful and not get carried away. I once ran across some Civil War letters and nearly frothed at the mouth over the stamps. Turned out, the letters themselves were more valuable.

Other Tidbits

Prices of old comic books, baseball cards, and other such humble collectibles are sometimes awesome. It pays to have at least a slight familiarity with these genres, because these are items you have a greater chance of encountering. An early Superman comic or one of Pete Rose's earliest baseball cards might buy you a very nice vacation. The key to any collecting is the condition your find is in. You could find a valuable comic book in a paper drive, but if the cover is torn or missing, it's worth zilch. The same is true even more so with stamps and coins.

COLLECTING BOOKS

Condition is all-important in book collecting, too, and book collecting is the recycling hobby that I think holds the most promise for a moneysaver willing to do a little homework. Books are everywhere. And it *is* true that you can run across a $10 or $20 book sometimes for 50¢ at a library sale. Even if the books you collect turn out to be nothing more than interesting to you, you at least get the satisfaction of reading them. Since there are all kinds of collectors collecting all kinds and categories of books, it is difficult to gauge market values. What I do is subscribe to a book dealer's catalog—Antiquarian Books, Box 188, Carey, OH 43316. The dealer, Robert Hayman, is renowned in the trade and also is a friend of mine. There are many other catalogs available, but I like his not only for the humorous quips he spices the book descriptions with, but because he deals mostly in books *in my part of the country*—Ohio and the states around it—the kind of books I might have a chance of accidentally finding myself.

I study the catalog, paying particular attention only to those books he prices over $100, which may be only a dozen or so in each catalog. I can't remember even these specific titles, but over the years I do get a feel for what kind of book might be rare enough or historically significant enough to command that kind of price. So armed, I can glance over the books at garage sales, flea markets, the giveaway shelf at the library, antique stores, the Saturday night auction house where I worked once, and farm sales, and make a fairly educated guess about whether it is worthwhile to wait around and bid on them. I've never yet scored big, but preparing myself to do so makes life so much more interesting. And I may rescue a truly valuable book that belongs in a rare-books library from going to the dump. And that's *real* recycling.

BARBED WIRE AND OTHER "NEWER PRIMITIVES"

The moneywise recycler needs to be aware, too, of the many unusual collecting hobbies some people follow. At least one collection of brass checks (or bawdy-house tokens) exists and is considered very valuable (see *Incredible Collectors, Weird Antiques and Odd Hobbies* by Bill Carmichael [Prentice-Hall, Englewood Cliffs, N.J., 1971]). More accessible if not acceptable to the casual stroller, bicycler, or traveler is barbed wire, which has been avidly collected for over a decade, believe it or not. Unlikely as it might seem, barbed wire has been manufactured in many types since about 1867. But I think its popularity stems from the fact that you can still find it for free. The older desirable types are seldom in use any more but are found rolled up in fence corners or sticking out of old trees in fence lines. In the latter case, the wire was originally nailed to a young tree that promptly grew around it. Later on, a second strand of barb may have been nailed to the tree, and it, too, was eventually enveloped by the tree trunk. I have seen trees with as many as three different kinds of barbed wire sticking out of their trunks. Collectors say that the wire inside the tree trunk is sometimes in almost mint condition, unlike the rusty stuff exposed to the weather. But one is not often in a position where he can cut down a tree and slice out the barb.

The best hunting is in the West, where more barbed wire was used than anywhere else and where the dry climate preserved it better. One rich collector supposedly hunts the stuff with a helicopter and spyglass. Pieces 18 inches long are collected, though if very rare and unavailable in that length, shorter strands will do. For what you will probably find, figure top value at $3 to $20 per strand.

Old barbed wire might be found in a barn or line shack, long abandoned, which brings up another kind of landcombing. Abandoned homes and homesteads, barns, camps, ghost towns, bunkhouses, city slums, and so forth, can be sources of collectibles that only a few years ago were considered worthless and are still rather undervalued. Western Americana and primitive farm tools (the traditional farmer is disappearing just as surely as the traditional cowboy) can still be picked up cheaply or for free, especially the latter category. For example, Les Beitz, in his *Treasury of Frontier Relics: A Collector's Guide* (Edwin House, New York, 1966), treats the old hub wrench or wagon wheel wrench as something special in western relics, but nearly twenty years later, I have seen these wrenches hanging neglected in *eastern* barns at farm sales, no effort made to sell them, because they are considered valueless. Also ignored are miscellaneous old pulleys, stirrups, open-end wrenches, harrow teeth, cultivating disks, tobacco tins, nail boxes, hinges, odd bolts, and machine parts, all of which will someday be collected or are being collected now in other parts of the country. (Remember my parable about the orchids in the lawn.)

At farm sales, I comb through the barns for such items and if I see something interesting I try to buy or beg it from the owner or have the auctioneer bid it off. In more southern regions, I keep a sharp eye for old tools and paraphernalia connected with tobacco farming, still largely a handcrafted process but on its way out, too. The West is an even more lucrative place to hunt because of the popularity of anything connected with our mythic hero, the cowboy (who was actually not very heroic at all). A search around abandoned ranchhouses and bunkhouses is likely to turn up bootjacks, spurs, stirrups, horse bits, and whiskey jugs and bottles.

FREE FRUIT TREES AND OTHER WILD PLANTS

Wild plants offer another kind of moneysaving or moneymaking opportunity for the casual landcomber. In my orchard there's a pawpaw tree I paid $10 for, if I remember correctly, but it cost Corwin Davis, the man who sold it to me, only his time. Davis is a well-known hunter of high-quality wild fruit trees and a member of the North American Fruit Explorers. Members make a habit of spending leisure time sauntering through the woods or along the roadsides tasting various wild fruits. What they know, and what is not generally known, is that quality varies from tree to tree of the same species. What Davis found in a lifetime of hunting pawpaws was that there are about six trees with much-better-than-average-tasting fruit. He grafted these to seedlings and sold them, or sold seeds from them, turning his miles of adventuresome hiking into a little sideline business. The grafted trees sell for a high price because of the added labor and because they can be guaranteed true to the name, unlike seeds, which will not necessarily come true to the parent and so sell cheaply. But seeds are easier to send. Members of the organization are constantly trading or selling seeds and scions among themselves, and you can be a part of it. Just write to membership chairwoman Mary Kurle (10 S. 055 Madison Street, Hinsdale, IL 60521).

Some "fruit explorers" hunt for old, abandoned homesites and study the trees in what remains of the old orchards. If an apple tree is in fairly good health, though it has been neglected for years, the assumption is that it will not need constant spraying. If, in addition, the fruit is good tasting, the tree is considered a great find and the explorer will graft scions of it to his own orchard trees, thus rescuing it from extinction. Two of my best apple trees come from a wild fence row tree, and I didn't have to graft them. I simply dug up root sections that had sent up sucker growth and transplanted them.

Several years ago Douglas Campbell, then president of the Northern Nut Growers Association, led a party of plant explorers on an expedition to discover the northernmost pecan tree in the United States. They found a grove on an island in the Mississippi River in the region of Dubuque, Iowa—rather far north for a pecan. Nuts from the tree have been sold to growers all over the country since then. If your interests are inclined in that direction, can you think of a more delightful way to spend a vacation and possibly make money, too?

Just by paying attention to the fruit and nut trees of your own area, you can establish your own carefree orchard at practically no cost at all. I have never had much luck grafting nut trees, but planting their seeds is easy, and I now have started, for free, the best hickory, black walnut, and wild hazelnut trees in the county. I have a pear from an old homestead tree that was the only one in the orchard on which the fruit buds did not freeze in our bad winter last year. I have two apricots grown from seed of an heirloom variety from Wisconsin. It has been grown there for a century and comes true to seed. Peaches often come true to seed, too, and I have several such seedlings from seed begged from other growers. After I had given up trying to grow serviceberry (sarvistree, shadbush, *Amelanchier*) in my orchard (the trees would just die), I found a bushy type growing in the nearby woods and transplanted it to the orchard. My goal is an orchard of fruit so acclimated to this area that it will require no spraying—and that will be a moneysaver indeed.

Wildflower Seed

If you have checked the prices on wildflowers, you may be ready to start gathering the seed yourself. This is a much better way to get the plant started on your property—you don't run the risk of digging up a plant only to have it die, a sad but common occurrence with wildflower pirates. Mark the spot where you find the plants blooming. You might even tie a bit of thread around the plants to identify them because when you return to gather seed, the plants will be hard to recognize. The early spring flowers in particular, such as bloodroot (*Sanguinaria canadensis*), begin to fade away rapidly by late May. Experience will teach you the gathering times—a short period in late spring for the early plants, and a longer period lasting all of late summer and early fall for later plants. Among the easy and practical flowers to collect are:

Trout lily	*(Erythronium americanum)*
Virginia bluebells	*(Mertensia virginica)*
Bloodroot	*(Sanguinaria canadensis)*
Butterfly milkweed	*(Asclepias tuberosa)*
Spiderwort	*(Tradescantia virginiana)*
Wild columbine	*(Aquilegia canadensis)*
Jack-in-the-pulpit	*(Arisaema triphyllum)*
Evening primrose	*(Oenothera biennis)*

Recycling Weeds

Shirley and Dave Gibson's garage in my hometown is like no other garage I've ever seen. Instead of being occupied by a car or the usual lawn and handyman tools, this one is festooned with gorgeous bunches of drying plants. They hang from the ceiling and on the walls, and stand in baskets and crocks on the floor, giving off heavenly aromas and imparting to the room a magical quality. A visitor feels he has stepped suddenly into a forest glen. After the plants dry properly, Shirley makes wall decorations, table arrangements, and wreaths out of them. Or, as in the case of the red clover blossoms, she uses them as ingredients in potpourri.

What is most fascinating about Shirley's hobby is that at least half of her drying plants are common roadside weeds, available free to anyone who, in her words, likes to "tramp the roadside." I regard narrow-leaf dock in my fields as an enemy, but those rusty red

seedheads in a dried-flower arrangement, along with yarrow and a few stems of ripe wheat, look marvelous. A crock full of mullein seedheads seems transformed into exotic desert plants. Tight round branchings of pepper grass, so common in the fields, appear in a vase to have changed, Cinderellalike, into a rare bouquet.

It would seem, from the array in the garage, that the Gibsons are in the dried plant business. "We could be," says Shirley, "but I prefer to do it just for fun. I'm not a very competitive person. But for several years we did have an annual sale of what we collected and arranged. *Last fall we sold $500 worth in forty-five minutes."*

The Gibsons' moneysaving and moneymaking hobby turns their

every walk or drive into an adventure. "I'm always telling Dave not to drive so fast. I get cross-eyed trying to focus on every plant we pass," says Shirley.

I asked her how she could tell ahead of time which weeds would look nice when dried and used in flower arrangements. She shrugged. She explained that it's a matter of experimentation—trial and error. Some things dry nicely and hold color and some don't.

But I think it takes a special kind of imagination to bring beauty out of the commonplace. For example, just inside the garage door sits a basket of red corncobs. They look singularly attractive to a person who has been kicking corncobs across barnyards for years. Who would have predicted that result? The same feature distinguished her wild grapevine wreaths: The bunches of grapes, dried, were still attached to the vines. Such wreaths would sell easily for $15 to $20, yet the materials are free to the woodland stroller.

There are only a few hard and fast rules when gathering plants for drying. The plants should not be wet from rain or dew. It's best to pick during the heat of the day unless it is so hot the plants are wilted. The rest is a matter of timing and what you want. If the flowers are important, the plant should be picked at the peak of bloom, not after the flowers have started fading. Wild white yarrow blossoms, for example, will not hold together if picked too early or too late. But the gatherer should always be aware, like the gardener, that no two years are the same. Maturity may come earlier or later than "normal" from one year to the next, and usually does. And not all collectible plants mature in the fall. Some are ready in summer. Seedheads or pods should be gathered at whatever stage of maturity you desire. For example, if you want green seedheads on sourdock, cut the stems when the seeds are still green, and they will keep their color upon drying. If you want rusty red seedheads, wait until the heads mature to that color. Teasel can be cut when in full bloom to preserve a pinkish purple color in the head, or left until the plant dies in the fall for a silvery color. Some arrangers then spray-paint the teasel.

Advice on drying does not hold true for every arrangement in the Gibson garage. There is one wreath on the wall, held together with plaid ribbon, that is composed of a rusty roll of—what else—barbed wire! "I've had many offers for it, but I really want to keep it," says Shirley. "It's sort of a gift from my brother. I told him one day I thought a roll of rusty barbed wire might make a nice wreath if it wasn't too difficult to roll some up. He snapped his fingers and said, 'No problem. I know where there's some hanging on a fence post already rolled.'"

Here's a list of roadside and brushland plants that can provide material for wreaths and arrangements, and most likely you will discover more on your own.

1. Red clover blossoms for potpourri: The dried blossoms will absorb and hold aromas of herbs and spices mixed with them.
2. Cattail stems: used for decoration when large and small.
3. Black walnuts: dried *hull and all* and displayed in basket or pan.
4. Catnip: used to scent a wreath or for potpourri (or for tea). Pennyroyal and sweet cicely are also aromatic.
5. Tassel-headed stems of tall wild grasses that resemble pampas grass: used in arrangements.
6. The tall, dead podded stems of evening primose: collected late in the fall and used in arrangements. (The pods will still be full of seed if you want to collect that, too.)
7. Corn husks: used for decoration after corn harvest in the fall.
8. Butterfly weed (orange glory flower): Left to go to seed, the plant sports longish, canoe-shaped pods good for decorative arrangements.
9. Seed balls from sycamore and gum trees: collected late in the fall and used for Christmas tree ornaments.
10. Bittersweet: harvested when berries are orange but leaves are still green, and used for wreaths and arrangements.
11. Sumac seedheads: used for wreaths and arrangements. (Be sure you know the difference between these red seedheads and the white drooping heads of poison sumac. Also be aware that white-berried vines in a fence row are probably poison ivy vines.)
12. Tumbleweed: sprayed with silver or glitter and hung up for holiday decorations.
13. Timothy: woven into wreaths or coils for basket-making.
14. Limber roots: coiled into fantastically shaped baskets and then dried.
15. Pine cones: used in wreaths and for decorations.
16. Buckeyes: very beautiful when arranged in a basket. They also seem to work as a substitute for mothballs.

Grace Caldwell of Mansfield, Ohio, gathers herbs and plants for drying, too, but she also combines this hobby with another: leaded glass. She turns recycled scraps from both hobbies into key-chain tabs by sandwiching flower, leaf, and stem bits in artistic arrange-

ments between two pieces of scrap glass. Almost any kind of glass will do, even if slightly curved, as from a bottle. The edges of the glass are ground smooth on a glass grinder or with a file, the plant material is arranged between them, and then the two pieces are soldered around the edges with lead came, as is done in any kind of leaded glass work. Caldwell gives the key chains as gifts. The one in the photo contains a little fleabane blossom, a bit of fennel stem, and a hyssop flower. This technique could also be used to make larger wall hangings, windows, or other objects in leaded glass.

TRAMPING RAILROADS

Roadsides are not the only publicly accessible places for an enjoyable landcombing tramp. Railroad right-of-ways are lucrative, too, and not just for plants. Very often, electrical and telephone lines run alongside the rails, or they used to. This means it's a good place to find old glass and porcelain insulators, which are popular with collectors. Even if the lines and poles are now gone, insulators often lie half-buried in the weeds and cinders at the foot of the railroad embankment.

As you walk along, you can scout for railroad ties, too. Often as not these days, rail officials will not give away or even sell old ties to individuals. If partially decayed, the ties are sawn into three pieces and burnt. You may run into a mile-long section of track where the sawn ties are piled along the rails waiting to be hauled away.

FINDING AND SELLING WORMS AND BUGS

While some people may be a bit squeamish about fingering worms and bugs, it can be a very profitable venture. Fishermen are always on the lookout for a good supply of worms and other live bait, and there are plenty of gardeners out there looking for "good" bugs to control the destructive ones in their gardens.

Live Bait

Fishing worms can be a backyard source of "free money," but you don't have to raise them—just pick them out of the grass at night. Lawns not soaked periodically in poisons often support large populations of "nightcrawlers." After dark, walk softly and very slowly, crouched over, with a flashlight. The crawlers extend themselves several inches from their holes but will zip back in at the slightest provocation. Therefore it takes a fast hand to catch them, then to gently pull them from the ground without injuring them. The worms keep well in cool, moist moss, sawdust, mulch, or grass clippings until advertising or word of mouth brings fishermen to buy them.

Hellgrammites, the larval stage of the dobsonfly, are excellent bass bait and sell quickly. When I was a boy, my friends and I used to catch them by turning over rocks in the river rapids. Sometimes the larvae would still be hanging onto the rock, but most often, a second person stationed a bit downstream caught the aquatic insects in a fine-meshed net—a piece of window screen stapled to two sticks will do. We also netted crayfish, which in the soft-shelled stage make excellent fish bait. Bait houses may have a good supply of worms and minnows, but they seldom carry hellgrammites and soft-shelled crayfish.

Beneficial Insects

Buying praying mantis egg cases for your organic garden can become an expensive proposition, so gathering the egg cases for your own use or selling them to gardeners or to the markets that provide them to gardeners is another possible source of "free" money. The tan, tough, leathery cocoons, about the size of a human nose, can be found in the fall attached to shrubs and low-growing weed stems. If mantises are established in an area, these cocoons can be quite common. I value them too much to sell but often clip off the stem they are attached to and tape the stem to a bush or low tree twig in my garden or orchard. When the mantises hatch out in the spring, I hope that they hang around the garden awhile.

The most unusual money-making project I've ever heard about is collecting wasps and hornets. Not many people will want to try, but the very idea of it stretches the mind to the infinite possibilities the world offers us. Vespa Laboratory, in Spring Mill, Pennsylvania, extracts venom from wasps for use in desensitizing people who are especially allergic to insect stings. So far as I know, Vespa is the only laboratory that does this, so obviously the market is limited. Yet USDA Extension Service entomologist Bill Lyon says that in recent years prices paid per pound of frozen yellow jackets were as high as $360 or more, and female paper wasps sold for $600 a pound! Limited or not, *somebody* pockets this money, and in fact the Extension Service entomologists provided a list of professional collectors who do.

I called one of the collectors, Greg Lamp of Oregon, Ohio. He was not very encouraging. The work can be dangerous, as when removing a yellow jacket colony from a house. He told me that only about one in ten beekeepers have the cool to do the job. He uses a vacuum pump, much like a household vacuum cleaner, to suck the insects up gently without injuring them. Of course it takes a heap of yellow jackets to make a pound, but with the experiences I have had with so many colonies in my lawn, I don't think it would be too dangerous to capture them off their entrance holes. Certainly it would be better to recycle them in a way beneficial to man than just to pour gasoline down their holes, which is what I've been forced to do occasionally, when a nest is in a place where children and others are endangered. I hesitate to give the names of current field collectors connected with Vespa since they may change by the time you read this and since they don't want competition anyway. The laboratory itself discourages direct queries. Your best bet is to get information where I did: from the entomology departments at Ohio State University or the Pennsylvania State University.

As biological control methods for insect pests grow in practicality, there may be other markets for insects opening up—such as the laboratories that provide control services. These will always be small, limited markets open only to a few meticulous and painstaking collectors. But remember that anything that is too easy to produce and market is always in surplus and therefore profitless. *Any* worthwhile collection must, by definition, be difficult to obtain.

BEACHCOMBING

The possibility of finding a small treasure still awaits the conventional beachcomber. Late-summer vacationers on the southern Atlantic seaboard tell me that despite the crowds, the seashell and sand dollar hunting was exceptionally good in 1985, due to an early, violent offshore hurricane that whipped up the water and uncovered troves of shells. All around the Gulf of Mexico it's possible to discover ancient gold coins, washed ashore from the now much-publicized wrecks of Spanish galleons. And there are still Mississippi rivermen who drag the mussel beds and sell the shells, hoping, always hoping, to find in one of them a big river pearl like those more or less common 100 years ago in the heyday of the pearl button trade. And such pearls *are* still found occasionally. (See "Mississippi Shell Game" by John Madson in *Audubon* magazine, March 1985.) Most of our inland rivers from the Mississippi Valley eastward are potential freshwater pearl grounds, if not because of the live mussels still in them, then from the billions that have lived and died there from time immemorial.

CHAPTER 8

Lengthening the Life of Your Possessions

M aintenance is what you do to avoid making costly repairs. Repair is what you have to do if you don't maintain properly. When something finally gets so old it must be repaired if it is to continue to be used, and especially if that old thing has antique value, then the repair becomes known more glamorously as restoration. In keeping anything in use over a long period of time, maintenance, repair, and restoration coalesce into one extended process rather than three distinct operations. Whether the object in hand is an electric motor or an old chest of drawers, you must clean it, replace or fix broken parts, and then decorate, paint, lubricate, or otherwise protect its surfaces from excessive wear to lengthen its life.

Extending the life of any tool, appliance, piece of furniture, building, or automobile can be enormously profitable, especially if your own labor is used. Even where you must involve the expert labor of another, such as a good auto mechanic to install a rebuilt motor in a car, considerable savings are possible. For every year of life you can add to an item, you add to your income a hidden profit equal to the interest on the money you would spend to replace that item with a new one. If, finally, your maintenance and restoration preserves an item that has antique value over and above its actual use value, you will have "saved" or acquired more hidden profit, sometimes quite significant amounts. A properly preserved wrought iron fence, for example, may take on a value all out of proportion to its use value compared to a chain-link or wood board fence, solely because of its popularity as an antique.

RESTORATIVE CLEANING

Moneysaving maintenance and restoration begins with cleaning—and sometimes that is all that is necessary. A wood floor may need only a good washing with Murphy's Oil Soap to restore it to a pleasing appearance without refinishing at all. A brick wall may need sandblasting (don't sandblast wood unless you like the weathered, driftwood look). A local restorer of antique engines and tractors says sandblasting is by far the most effective way to clean up old motors and engine frames and bodies. "It takes about five hours of very dirty work to do an old tractor or truck but is well worth it," he says.

Regularly cleaning or replacing dirty filters on furnaces, motors, and so on will prolong the life of the machines and save money in operation. Filters on hot air furnaces are easy to change but easy to forget about. The money a homeowner thinks he is saving with added insulation might be lost by inefficient operation of a furnace with a dirty filter. And it often turns out that dirt is the reason an item, especially an electric motor, appears to be "broken." When one of our window fans decided to quit running, I, the nonmechanic, was ready to junk it. My son, poorer but wiser than I, took the housing off the motor, cleaned the dirt of a decade from around all those coils of wires that surround the armature, then cleaned the grease and dirt choking the motor shaft, and the fan ran like new.

The first step to good cleaning is to take the item completely apart, or as nearly so as possible. This applies to almost everything, including furniture.

Bottles and Glass

Old bottles sometimes have a whitish film on their innards that is difficult to remove. As a collector myself, I don't like to remove all of this film because then the bottle looks like new. A brush, detergent, and persistance will remove enough to suit me, but some people want their bottles ultraclean. Sand is, in that case, more effective than a brush, especially in hard-to-reach areas. Put a handful of sand in the bottle along with warm water and detergent and swirl vigorously. I've used pebbles and shotgun pellets, too, but these may scratch the glass. In really grim cases, soaking the bottle overnight in a 5 percent solution of caustic soda should do the trick. Ammonia and water

overnight sometimes works, too. Suzanne Beedell, in her book *Restoring Junk* (MacDonald, London, 1970), says that a 5 percent solution of nitric acid will remove wine stains from glass. She also reveals a little-known secret—you can sometimes rub a shallow scratch out of glass by polishing it persistently with jeweler's rouge, because glass actually flows slightly under pressure, and vigorous, steady rubbing causes it to fill in the scratch! On exterior glass surfaces, stains that won't come off with a good glass cleaner will sometimes yield to a metal polish, without hurting the glass.

Coins

You can lower the value of a rare coin by cleaning it. New, uncirculated coins should be protected from tarnishing by wrapping them in aluminum foil and placing them in a tarnish-proof envelope, available from stamp and coin dealers. Ordinary paper contains sulfur, which tarnishes coins. (Rubber, by the way, will tarnish silver black.) Handle a coin only on the edges. If you must clean an old silver coin, do not use abrasives—a paste of baking soda and water is the safest. Gently rub the paste over the coin with your fingers, then rinse, and dry it on a blotter. This procedure won't work on copper and brass. If you use metal cleaners on a copper or brass coin, you will brighten only high parts of the coin and its value will be lessened. Acids and buffing will not restore the original lustre to these coins— it's best not to clean them. Sell them at a good price to a collector who is expert in these matters, or who thinks he is, and let him ruin them.

Tin, Silver, and Pewter

To clean tin, an old household remedy says to bring water and wood ashes to a boil, then dip the tin in, and wipe it bright with a rag. Really dirty pieces should be soaked for ten minutes or more and then rubbed with emery cloth.

I once bought an antique tin cigar box that was very brightly painted. I decided to get the remains of a tobacco stamp off the exterior with soap and water. To my chagrin, the painted decorations started coming off, too. The moral of the story is obvious. However, my wife did manage to brighten the faded paint considerably with a coat of vegetable oil.

If you're trying to re-create old tin rather than clean up the real thing, here's a neat trick: To mimic the old painted toleware with its black background, paint a flat black paint on the tin and cover with a coat of shellac. Then paint colorful designs over the shellac. George Grotz, in his wonderful book *The Furniture Doctor,* offers a recycling trick to obtain a good black shellac. Dissolve old records, which were made of shellac and lampblack, in alcohol. But before you do this, make sure the old 78-rpm records you have in mind have no value for collectors.

When cleaning silver or any metal with abrasive metal cleaners, you remove a bit of the metal with the tarnish. Be especially careful around the numbers imprinted on silver—the hallmark—which dates the piece and sometimes gives the grade of the silver. Rubbing and polishing too hard over the hallmark will diminish it over time and greatly lower the value of the piece.

A traditional technique for cleaning pewter calls for boiling it with hay in the water, although what kind of hay is anybody's guess. If you're not up for gathering hay, try washing the pewter in warm water and mild soap. Don't *ever* put pewter in the dishwasher—it melts very easily. Keep this in mind when you're repairing it, too, such as when soldering a broken piece. Keep the area around the hole or break cool by leaning it against a wet sponge or any cool object you can rig up. Use soft solder only.

REPLACING OR REPAIRING WORN-OUT PARTS

Once you've taken an item apart for cleaning, you'll be able to see if there are parts that are broken or suspected of being worn out. Some parts are supposed to wear out and be replaced to save wear and tear on the rest of the machine. Thus, in hot-water heaters there is a metal rod of magnesium that corrodes quicker than the tank metal, the theory being that this will add longer life to the tank. The rod goes by the unlikely name of "sacrificial anode," though I have never heard a plumber get that poetic. When the rod deteriorates down to about the size of a length of wire, you are supposed to replace it with a new one. The problem with these rods is that in certain kinds of well water, like ours, they cause the water to smell unduly like sulfur. When we told our plumber about our water problem after he had installed the heater, he removed the rod. End of smelly water. Perhaps our tank will not last quite as long, but I'll trade that for clean-smelling water any day.

Gaskets are also made to be replaced. You can save money by buying a sheet of the right gasket material and cutting out your own, using the old gasket as a pattern. The restorer of old tractors mentioned previously uses the waistbands of worn-out underwear as cushion gaskets between metal straps and the gas tanks, hoods, and so on that they hold in place. "These bands look like the original strips and work just about as well," he says.

Working with Wood

Replacement parts of wood are comparatively easy to make in home woodworking shops. But once you get down to the actual repair, you need not only your wood pieces but good glue as well. Of the hundreds of glues on the market, most of the common ones and the old standbys fit chemically into one of the three categories listed below. (Not included are specialty epoxies, hot-melt glues, contact cements, and cyanoacrylates that are seldom used around the house.)

Animal protein glues: hide glue and casein (or milk) glue. Hide glue is used for gluing musical instruments, paper, and sometimes furniture. Gummed labels usually have hide glue on them, because it is nontoxic. Hide glue sands without gumming up the sandpaper. It is neither heat- nor water-resistant, but the fact that heat melts it is advantageous to a woodworker when he needs to take a piece of furniture apart again. Casein glue is more water-resistant than hide glue and works better in cool temperatures. It is water-resistant but not waterproof and is good for gluing oily woods such as lemonwood and teak.

Polyvinyl acetate glues: common white and yellow glues. White glue is the all-purpose household glue such as Elmer's Glue-All and Weldbond. White glue will hold wood, fabrics, and pottery. It is not very resistant to moisture, however, and is a bit gummy to sand. It dries clear, is nontoxic, and is very strong. Yellow glue is preferred by woodworkers because it sands better, gets tacky more quickly, and sets up more slowly. There are many brands.

Urea-formaldehyde and resorcinol-formaldehyde glues: the newer water-resistant and waterproof resin glues. The urea type is highly water-resistant but not quite waterproof. Weldwood and Wilbond are common brand names. It does not dry clear and won't hold oily woods, such as teak, very well, but it can be used on objects that remain outdoors, as long as they don't frequently get rained on. The resorcinol type is waterproof and useful therefore for lawn furniture, boats, and other outdoor items. It will withstand the most caustic chemicals. Caution is advisable with these two glues because they release formaldehyde, a suspected carcinogen, as they dry.

Of course, gluing will be ineffective if not done under pressure. Clamps of all kinds are handy and eventually moneysaving if you use them. In a pinch, you can make "clamps." I have used everything from cement blocks to old typewriters to weigh down glued surfaces. When gluing two boards together on adjacent edges, a neat trick is to lay them on the workshop floor with the edges to be glued touching. Put the outside edge of one board against a wall or against a length of wood nailed to the floor. On the outside edge of the other board, nail

---

GLUING HINTS

To glue glass or pottery, use epoxy resin glues sold for that purpose. Make sure the joints are very clean and dry. Apply glue *thinly,* press the parts together as hard as you can without breaking them, and tape together. In gluing up furniture, especially chairs and stools, glue *all* the parts together at the same time, set the piece on the floor, and wiggle it before the glue dries to make sure all the legs touch solidly. If you glue only two pieces at a time, invariably when you get to the last piece, it won't fit properly, or the legs won't be quite true to the floor, or a rung will be askew.

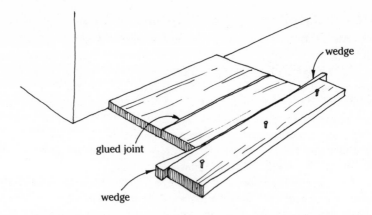

wedge

glued joint

wedge

another length of wood to the floor, leaving just enough space between it and the board to enter a wedge at either end. Glue the boards,
place in position between the piece of wood and the wall, and tap in
the wedges. This arrangement could be set up on a bench, too.

A pair of threaded rods and two pieces of inch board can also act
as a clamp. Drill two holes in each board for the rods. The boards
become the vise or clamp jaws when burrs tighten them against the
object to be clamped.

Working with Metal

Just about every local area has at least one metalworking shop where
metal replacement parts can be machined. For automotive parts,
restorers haunt junkyards and collect parts catalogs. In dissembling
old parts from any piece of machinery, be sure to use wrenches and

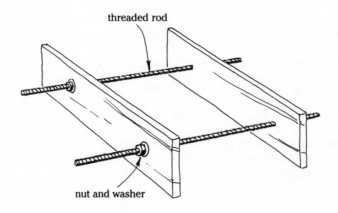

threaded rod

nut and washer

screwdrivers that are precisely the right size for the job. If a screw-driver is too small for the screw slot, it will tear out the slot when you try to turn a rusted screw and then you can't get the screw out even with the right screwdriver. You'll have to drill it out, which is not easy. For bolts, have a can of rust solvent, like Liquid Wrench, handy and let it soak into rusted threads for a few minutes before you try to turn the bolt loose. Lightly tap the bolt with a hammer after the solvent has soaked in. Old muffler and tailpipe assemblies are often so difficult to remove that it is worthwhile to drive to a service station where power cutters make the job comparatively easy.

It often happens that when a riding mower has come to its last days, it is only the motor that is worn out. On some mowers, it is fairly easy to remove the whole motor and replace it with a new one your-self. You gain the equivalent of a practically new machine for much less than half the cost. In shopping for mowers, moneysavers should look for this easy motor replacement. If you can deal directly with a distributor of the motor itself—such as Briggs & Stratton or Tecum-seh—rather than the mower dealership, you may get a better price on the replacement motor.

PROTECTING SURFACES FROM FURTHER WEAR

It is amazing how often "worn out" machines just need lubrication, or how much longer tools will last if given a coat of used oil or grease when not in use. It is not much trouble to keep a bucket of used oil in the corner of the garage to dunk garden tools in and a grease rag hanging nearby to wipe over your carpentry tools that are prone to rust.

Steel lintels above door and window frames on brick and ma-sonry houses are often-overlooked locations of destructive rust, as is the flashing on roofs. Paint them periodically with a rust-inhibiting paint like Rustoleum. I like to paint the metal parts of old lawn and field equipment with Rustoleum, too, after first wire-brushing away rust. If you want a nice smooth finish on old metal, cover it with a coat of body putty—the amazing stuff used on rusted car bodies—and then spray with lacquer, same as you would when repainting a re-stored car.

Motors around the house, like those on hot-air circulators, need to be oiled two or three times a year. There are little caps on the motor shafts to fill with oil. Use a very light oil and do not overfill the well, as the oil might overflow onto the commutator or brushes and prevent good electrical contact or encourage dust to build up. Sewing machines also need to be oiled—look at the directions that come with the machine.

Furniture

Furniture surfaces need to be "oiled," too, to protect them through the years, especially if they are valuable antiques or could become such. Furniture doctors argue among themselves as to the best way to preserve finishes on wood—whether with an oil or a wax polish. A good wax (one with some hard wax like carnauba in it) requires elbow grease to rub in and shine well, but will last a year. Oil polishes go on with a swipe of the rag but need to be renewed weekly. Wax protects better, but builds up and needs to be removed about every five years (with mineral spirits). Oil catches dust, which inadvertently is worked into the finish. Oil darkens wood quicker than wax, and the darkening is not so easily removed. Oil polishes are mostly mineral oil with lemon scent. You can use plain old mineral oil (which is nothing more than a light lubricating oil) to polish furniture more cheaply and protect the wood just as well. After all, who wants lemon-scented walnut furniture? Linseed oil is a better surface protectant but darkens the wood much faster. Some people give a coat or two of linseed oil to new wood, then use regular mineral oil polishes the rest of the time.

All in all, hard wax, like the good old Simoniz used on cars, is still the best polish for furniture, but the oil polishes usually win out in popularity because they are easier to apply.

Removing Paint

In most wood restoration, coats of paint or varnish have to be removed prior to refinishing. Humans go through various historical (and hysterical) moods about wood. At one time they preferred the real wood grain. Then they wanted it stained. Then they wanted a fake grain. Then they wanted to obliterate the grain altogether with paint. As styles and moods change, fingers get worn to the bone removing the styles and moods of yesteryear. We are still in the midst of removing paints from Early American furniture, or its reproductions, while on the horizon, painted furniture appears to be coming back in style again. Ho hum.

No matter how you look at it, removing paint is a real pain. If you are dealing with one coat, you can proceed as with varnish and use one of the liquid strippers on the market. If the wood has many coats of paint, as it likely will, lye, while dangerous, will work, although it's

HOW TO MAKE FURNITURE DENTS DISAPPEAR

To make a dent in wood almost disappear, first remove any wax (with turpentine) from the dent. Then soak the wood with a sponge or wet pad or blotter laid over the dent for several hours. Then remove the pad and heat the wood with an iron set on the lowest heat setting. It is best if the iron does not contact the wood directly. Lay a safety pin or bottle cap open side down over the dent and under the iron. Keep checking until wood swells and more or less fills out the dent. In hardwoods, a few pinpricks into the wood will allow for better water and heat penetration for more effective swelling.

not something I would recommend. Take the piece to a commercial stripper whose vat is full of a substance so caustic it will eat a hole in your hand in seconds (I am not exaggerating). Electric paint removers, such as blowtorches, use heat to soften the paint for scraping off, but despite what you might read elsewhere, they do not make the job much easier and can actually singe the wood or, worse, burn the house down. If you decide to use an electric paint remover, keep a fire extinguisher handy. Beware of fumes and keep children away—the paint might be lead based if it's old. You'll need a drop cloth on the floor under the work, preferably of nonflammable material. The paint that drops off the scraper will be hot.

The proper procedure (if there is one) with liquid paint removers is to put the stuff on thickly with a brush. Let it soak until the paint is loose, then scrape off with a scraper. Next clean with a wire brush and, finally, with steel wool. Before going to wire brush and steel wool, you may need to repeat a second application of the paint remover. A small pointed tool (a spike or an old screwdriver) might be needed to get paint out of nooks and crannies before wire brushing.

There are various strippers on the market for clear wood finishes, but before you invest in them, determine what the finish is on that old piece of furniture. Most old furniture was finished in shellac or lacquer. Shellac comes off easily with denatured alcohol. If the alcohol dissolves the shellac only to a sticky consistency that's hard to wipe off, add lacquer thinner to it—1 part lacquer thinner to about 4 parts alcohol. Lacquer thinner will, of course, remove lacquer. Add a little alcohol to it to make the job go faster. Half lacquer and half alcohol will take off some varnishes, but in this case one of the commercial liquid strippers works a little better. The fastest and most effective way I have seen varnish removed from a flat surface is with hand scrapers, the kind used by woodworkers. It takes strong fingers and this trick: Bend the scraper (which is just a flat, square piece of metal with a sharp burr ground on the edges) slightly convex, then push the edge against the wood, with the convex surface away from you, in short powerful strokes across the wood surface. Polyurethane varnishes pop right off.

MAINTAINING HOUSEHOLD APPLIANCES

Keeping refrigerators, washers, dryers, and so on working much longer than they're warrantied for means you must regularly clean the appliance, replace its worn parts, and protect its surfaces. A dishwasher's strainer screen, for example, needs to be cleaned out regularly, especially if you are sloppy about scraping plates before putting them in. And a water heater thermostat that allows water to get too hot needs to be replaced. (A water temperature of 160°F is plenty hot for any household.) Proper water pressure in the house—50 to 60 pounds per square inch—will prolong the life of appliances, too. You can buy inexpensive pressure gauges at hardware stores that screw onto faucets or hose connections.

A dishwasher will work efficiently (and therefore save money) if your household water is between 140° and 160°F. Any hotter, or below 140°F, and dishes won't clean properly. A clothes washer works best at 140° to 160°F, too. But water temperature isn't the only factor in lengthening the life of your appliances. Detergent can be critical in a dishwasher. If it won't dissolve readily in 150° to 160°F water, it is too old or the box has been open too long, and it won't clean well. Try to use up an opened box within a month.

Toasters, Irons, and Can Openers

Some appliances have built-in features that make maintenance relatively easy, if you know what to look for. Toasters, for example, have crumb trays in their bottoms. (I confess I didn't know this until about a year ago.) To clean out a toaster, you are *not* supposed to turn it upside down like I did and let the crumbs dribble out all over and possibly gum up the heating elements so they burn out. After unplugging the toaster, clean it by brushing crumbs, sugar, or whatever with a soft brush down onto the crumb tray. Then empty the tray. On toasters and any other appliances that you frequently plug and un-plug, the electric cord right behind the plug often breaks after pro-longed use, tempting you to believe the toaster is broken. Be sure to check for frayed cords before giving up on the appliance.

Ports in electric irons sometimes get plugged with minerals from your water. Clean them with a piece of wire. A solution of half vinegar and half water in the iron's holding tank will also clean it out. Set the iron on steam and let the mixture steam away.

If you have an electric can opener that will no longer hold a can or lid properly, dirt has probably built up on the cutter. Clean the cutter with soapy water and a toothbrush, carefully scraping away any hard crust with a knife. Then remember to perform this maintenance regularly to keep the cutter clean.

There are commonsense ways to lengthen the life of your appli-ances, and at the same time save money, that have nothing to do with maintenance. For example, if you have a yard, give your clothes dryer a rest and dry your clothes outside when the weather is nice. The fresh clean smell this will impart in your clothes is alone worth the effort, not to mention the energy dollars you will have saved. Don't overtax your washing machine by overloading it, and don't waste energy by doing only half-loads, unless your machine has a low-water-level setting. Most washers today have cold-water wash and rinse settings—use them. Just be sure to use a detergent that is made for cleaning in cold water. Likewise, don't overload or underload your dishwasher, and open the door when your machine reaches the dry cycle and let your dishes air dry rather than waste energy with the heat element.

TAKING CARE OF BOOKS AND PAINTINGS

It's funny how when people buy books and paintings, they tend to quickly put the books on a shelf and hang the paintings on a wall, and soon forget about them. But books and paintings need to be cared for in the same way that other possessions do in order to keep, or even enhance, their value.

Protecting Books

Not until I worked in a museum did I learn how crucial temperature and humidity are to the lasting qualities of organic materials such as paper. An environment comfortable for humans is good for books, too, with enough air circulation to ward off mildew. High humidity encourages mildew and will destroy books in a couple of generations. And contrary to what many people believe, glass cases are the worst place to keep books, not only because the air inside is stagnant, but because such cases discourage handling. Handling books is good for them—turning the pages provides needed aeration. Bookshelves should be open and books not pushed against the back wall, but space left for air circulation. Dust should not be allowed to build up on the top edges of shelved books. And be on the lookout for silverfish. They will eat paper as well as rug backing. Insofar as books represent quite an investment nowadays, and often an investment that grows in value, caring for them is money in the bank.

Cleaning and Restoring a Painting

When it comes to cleaning any painting of value, chances are you would call on an expert. But if you buy a painting, say, at an auction because you like it, not because it is valuable, you can clean it yourself if you are careful, and that may be all the restoration it needs. But don't do anything to a painting until you test the procedure on one tiny spot—if possible at the edge where the frame will cover it. Even after you start in on the picture, do only a small spot at a time. If color comes off on the pad you are dabbing with, stop immediately and wipe off whatever solvent you are using with another medium that will stop its action—turpentine or castor oil if you're using alcohol for your solvent; kerosene if you're using acetone. But be careful of the kerosene, because it might harm the oils in the painting.

A painting is generally composed of three layers. The bottom coat is gesso, upon which the oil is painted. The oil is usually covered by a clear finish—shellac or varnish—to protect it. The very top film of the varnish gets dirty and if you can't get just the dirt off, you'll have to take off some of the protective coating that is darkening the picture. You might have to take off all or most of the varnish, and that's where the tricky part comes in, because you don't want to clean *through* the varnish and get into the painting itself.

First just wipe off the painting gently with a soft pad and a bit of water and ammonia—½ teaspoon of ammonia in a cup of cold water. Then wipe on a good wax polish and shine. The polish will remove dirt, too. If this does not make the painting bright and clear enough to suit you, sponge the painting lightly with turpentine. (Remember, do a test spot on the edge at every step.) Then start dabbing, a little spot at a time, with a mixture of half turpentine and half alcohol. If nothing much happens, increase the amount of alcohol. Keep watching your dabbing pad. If it shows color, stop immediately and dab with castor oil or pure turpentine to stop the solvent power of the alcohol until you can carefully wipe it up. When finished, sponge off the whole painting with pure turpentine again. If there is a whitish cast on parts of the painting, it can sometimes be removed with mineral oil. Some recipes for picture-cleaning add acetone (ethyl acetate) to the alcohol/turpentine mix. At any rate, don't overdo it. Be content with a fairly bright picture rather than go through the varnish and ruin the painting.

After the cleaning is finished, the painting can be given a coat of shellac or picture varnish, available from an art shop.

Watercolors are very hard to clean. Don't use water, of course. Gasoline won't hurt the watercolors if dabbed carefully with a brush, and it can be used to lift grease marks and then left to evaporate.

Other watercolor discolorations are often due to some form of mildew generated by the glue in the backing. Unless you have experience in the tedious job of removing backing, you'd best take your painting to an expert.

TAKING CARE OF LEATHER

Leather is only expensive if not cared for, in which case it will not even last several human lifetimes. Leather-bound books ought to be treated with saddle soap, or handled frequently—the oils from the skin then perform the same service the leather dressing does. Leather boots and shoes should be cleaned with saddle soap, not detergents. To condition them, use a leather dressing such as neat's-foot oil. Do not try to waterproof leather with paraffin-based waxes, silicones, water repellents, or ordinary oil or grease. Leather must breathe to stay healthy. If you want boots to shine, use a leather dressing that contains lanolin. Mildewed leather can be cleaned with a mixture of 1 cup chlorine bleach to 1 gallon of water or equal parts of water and denatured alcohol, but saddle soap will usually work better.

KEEPING YOUR HOUSE INTACT

One of the most important possessions you will ever maintain is your house. Lengthening its life by proper maintenance and repair not only gives you added years of comfortable living but also increases your home's value. There are all kinds of tips for taking care of a home, but here are two areas of particular concern.

How to Have a Dry Basement

Basements are almost always mildew-makers, even when they appear to be dry. Furnace, stove, or fireplace heat might keep the basement dry in winter, but in summer a dehumidifier will almost always be necessary, especially where a basement is finished off with rugs, woodwork, and so forth. Even if the room is only partially underground, as in a split level, mildew will invariably form on back walls.

Before a dehumidifier will do a good job, though, the basement walls must be properly waterproofed. The outside wall must have a tile along the footer to drain away ground water. If you are having trouble with leaky basement walls not so tiled, do that first. Otherwise water will stand along the wall no matter how well the outside surface slopes away. Walls, especially of cement block, ought to be waterproofed on the outside. Tar or asphalt is often used, but cracks will open up in it. A cement-based sealer, such as Thoroseal Products' Foundation Coating, is better. You can also coat inside walls with products like Thoroseal to make an even drier basement. Also check around the outside of the house to make sure the soil surface slopes away directly from the wall. Otherwise, water dripping down the walls in heavy rain will have a tendency to stand against the wall too much, even if a drain tile has been installed.

Brick walls are almost maintenance free, but old ones will have deteriorating mortar here and there. Chip out loose mortar, flush with water, then tuck-point with one of the new nonshrinking mortars. To protect old masonry or stone surfaces without hiding their beauty, use a clear silicone water repellent made for masonry and apply it like paint. (Thoroclear from Thoroseal Products is one brand name.)

If your house does not have an interior vapor barrier like it should, you can alleviate some mildew and flaking problems on the outside by using oil-based paint, or on the inside by hanging vinyl wallpaper on interior walls, or polyethylene film under paneling or wallboard.

Basement walls aren't the only places to look for cracks—in time, chimney caps, too, will invariably crack. If you haven't checked yours out in a while, do so. If you find cracks, fill them with 3 parts fine sand and 1 part cement. For cracks in plaster, chisel out holes or cracks to about ¼ inch deep and wide, and apply a nonshrinking hydraulic cement.

Weatherstripping Secrets

The experts all agree that dollar for dollar, weatherstripping pays back more than any other home improvement. The reason this is true is not only because the stuff is relatively inexpensive, but because the homeowner can do all the work. In an admirable project in Louisville, Kentucky, high school freshmen without any previous training are weatherstripping homes of the elderly. It's simple once you wade through the bewildering choice of materials available. The more permanent types of weatherstripping cost more and are worth it, but cheaper, temporary types of stripping have their place, too. I hate to admit it, but in emergencies (like 20 below zero and a door warped beyond the help of any permanent stripping) I have used varying layers of paper tape over cracks. It was rather effective, too, and we could still open the door if necessary and the tape would restick on closing. It was ugly, but definitely warmer. If ugliness doesn't bother you, duct tape is a more effective temporary draft-stopper than paper tape is.

I would not have had to resort to tape if it had not been for my dear wife, who is not known to give up easily. She liked her wood front door so much that she refused to have it obscured by any storm door we could afford to buy. The poor wooden door, facing heat up to 88°F on the inside, thanks to an overzealous woodstove, and −20°F on the outside, cringed into a nice little bow, opening a crack through which we could watch the sun go down. Even worse, the sun quickly wreaked havoc on the door's exterior finish. Years passed before she gave up and ordered a storm door (there are full glass ones now that are hefty enough to suit her and not too expensive). The second time around she also relented on the door's finish and redid it with an exterior marine spar varnish that previously had been vetoed as being "too shiny." We hope this shiny spar varnish will handle the sunshine better.

Rope caulking or tape caulking seals out cold better than tape, but of course can't be used on a door or window that has to be opened. The same is true with transparent caulking compounds. But these materials are low-cost ways to seal a window you don't open during the winter, or ever.

Plastic window inserts have barbed fins that are supposed to spread out and fill a crack into which the strip is stuffed. These strips can be used over, but once placed between door and frame, the door can't be opened or you have to reapply the strip.

Plastic foam and rubber foam strips have adhesive backing and are glued to the door or window frame so that when the door or window is closed, the stripping is compressed, blocking out air movement through the crack. In about a year or so, the strips start coming loose or begin to deteriorate and need to be replaced, but replacement is very simple.

Self-adhesive door bottom strips also come loose fairly soon. Instead, use the kind that attach with screws—the metal-backed sweeps of plastic strips or nylon bristles. Sweeps can be adjusted so that they give a snug fit over the threshold but are still high enough to clear rugs.

Threshold gaskets fit under the door. Use the adjustable kinds that can be fitted to an uneven door bottom.

Felt strips are tacked into place. Hemmed felt has a rigid backing to make the strip easier to mount. Many other kinds of gasket stripping are made, all designed to be installed more permanently than adhesive-backed strips. But remember, the more permanent the stripping, the higher the cost.

If the weatherstripping on metal storm doors, windows, and patio doors wears out, you can buy replacement strips that snap into place when pressed on the edge with an old screwdriver or similar tool.

Magnetic weatherstripping, interlocking metal strips, and other permanently installed metal-backed gasket strippings are the most expensive and long lasting. If not more or less hidden from view, they at least are not unattractive to the eye.

In an article in *Rodale's New Shelter* magazine (October 1985), David Sellers and Craig Canine give some rarely told tips on installing weatherstripping: First, don't stretch flexible strips to make them fit. Cut them accurately. The tension of stretching will make them come loose quicker and deteriorate faster. Second, on doors, accurately measure the gap to be closed and use a gasket of appropriate thickness. If the strip is too thick by even a little, the door will be hard to close. Third, when installing tension strips, pay attention to gap size, too. A standard plastic V strip works best in gaps of $\frac{1}{16}$ to $\frac{3}{8}$ inch, Mylar strips in gaps from $\frac{1}{32}$ to $\frac{1}{4}$ inch, and preformed brass tension V strips in $\frac{3}{32}$- to $\frac{5}{8}$-inch gaps. And finally, when buying stripping, a standard kit may not contain enough for a whole window or door, so measure carefully and buy accordingly.

EXTENDING THE LIFE OF YOUR CAR

Your automobiles are your second most expensive investment in life (after housing). Cars can be repaired on the inside nearly forever, but used-car prices generally rise and fall on the condition of the exterior. Salt, humidity, industrial pollutants, dirt, and even trees are the great enemies of your bank account in this regard. (When certain aphids attack trees, the leaves drip a sap and honeydew mixture which, along with bird droppings, produces a fallout that can cause paint to degrade on cars parked below.) A frequent washing with soap and water is the best defense against all these threats. A good waxing with hard wax (something with carnauba in it) is the next line of defense, unless your new car has had a Teflon-based product applied to it (or applied by you), in which case waxing is not too important. Scratches can be cleaned up with a pre-wax cleaner and then retouched with paint available from your dealer. Be careful with the pre-wax cleaner. You can rub right down to metal when all you want to do is smooth out scratches in the *paint*. If the scratch goes to bare metal, and/or rust has appeared, rub away rust with an emery cloth, then dab on primer and then the proper paint. If you are using a glazing putty on a dent or scratch, primer is not necessary. This putty is used to fill *small* dents and holes.

Most cars come undercoated from the factory, and if you live where salt is applied to roads during winter, undercoating is a necessity. As an additional measure, I apply used oil from a squirt can all around the bottom inside edge of a new car, where mud and moisture gather and where rust makes its first inroads. Those drain holes along the bottom of the car body should be kept open, not allowed to get plugged with mud. If that inside lip around the bottom of the car is thoroughly cleaned every year and used oil applied, you can stall off rust much longer than usual. A lot of the young people in our area who fix up old cars and trucks go a step further. They park their restored vehicles inside from December to March, and buy old, rusty-but-running models to drive to work during the salt and ice months.

Repairing Dents and Removing Rust

Most dents, holes, and rust spots can be healed fairly easily in the home garage if they are not too large. If the rust is on the surface only, it can be removed with rust remover or with sandpaper. If the rust goes all the way through, you have to carefully cut and scrape it all back to bare metal, apply a rust inhibitor (these products are all available at automotive supply stores along with detailed instructions on use), then plastic filler. If the hole is fairly large, you will have to back it with a piece of fiberglass screen to hold the plastic filler in place until it hardens. First you apply the filler around the edges of the hole and edges of the screening to cement the latter in place. Then fill the hole. Apply the filler so that it is just a bit higher than the surrounding surface and then file it down almost flush after it is dry. Directions with the filler explain this procedure in detail. After you've sanded the filler perfectly smooth, prime and paint.

The hard part of fixing minor holes or rust spots is in remembering the basics that are often overlooked: having the surfaces clean and dry so that whatever you're applying adheres well, and sanding or feathering the sides of the hole or dent so the new paints adhere to the old and blend into a smooth finished coat, without leaving a little crater with a definite edge to it. Work from the outside to the inside of the repair spot, sanding a gradual slope from outer edge to center. The outer edge should show a band of exterior paint, a band of primer, and then bare metal. The wider the bands (up to about 1 inch), the more gradual the slope and the better the new primer and paint will adhere and produce one smooth surface.

Replacing a Windshield

Because insurance takes care of most broken windshields and their replacement, no one ever thinks of replacing one themselves. But there is no law against doing the job and having the insurance company pay you if you have the low bid. You save money and so does your insurance company. At any rate, you may some day have to replace a windshield and if so, you should know that it is really a simple job. I should know—I watched a repairman do it.

This particular windshield was one of the "glued in place" kind that is most prevalent these days. Those that are sealed shut with rubber gaskets are even easier to replace, the repairman said. He started by removing the windshield wipers and the rearview mirror from the old, broken windshield. Then he snapped off the chrome strip around the edge of the windshield that helps hold it in place. There are little metal fasteners at regular intervals around the windshield. These just have to be pried up gently with a screwdriver. With the chrome strip removed, all that holds the windshield in place is a bed of butyl plastic, a gummy sealant around the edges of the glass. To separate the glass from the "glue," the repairman had a special tool with a pointed metal hook that he inserted between the glass and the butyl plastic. Then by pulling on a short cable attached to the tool, the little hook could be slid around the window edge, separating the glass from the putty. In the absence of this tool, the repairman said he would insert a length of wire he called piano wire—a fine spring steel wire—between glass and putty and draw it around the edge, separating the seal. In a pinch, a table knife could do the job, but it would take more time. Sometimes the glass breaks if it is laminated glass. If it is tempered glass, you generally don't have to remove the windshield because when it breaks, it shatters into millions of little pieces.

The repairman then lifted the old windshield, or pieces of windshield, out of the frame. With a large screwdriver (a heavy putty knife or similar tool could also be used), he removed the old butyl plastic putty from the frame. The stuff is gooey and comes off easily. It's not necessary to remove every last bit of it. The repairman next laid down a new application of the putty. It comes in coils from glass and auto repair suppliers, with the coils separated from each other by a strip of paper. He unrolled the coil in place around the window frame where the old putty was, being careful not to cover the little fasteners to which the trim snaps in place. With the putty in place around the frame, he next added a bead of windshield sealant all around the outer edge of the coil of putty with a putty gun. The sealant is the same material as the coil, but a little runnier and a little more pliable so that it will work into any tiny crack or deformity in the glass to ensure there will be no leaks. Some repairmen add this thinner putty after the window is in place, my source informed me, but the majority believe it seals better and easier if applied as described.

Next he laid the new windshield in place and pressed it down onto the coil of putty, spreading the putty out somewhat. He cautioned that one should always press on the glass with the whole palm of the hand, equalizing the pressure through all the fingers and the heel of the hand. If you press too hard with the heel of the hand only, he said, the glass might break. With the windshield firmly in place, he took a small triangular putty knife and pushed and pressed the thinner sealant in and around the outside edge of the glass and down into any would-be hairline openings between the glass and the coil of putty.

Then he snapped the chrome strip back in place, mounted the wipers outside and the mirror inside, and the job was done.

With rubber gaskets instead of glue, all you need to know is how to remove the gasket from around the edge of the glass—usually it just hooks into a metal lip.

For some reason, automotive books for the do-it-yourselfer seldom describe how to replace a windshield. But now you know.

The Proper Way to Paint

You can paint a whole panel (or a whole car for that matter) on your own, although most people prefer to have a professional do the job. If you decide to do it yourself, sand your car first. Not everyone does it, but if you want a really good finish, you must. After all the dents, holes, and rust spots have been filled, sand the whole car. This is best done with water and a sanding block. Hold a garden hose in one hand and let water flow over the area you are sanding. Sand in one direction, not in circles. Be careful near chrome or glass because the sandpaper will scratch these materials. Use 220-grit wet sandpaper first, then 320—both are available at automotive stores.

That finished, you next must tape up *all* areas of the car you don't want to get paint on. This takes longer than the painting. It is an excellent idea to watch a professional do this first, as well as watch him or her paint. Painting is always done with a power sprayer for a good job, and for beginners lacquer or acrylic are far easier to work with than enamel. (If you are going to spray lacquer or acrylic *over* enamel you may need to spray on a sealer first. Ask a professional painter.) Before you start spraying, practice. This is one good thing about the primer coat. It allows you to continue practicing right on the car, because the primer coat is not as critical as the final coat of paint.

Learn how to use the spray gun's controls to vary the spray pattern. Spraying is done by swinging the gun back and forth in about a 2-foot arc or swath over the surface, the edges of each swath lapping slightly over the preceding swath's edge. For most painters, spray guns are best held about 8 to 12 inches from the surface being painted. This will throw a pattern that is neither too thick, which causes running of the paint, nor too thin, which causes the surface to dry grainy. When applied correctly, the lacquer or acrylic will be momentarily grainy when it hits the car surface, then will flow together smoothly. By the time you get the primer on, you should have just about mastered the basic skill. Of course, your first job is not going to be great, but it can be passable.

Lacquer dries immediately and you can spray a second coat. Acrylic needs to "flash," as the pros say—that is, surface-harden a bit before the next coat is applied. Apply a very light coat the first time and allow the surface to harden a bit before applying a second coat. Enamel is slow-drying, tricky, and definitely should not be put on in one coat unless you are a master. Let me add that I am not a car painter. But my neighbor is a pro, and I watch him and listen to his wisdom. He says one thing I have never seen written down anywhere: Don't paint lacquer in very humid weather. If you do, it's liable to have a whitish cast to it.

Lacquer and acrylic can be sprayed outdoors, but pay attention to the temperature requirements on the label. A car body can get very hot in the sun, maybe too hot for the paint. On the other hand, it is best to plan painting so that it is finished a few hours before sunset, to take advantage of warm drying time. If temperatures are below 60°F, painting is not a good idea.

CHAPTER 9

Voluntary Simplicity and the Good Life

A book such as this, full of practical suggestions and tips about saving money, may convey the notion that frugality is an end in itself. But seldom, if ever, does piling up money—even a big pile—bring much real satisfaction. After all, miser and miserable come from the same root word. Or as Edmund Burke put it so well, "Mere parsimony is not economy. . . . Economy is a distributive virtue and consists not in saving but in selection."

In other words, wise humans save money one way so that they can use it in another way to bring more quality to their lives. Perhaps you've wondered how your neighbors, whose income is about the same as yours, can afford a trip to Europe while you can't. It could be because the neighbors drive a 10-year-old car, mow with a $400 walk-behind model (not a $3,000 rider), and are still using their 20-year-old stove and refrigerator. Or how about the people who dine frugally all week so they can afford those nights out at fine restaurants?

Such practices are examples of voluntary simplicity. The emphasis is not on giving up something but in choosing something else. The better the choices, in terms of long-range benefits to the chooser, the wiser his or her life-style is considered to be. Voluntary simplicity allows one person to live quite elegantly on an income that another considers near poverty level. And we all know examples of people with high incomes who live constantly in heavy debt because they choose not to make choices, not to practice economy.

A MODEST, YET ELEGANT, EXISTENCE

The most deliberate form of voluntary simplicity I know is that practiced by Skip Stauffer, who resides near Ada, Ohio. Skip lives in the nineteenth century as much as she can and lives quite elegantly that way. Her and husband Mick's Primitive Acres Herb Farm is remarkable enough if you know what you are looking at, but the nest gardens of esoteric herbs give barely an inkling of the wonders that lie behind them. Skip herself would seem no more unusual than any other vivacious, bustling gardener in her middle 40s—if the year were 1886 instead of 1986. She wears a long skirt not unlike the peasant skirts popular a few years ago, only this one is made of homespun. A ruffled petticoat peeks out from under it. Over it and her long-sleeved blouse is a full-length apron, stained from the tomatoes she is canning. She is barefoot. Except for the absence of the high-buttoned shoes she wears when the weather is cooler, this is the way Skip Stauffer dresses all the time. Her heart lies back in the nineteenth century. And because of that, hundreds of urban and urbane visitors flock to her door, seeking, well, who knows exactly what? They look around with utter fascination, then carry home Skip's philosophy and her herb wreaths, as if somehow her spirit of simplicity will soothe and calm the hectic pace of their own lives.

In the dooryard next to the summer kitchen stands a wooden food dryer, no larger than a refrigerator, with a tiny woodstove in the bottom of it. Mick built the dryer. (Skip envisions the nineteenth century and Mick renders the visions into wood and metal.) Skip dries much of her fruit and vegetable crop in it. The dryer comes straight out of the late 1800s, a time when people learned that in the whimsical weather of the Northeast, the only kind of solar heat you could rely on for quality food drying was the kind stored away in wood.

Next to the dryer, a pot hangs suspended from a tripod. Skip does much of her summer cooking in the pot. Next to the tripod, a steel griddle straddles a fire and holds the boiler for the jars of tomatoes she is canning. "Much faster to bring water to a boil outside like this than on a stove," she points out. "Cheaper, too, if you have any wood scraps around."

A walk with her through the extensive gardens surrounding the house becomes a commentary on moneysaving ways. The birdbath is a big sandstone rock, hollowed out with a stone chisel to hold water. Her gazebo, which she calls a tearoom, is the simplest of structures: four posts forming a square about 12 feet on each side, connected at their tops by 2 × 6s, over which rests a heap of tree branches casting dappled shade into the shelter. "We have tea here every afternoon in the Colonial manner," she says. "This type of structure was common a century ago, especially in the South. Shade houses were built next to the gardens and fields, handy for workers to rest and cool off in on hot days—better than air-conditioning."

She names the herbs as she passes them. "That big green stuff is annua, very fragrant, but spreads like a weed. So we've confined it in a bed surrounded by 3-foot walls of railroad ties, as you can see. That silvery stuff is silver king (artemisia), marvelously aromatic. It makes wonderful wreaths that sell well to the city market. What I like about it is that it will grow on that gravelly, sandy bank where nothing else will. By your foot there, that's tansy. If you get ants in the house, spread some tansy on the floor and they'll go away. Over there is chamomile. Chamomile tea will help you get to sleep. And next to it is sage. We drink sage tea for colds. Mind you, I'm not prescribing. Just telling you what works for me. And those are all different kinds of mints. We think they make the most refreshing cold teas on hot days."

But it is only when you step into the tree-shrouded house, past the giant basket made of vines, past the homemade twig broom, through the door with a handle from a curved, weathered section of tree branch, that you begin to grasp the true spirit of Primitive Acres. You must pause at the door to allow your eyes to grow accustomed to the dark interior. There are no overhead fluorescents to switch on— the only lamps are kerosene. A skylight sends a shaft of light down onto a braid of red onions and several bunches of herbs drying on the wall. At the far end of the room glows one tiny electric bulb, all that Skip allows in her domain, except in the bathroom. "Mick insisted on a bright light to shave by," she says. "But then he built a wooden seat up around the toilet, so it would look like an outhouse."

It is not that she avoids electricity, but she uses it only where it can really count: a deep freeze, a refrigerator, and a washer. Food is prepared in the big walk-in fireplace, or on the woodstove, or on the kerosene range when the tripod arrangement outside is not practical. As your eyes become accustomed to the soft glow of candles (hand-dipped by Skip), the whole world of nineteenth-century cooking takes shape in the house: tinware, pewter, pots, pans, iron skillets, Dutch ovens, a "tin kitchen" for cooking in the fireplace, rolling pins of enormous size, woven baskets, wooden spoons, wooden bowls. "A spoon and a bowl are the closest thing I have to a blender," she says.

Off the kitchen on a lower level is the buttery, which is unheated except for what warmth may be allowed to flow in from the kitchen. Here the family's food is stored—canned goods, potatoes, bins of flour and meal, baskets of fruits and vegetables. She takes grain, 100 pounds at a time, to be ground at Clifton Mills, a water-powered flour mill still in operation.

In another part of the house sits a loom with a rag rug partially finished on it. Nearby stands a spinning wheel. Here Skip works in winter when there is time. The room is cluttered with more antiques than a museum, especially dolls, toys, and tiny sets of play dishes. A visitor muses at the havoc a child might wreak in the room. "Oh no, not my children," replies Skip. "Nor my grandchildren. A child raised in this kind of atmosphere does not tear things up."

The bedrooms appear to be right out of a museum, too. The beds have big feather ticks mounded over them. "Those feather ticks are warmer than electric blankets," says Skip.

The kitchen and buttery form the original house, built more than 100 years ago. The rest Mick added on, using old barn timbers for framing. The floors look like old hardwood boards to match the kitchen, but they are really new pine aged by the Stauffers' own discovery. "We couldn't afford a real hardwood floor," says Mick. "The lumberyard said soft pine would never do. But Skip saved all the old vegetable oil she cooked with, strained it, and put a coat of it on the floor regularly. It soaked in enough to give pretty good moisture protection, and after a while produced an almost perfect patina of aged wood."

The summer kitchen was a later addition and not exactly what Mick had in mind. He thought he was building a garage, a notion that did not harmonize too well with Skip's visions of the nineteenth century. When the garage was almost finished, needing only a concrete floor to be poured, Skip had an inspiration. As soon as Mick left for work one morning she began to work furiously, hauling bricks scavenged for another project to the garage by the wheelbarrow load, and laying them down for a floor. That finished, she furnished the room appropriately and when Mick arrived home, his garage had been transformed into a summer kitchen. He objected. She implored. They compromised—the room would be a summer kitchen in summer and a garage in winter. That was several years ago. The cars are still parked out by the pasture field fence. "I can be very persuasive," says Skip with an almost wicked grin.

The summer kitchen becomes a salesroom in September and October when Skip sells wreaths, swags, potpourri, and other items she makes from her herbs. Occasionally she gives lectures, but because she doesn't drive, such events are few and far between. "Mostly I stay home," she says. "I have created my own world here and I'm happiest when I'm in it." Not that she needs to travel much. Although she lives in a manner few would closely follow, it's ironic that the world beats a path to her door, fascinated to learn from her.

Observing voluntary simplicity in one's life need not follow Skip Stauffer's arduous path. Simplicity does not mean privation or poverty, nor does it result in an inelegant life-style. On the contrary, simplicity is the essence of real wealth—real economy in the classic sense of the word. I thought of this as I watched Danny Downs, the young blacksmith I spoke of earlier, turn a piece of old wagon wheel rim and a cast-off length of junked steel into a breathtakingly beautiful Damascus steel knife. Damascus steel, highly prized since at least the Middle Ages, is very simple to make. There need be only the smallest of cash outlays to produce it. *What is needed to make the metal is ample time and knowledge, which are the fruits of simplicity in life-style.* Every craftsperson knows that on the way to the production of the highest quality goods and services, a simple life-style—sacrificing income to gain time and knowledge to produce good work—is a prerequisite. Even after the world rewards their sacrifice with high commissions, most craftspeople and artisans continue to live relatively uncluttered lives, because otherwise, as Andrew Wyeth once said to me, "you couldn't get any work done." Work, not play, is the joy of life. Or, when one's work becomes one's play, then life becomes a joy and the ultimate simplicity has been achieved.

A FEW STEPS TOWARD SIMPLICITY

Simplicity allows us to cut the fat from our budgets and lives, and there is plenty we could dispose of and hardly notice. For instance, other than status, does one suffer anything from driving an $8,000 car rather than a $14,000 one? Or from wearing lower-priced "regular" clothes rather than "designer" ones?

I have a friend who trained his children to walk on the outer parts of the carpeted steps rather than the middle so the carpet would last twice as long. Well, why not?

Such simple habits as making better use of the shoe repair shop can save hundreds of dollars in a lifetime. Or make it a habit to carpool. It may seem a bit bothersome in a way, but bother doesn't cost money and think of what a nice contribution the companionship makes. Of course, if you are close enough to walk to work, then do so. You'll save on transportation costs, plus help keep yourself fit.

Try to stay away from gadgets: A gadget spurned is at least $30 earned these days. The number of nominees for the yearly "UI" award, as we call it (for the Ultimate Insanity), continues to grow. Last year, power leaf blowers won the coveted honor, and the year before that, flame-throwing sidewalk de-icers. The UI tragedy of the year was the elderly gentleman who died of a heart attack while removing snow during a snowstorm. He was not *shoveling* snow as you might surmise, but *trying to start his snowblower.* In a rage, he kept pulling on the starter rope until he did himself in. (We will, as a result, probably see safety legislation introduced requiring manufacturers to make starter ropes that will break if pulled more than twenty-seven times in quick succession.)

It is no longer environmentally chic to make fun of electrical gadgets since the environmentalists finally realized that preaching the curtailment of the luxuries of life meant they had to do so, too. But like my Amish friends say, once you decide that electricity (as one example) is wonderful stuff, then you face each application of it with less and less choice and less and less sense of what you give up, in money and in simplicity of life. I hear parents stoutly maintain that they would never give up their dishwashers and then just as stoutly complain that there is no work for children to do around the house anymore. And despite protestations to the contrary, I have never known a family who could effectively control the amount of time spent watching television, talking needlessly on the phone, or unnecessarily bathing and laundering. "Well, I'd rather have her washing her hair twice a day than not at all, like it was a few years ago," one despondent father told me.

Young people are no different than adults: Humans can't just use technology; many times they also abuse it. We used to complain because we had to wash and wipe dishes. Today's child complains when he has to scrape off his plate and stick it in the dishwasher. Tomorrow's child will protest the time it takes to punch the buttons that deliver his food.

One of the other ironies of the human condition is that people who might benefit most from the moneysaving opportunities of embracing a simpler way of life attempt to spurn such practices as heedlessly as the very rich. An Agricultural Extension worker at the University of Kentucky once told me that she could only persuade some low-income families to plant gardens after she passed out gaudy garden magazines proclaiming the fact that well-off people plant gardens, too. These poorer people, she found, associated gardening not with voluntary simplicity but with involuntary servitude. Such people were also surprised to learn that woodstoves could be found in expensive homes—they had been brought up to believe one burned wood only if one could afford nothing else.

Sociologists could give all kinds of reasons for this way of thinking. Perhaps a person will follow voluntary simplicity if it's his own idea, but not if it's someone else's. Or maybe it's because people save money only in hope of thereby bettering themselves, and the poor have no such hope. But mostly, I think, moneysaving is a matter of habit handed down in some families and not in others. I never even heard the phrase "voluntary simplicity" until three years ago and yet when I look around my office, I must have been practicing it all along. There's a couch I made from some scrap walnut wood that was given to me, and my wife made the cushions. The rug on the floor was bummed from a sister who was getting rid of it. The pictures on the wall are framed with barnwood from a scrap pile. A friend gave me a stuffed chair when he moved. My swivel chair sits on a piece of plywood rather than one of those nice lucite pads. I bought my desk secondhand years ago. Instead of a $3,000 word processor system I'd like to have, I process words on an old, used Remington Standard I bought twenty years ago for $35. Though it is used I daresay more than most typewriters, it has never once needed repair. Bragging about this typewriter gives me more satisfaction than a word processor would.

RECYCLING YOUR SAVINGS

No one can tell you the best way to invest your savings, although there are plenty of experts who want to try. Some of the worst ways, according to the experts, might turn out to be the best. When the government took the silver out of our coins, I wanted ever so badly to convert my savings into silver 50¢ coins and bury them in the yard. Had I done so, I would have made a fairly handsome investment, but I didn't have any savings then. If I had, I would not have known the proper time to sell my hoard and so a good investment might have turned sour.

The point is, no one knows the future so no one knows the best way to recycle savings. For most of us who do not like to gamble, a savings account is probably as good a way as any. You can't brag about a savings account the way you can about a stock portfolio or a hot property, but a lot of that bragging is hot air anyway. If someone tells you about how the value of his stock doubled in ten years, just remember that money in the bank at 9 percent interest doubles in a little over eight years. Of course, investments can grow in value faster than that, but generally speaking, such investing takes lots of personal involvement. People who really make money on the stock market spend much time studying it. Others buy stocks with the same kind of bravado they use betting on horses. Amateurs tend to do better if they buy a sound stock and then leave it alone as if it were savings in the bank. It might grow faster than money in the bank, or it might not, but it is best to just leave it there, ignoring the daily ups and downs of the market. And remember the old saw: Don't play the stock market with money you can't afford to lose.

Right now, banking is not as rock-solid a proposition as it has been over the last forty years. Banks are in trouble. The largest banks lent billions to Third World nations that can't or won't pay it back. Because land and real estate values are falling, especially farmland prices, many banks are stuck with bad loans made in inflationary times. And worst of all, our government is in such deep debt, no one knows whether an economic collapse can be avoided. Some financial experts believe that money value might better be "saved" if put into durable, income-producing tools, houses, equipment, or people. I don't know about such philosophies, but I can think of some examples that, no matter what state the economy would be in, could produce security equal to money savings. Finance a capable young man or woman through medical school or law school, or finance a new business in town. If you are young enough to still like to work hard in your spare time, putting money into income-producing hobbies might pay handsomely. If you can make good furniture, you can make good spare-time money, and if you become *really* good, the enterprise could work into a full-time business.

Skip Stauffer, in my estimation, has found a perfect way to invest savings. Since she was 16 she has been collecting primitive antiques. She did this not with the idea that the everyday things of the nineteenth century might become valuable, but because she wanted to *use* them for everyday things. But now these humble tools of yesterday *are* a good investment, financially, since the craze for the "country look" has swept urban and suburban America. And since most of these objects are almost indestructible, use only enhances their already growing value, like a good violin. Surely there can be no better economical way to invest savings in the good life.

Photography Credits

Index

18534

643
LOG

Logsdon, Gene

Gene Logsdon's
moneysaving
secrets

$18.95

DATE			

18534